THE **ADLARD COLES** BOOK OF

NAVIGATION

TIM BARTLETT

ADLARD COLES NAUTICAL
LONDON

Published by Adlard Coles Nautical
an imprint of A & C Black Publishers Ltd
38 Soho Square, London W1D 3HB
www.adlardcoles.com

Copyright © Tim Bartlett 1996, 2002, 2008

First edition published as
The RYA Book of Navigation 1996
Reprinted 1998, 1999 (twice), 2000
Second edition 2002
This edition published 2008

ISBN 978-0-7136-8939-6

The right of the author to be identified as the
author of this work has been asserted by him in
accordance with the Copyright, Designs and Patents
Act, 1988.

A CIP catalogue record for this book is available
from the British Library.

This book is produced using paper that is made
from wood grown in managed, sustainable forests.
It is natural, renewable and recyclable. The logging
and manufacturing processes conform to the
environmental regulations of the country of origin.

Typeset in 10pt Sabon
Printed and bound in Spain by Graphycems

Note: while all reasonable care has been taken in
the publication of this book, the publisher takes no
responsibility for the use of the methods or products
described in the book.

Contents

Foreword

Bill Anderson, in his Foreword to the original incarnation of this book as *The RYA Book of Navigation*, wrote 'The technology of navigation is under-going considerable change at the moment.'

He was dead right.

Already, we have seen the demise of three of the electronic navigation systems that were described in the first edition, published eleven years ago. Position fixes from the Global Positioning System (GPS), on the other hand, are nearly ten times more accurate than they were then, because the American government has removed the deliberate errors that were originally used to degrade the accuracy available to civilian users. Satellite-based differential systems promise even greater accuracy in the not too distant future, and it is quite likely that a European version of GPS will be operational within the next few years.

At the same time, the cost of electronic navigation equipment has fallen, and the level of sophistication available has risen. Chart plotters, in particular, have developed from being little more than toys to the stage at which they really can be regarded as serious navigational tools, with potentially life-saving advantages.

Despite these technological changes, of course, traditional navigation techniques survive. They may be less important now than they once were, but they are still available as backups to modern technology, and as a means of understanding or cross-checking the information available from the electronics... or even as an interest in their own right, that can be just as consuming and rewarding as boat-building, sail trim, or the racing rules.

Tim Bartlett FRIN

Foreword to the First Edition

Tim Bartlett's brief was to produce a navigation book to compliment RYA courses up to Yachtmaster Offshore. In some areas this book goes slightly beyond the current Yachtmaster Offshore syllabus. In particular, descriptions of electronic navigation systems are included to a greater depth than is strictly necessary for Yachtmaster candidates, but it was considered helpful to do this.

The use of radar for navigation and collision avoidance is included in the syllabus for the Coastal Skipper practical course (power) but not the equivalent sailing course. The book would have been incomplete without coverage of radar but it is not essential knowledge for all Yachtmaster candidates.

The use of a sextant for vertical angles, which is outside the scope of the current syllabus, is included in response to requests from numerous instructors who feel that a vertical sextant angle is a useful and simple navigational technique for measuring ranges.

The technology of navigation is undergoing considerable change at the moment. In November 1995 the UK general Lighthouse Authorities published a Consultation Paper Marine Aids to Navigation into the 21st Century. This proposed:

- The continuing provision of traditional aids to navigation for the next 25 years and probably beyond, with necessary planning changes due to:
  - the ongoing review of the mix of aids within that period
  - the acceptance of new radionavigation systems.

- Provision of an unencrypted and freely available DGPS service by 1996/97.

- Adoption of LORAN–C in 1997 subject to operational capability and adequate coverage of Britain and Ireland by the NW European LORAN–C chain (NELS).

- Withdrawal of the UK Decca Navigation System in 1999.

- Closure of the present radiobeacon service by the year 2000 or sooner.

- Sustained effort at the IMO for revision and modernization of chapter V of SOLAS 1974, ensuring that attention is given to rapid developments in marine navigation technology worldwide.

- Encouragement for the development and agreement of operational requirements for a civil satellite system for 2015 onwards and a strategy for international provision of such a system.

All of these are, of course, no more than proposals and several of them are subject to financial and political considerations before they can be implemented.

The other area of rapidly changing technology covers electronic charts. It seems likely that these will, eventually, become widely used by yachts, but with a number of competing systems at various stages of development it is almost impossible to forecast which of the systems will gain acceptance for small craft navigation.

Whatever new technology emerges it is unlikely that the basic principles of navigation will change or that the traditional skills will become redundant. Improved technology may give us potentially greater accuracy in position fixing but it is unlikely to replace the need for a skilled navigator who can evaluate the information and make sound and safe navigational decisions.

Bill Anderson

Acknowledgements
The author and publisher would like to express their thanks to all the following people and organizations who have assisted with the illustration of this book:

Photographs and equipment
Amberley Marine: pages 108, 109 and 110
Garmin: pages 38, 39 and 40
National Aeronautics and Space Administration: page 111
Raymarine: pages 41 and 106
Suunto: pages 24 and 27

Thanks also to:
Adlard Coles Nautical for permission to use the quotation from *Channel Harbours and Anchorages*
Bill Anderson
Linda Jermy
Hydrographer of the Navy for permission to use extracts from Admiralty charts and publications
Reeds Nautical Almanac for permission to use extracts from their publication
Alison Noice

Illustrations by the author

Introduction

We are all navigators. We have to be, because navigation is the art or science of controlling or directing travel. So as soon as we start learning to walk or crawl we also start learning to navigate. Of course, our first 'journeys' – from wherever we happen to be towards a favourite toy – are pretty simple; we can see our destination before we set off. Gradually though, we build up a mental picture or model of our surroundings until we are able to navigate to unseen destinations.

By the time we have grown to adulthood our individual territories are likely to have become quite large, but there will still be times when we find ourselves in unfamiliar surroundings. On holiday it might be quite fun to start the exploration process all over again, but in the hurry of everyday life we are more likely to ask someone else for directions. Following directions based on someone else's local knowledge can be very effective, and it is almost certainly the way many of the earliest seafarers 'navigated'. They engaged local pilots to navigate for them in unfamiliar waters, or used information handed down by word of mouth or in the form of written sailing directions. At sea, as well as on land, we still sometimes use these techniques today.

But simply following instructions is hardly navigation – there is no decision-making involved; you have no freedom to vary the route, and no real control other than to stop or go. More importantly it has serious limitations: handed-down instructions work only for one particular route, so you need different instructions for every combination of starting point and destination; they depend on your being able to recognize key landmarks from someone else's description; and they rapidly become useless if you get lost or have to deviate from the route for some reason or other.

To overcome these shortcomings, some of the old written sailing instructions were illustrated with drawings, then with simple maps or charts. The first recognizable charts were probably produced in China in about the tenth century AD, with Europe following suit two or three centuries later. In both cases, charts were developed at about the same time as the magnetic compass – and not purely by coincidence. Those early map-makers needed some means of measuring direction in order to produce their maps in the first place, and their customers equally needed the compass in order to use them to best advantage, because although maps may have been developed to overcome the difficulty of describing the appearance of a particular headland or the precise location of a rock, their big advantage was that they could be used as universal sailing directions. They gave navigators the information required to plan their own passages from anywhere to anywhere. It was this facility that made the compass so important. You can see why if you think of a simple land-based example. If you are following directions, 'turn left at the crossroads' is all you need, because whoever gave you the directions knows which road you are on in the first place. If you could have approached the crossroads from any direction, a much more positive indication is needed – north, south, east or west.

Art or science?

Whether navigation is an art or a science is a moot point, and in fact it is probably a bit of both. Like most other sciences it involves a certain amount of mathematics – nothing complicated, but the ability to do simple arithmetic and to draw and measure accurately are important – and it requires hard facts if it is to be put to practical use. Some of those facts have to be learned by heart, but others are too complicated or variable to commit to memory, so you need to know where to find the necessary information.

The scientific side of navigation can be taught in a classroom or learned from books. What makes it an art are those things that can only be developed through practical experience at sea – knowing how to get the best out of your equipment when conditions are against you; being able to make a 'best guess' when some key piece of information is not available; and being able to decide when – and when not – to use approximations and short cuts.

Electronics

Much of this book is concerned with what have become known as 'trad-nav' (traditional navigation) techniques. This is not just because 'they're in the syllabus', nor is it to pretend that modern electronics do not exist.

Increasingly, electronics have a part to play in sailing yacht navigation, and an even greater role in motorboats. But to depend on them totally not only means pinning your faith on the reliability of the equipment itself and on its power supply and aerial connections, but also on your own ability to operate it correctly. If you have ever dialled a wrong telephone number or recorded the wrong programme on your video, there is a sporting chance that one day you will make a similar mistake with an electronic navigator.

A good knowledge of trad-nav will serve as a backup in the event of electronic failure and serve as a double-check against operator error. No less important: it can be interesting and rewarding in its own right and form part of the reason for going to sea in the first place.

Charts and the Real World

Maps, or charts as they are called at sea, are the navigator's prime tool. They provide much of the information you require, serve as a work sheet for calculations, and as a temporary record of what has happened. First and foremost, however, a chart is a representation of part of the real world, so it makes sense to start by looking at the earth as a whole.

Our earth is an uneven, slightly flattened ball of rock spinning through space. To simplify the job of defining directions, distances and positions on its surface, it is divided up by a grid, or graticule, of imaginary lines of latitude and longitude. It is rather like the grid on a street map, but with the important difference that the grid of latitude and longitude is not purely arbitrary.

Latitude and longitude

The fact that the earth is spinning gives us two natural reference points, at the ends of the axis of spin, called the North and South Poles. Exactly midway between them, and at right angles to the axis, is the equator, running round the fattest part of the earth. Latitude can be defined as *angular distance from the equator measured at the centre of the earth*. Of course, lots of places are exactly the same distance north of the equator. If you were to join together all the points that are, say, 50° north, the result would be a circle running round the earth, parallel to the equator; so it is called a parallel of latitude (Figure 1).

Parallels of latitude are equivalent to the horizontal lines in the grid on a street plan,

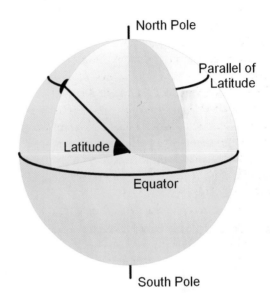

Fig 1 The latitude of a place is its distance from the equator, expressed in degrees, measured at the centre of the earth.

and appear as horizontal lines on most navigational charts.

The corresponding vertical lines on the chart are called meridians. They run from Pole to Pole. The equator was a reasonably obvious baseline from which to measure latitude, but you could draw any number of meridians between the Poles, none of which has any particularly strong case for being singled out as a starting point for measurements of longitude.

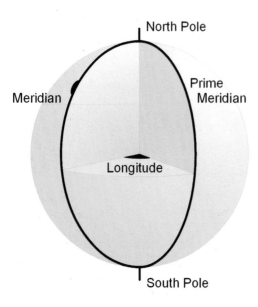

Fig 2 The longitude of a place is the angle between the meridian which passes through it and the prime (Greenwich) meridian.

For historic reasons, though, the meridian that passes through the Greenwich Observatory in London is internationally accepted as the prime meridian. So the longitude of somewhere can be defined as the *angular distance between its meridian and the prime meridian, measured at the centre of the earth* (Figure 2).

Latitude and longitude are both angles, so they are normally expressed in degrees. Latitude is measured as 0° at the equator and increases until it becomes 90° north or south at each Pole. Longitude is 0° at Greenwich increasing to 180° east and west. The earth is so big, however, that one degree measured at its centre corresponds to up to 60 miles at its surface. For this reason each degree is usually broken down into 60 minutes, while for even greater precision, each minute can be further

subdivided – either into 60 seconds, or into decimal parts.

Nowadays decimal parts are much more common, so you are likely to find the position of Portland Bill lighthouse, for instance, given as 50° 30'.82N 2° 27'.32W. Note that, by convention, latitude is always given first followed by longitude and that their directions (north or south, and east or west) are always included. They are important, because 50° 30'N 2° 27'E is a small town in northern France about fifty miles from the sea, while 50° 30'S 2°27'W is a remote and inhospitable spot in the southern ocean, some 2000 miles from Cape Town!

Geodetic datums

The working definitions of latitude and longitude given earlier in this chapter are something of an over-simplification, because the earth is not a perfect sphere and does not actually spin around a fixed axis. It is slightly flattened, uneven in shape and composition, and it wobbles. This means that it has several 'centres' depending on which part of its surface you are most interested in, so cartographers

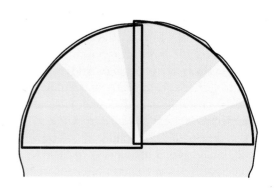

Fig 3 The earth is not a perfect sphere, so it has many possible 'centres', giving us many possible grids of latitude and longitude – or 'horizontal datums'.

use slightly different grids of latitude and longitude for different parts of the world (Figure 3). Until recently this was of purely academic interest to yacht navigators, but with the advent of satellite positioning systems it has assumed much greater significance.

Many charts of the British Isles, for instance, were drawn using a horizontal datum known as Ordnance Survey Great Britain 1936 (OSGB36), while those of our European neighbours and the Channel Islands are based on one called European Datum 1950 (ED50). Satellite navigators usually present positions based on a third grid – the World Geodetic System 1984 (WGS84). The difference between these three datums varies from place to place, but in the English Channel and North Sea it is typically in the order of 100 to 150 metres. Although this is enough to be significant when navigating close inshore, traditional navigators need not be concerned by it: they will be changing from charts drawn on one datum to charts drawn on another so far from land that the discrepancy will pass unnoticed. It is important, however, for those using satellite navigators; although most sets can give positions referred to any of the most widely used datums, they do not change over automatically: it is up to the operator to select the appropriate datum for the chart in use. Eventually, the problem will disappear. Most charts are now drawn on WGS84 or on a datum such as ETRS89 (European Terrestrial Reference System) which is effectively identical to it.

Direction

The grid of latitude and longitude also gives us a reference for our measurement of direction – *north* being the direction of a meridian heading towards the North Pole, whilst *south* is the direction of a meridian heading towards the South Pole. *East* and *west* are at right angles to these two, with east being the direction of the earth's rotation, and west the opposite.

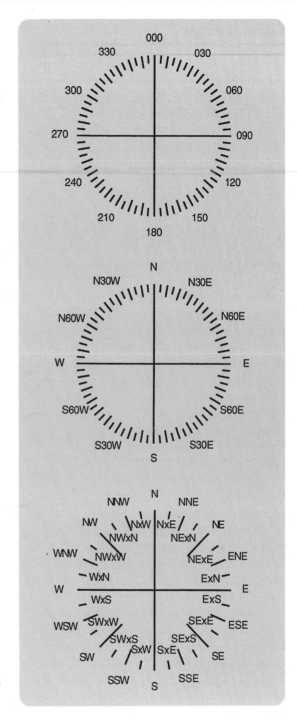

Fig 4 Direction can be expressed in several different ways: modern, three-figure notation (top); obsolete, quadrantal notation (middle); or traditional, points notation (bottom).

Cardinal notation

Directions between these four cardinal points can be given names too: the four half-cardinal points are called north-east, south-east, south-west and north-west. Continuing this process of sub-division produces eight quarter-cardinal points, each of which takes the name of the nearest cardinal point followed by the name of the nearest half-cardinal: north-north-east, east-north-east, east-south-east and so on. A third sub-division introduces sixteen by-points – so called because their names include the word 'by', as in 'north by east', meaning 'a little bit east of north'; 'north-east by north' meaning 'a little bit north of north-east' and so on.

This cardinal system served seamen and navigators well for centuries, but the names are unwieldy, and even using the full 32 points and by-points gives precision no better than 11¼°, so for most navigational purposes it has now been superseded. Cardinal, half-cardinal and even quarter-cardinal points still have their place in applications such as weather forecasts, where any more precise notation would give the listener a misleading impression of accuracy.

Quadrantal notation

One way of defining directions with greater precision involves using the four cardinal points to split the compass into four quadrants, then specifying the direction within each quadrant in terms of degrees, from north or south towards east or west. So 'north-east' became 'north 45° east'; 'south-south-west' became 'south 22½° west', and so on. This has the merit of precision, and was reasonably easily understood by seafarers who were used to the old points notation, but the names are still cumbersome, and any calculation which involves adding or subtracting angles is decidedly tricky.

Three-figure notation

Almost all navigators now use the three-figure notation, in which directions are referred to as angles, measured clockwise from north, so east is 090°, south is 180° and west is 270°. As the name 'three-figure notation' suggests, they are always written and spoken as three distinct figures, so you might say 'steer zero two zero' but never 'steer twenty degrees'.

Distance

The standard unit of distance used at sea is the *nautical mile*, now internationally defined as 1852 metres, making it about 15% longer than an English statute mile. It is not a purely arbitrary figure, but is based on another older unit of distance called the sea mile – which is the length of one minute of latitude at the surface of the earth. Unfortunately, because the earth is not a perfect sphere, the length of a sea mile varies slightly from place to place, ranging from 1843 metres at the equator to 1862 metres at the Poles. The discrepancy between these two and between the international nautical mile is so small that for most practical navigation purposes it can be ignored, and a minute of latitude taken to be a nautical mile. A minute of longitude is useless as a measure of distance because it varies from 1855 metres at the equator to zero at the Poles. So to sum up: when measuring distance in nautical miles, use the latitude scale down the side of your chart: eg 6 miles equals 6 minutes of latitude.

Distances less than a mile are nowadays often given in metres or sometimes yards, but you are still quite likely to come across distances given in *cables*. A cable is one tenth of a nautical mile or about 200 yards.

Speed

Speed, of course, is distance covered divided by the time taken, so at sea the most common unit of speed is a nautical mile per hour, known as a *knot*. The name, incidentally, comes from the days when speed was measured by throwing a 'log chip' overboard. The log chip was a small, flat piece of wood, ballasted so that it floated upright in the water to serve as a miniature sea anchor. Attached to it was a long piece of string with knots at 100 foot intervals. The number of knots that were dragged overboard in one minute as the ship sailed away from its log chip gave its speed in nautical miles per hour.

Navigational terminology

Direction is so important in navigation that navigators have many different words for it, just as Eskimos have many different words for snow. Each has a precise meaning, so they are not interchangeable:

Bearing is the direction of one object from another, eg 'the lighthouse is on a bearing of 270°', or 'the lighthouse bears 270°' means 'the lighthouse is to the west of us'.

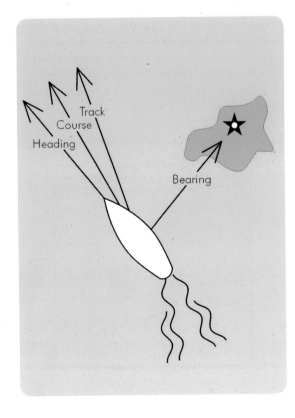

Fig 5 Navigators have several different words for 'direction', each with its own, distinct meaning.

Course is the direction in which the boat is being steered, and is ideally (but rarely) the same as ...

Heading which is the direction the boat is pointing at any given moment. So if the navigator asks the helmsman 'what is your heading?' he means 'what direction is the boat actually pointing now?' rather than 'in what direction is it supposed to be pointing?'

Track angle is the direction in which the boat is moving – as opposed to the direction in which it is pointing. The word 'angle' is often omitted. For some purposes it is useful to differentiate between the *water track angle* sometimes called the *wake course*, meaning the direction in which the boat is moving through the water, and the *ground track angle* – the direction in which it is moving over the seabed. The ground track angle is sometimes called the *course made good* (CMG) or the *course over ground* (CoG).

Charts

Every major maritime nation has a government department or agency responsible for producing official charts of its own waters, and in some cases of the waters around former colonies or dependencies. Their activities are co-ordinated (though not directly controlled) by the International Hydrographic Organization. Thanks largely to the efforts of the IHO, there is a fair degree of standardization amongst the official charts of different countries, so if you can navigate on a British chart you should not find it too difficult to operate on a French, Norwegian or American one. Whether you will ever need to is largely a matter of choice, because the UK Hydrographic Office is one of few that publishes its own charts of the whole world. Outside UK and Commonwealth waters, however, its policy is to provide charts that 'enable ships to cross the oceans and proceed along the coasts of the world to reach the approaches to major ports', so their coverage of small foreign harbours is generally less detailed than on charts produced by the country concerned.

In some respects the requirements of the yacht navigator are quite different from those of his counterpart on board a ship. In particular, a yacht may not have room to spread a full sized chart, nor the stowage space available for a large stock. For this reason, some Hydrographic Offices – including the British Admiralty – produce special small craft charts, as do commercial publishing houses. In the UK, Imray, Laurie, Norie and Wilson publish a range of charts covering the UK and near continental waters, as well as some popular but more distant cruising grounds such as the Mediterranean. An important feature of Imray charts is they often include harbour plans as insets on their coastal charts, so complete coverage of an area can be achieved with far fewer charts than when using the British Admiralty charts. This makes them a much cheaper option, though the detail of their information suffers as a result.

Chart projections

A chart is intended to be an accurate representation of part of the earth. Unfortunately, despite the best efforts of surveyors and cartographers, it can never be absolutely perfect, because the earth's surface is curved while a chart is flat. There are many different ways of projecting a curved surface on to a flat one, but they all introduce distortions of one kind or another, so which projection the cartographer decides to use is determined by which distortions are acceptable and which are intolerable. In other words, it is determined by the chart's intended purpose. On a political map of the world in a school atlas, for instance, the main requirement may be for the whole map to be at the same scale, so that all countries appear to be the right size compared to each other.

For navigation, the most important requirement is usually that direction should be undistorted, so that north appears to be in the same direction everywhere on the chart, and that a straight line (such as a bearing or a constant course) appears to be straight when it is drawn on the chart.

Although, strictly speaking, projections are defined mathematically it can be quite useful to visualize them as the picture that would be cast on a sheet of paper wrapped round a transparent globe with a light somewhere in the middle.

Mercator charts

One of the most useful projections for navigation is the Mercator projection, which – using the globe and paper analogy – would be the result of rolling the paper into a cylinder, centred on the earth's axis so that it touched the globe only at the equator, while the globe is lit internally by an all-round light at its centre (see Figure 6). The effect is to make meridians appear on the chart as vertical parallel lines, and the parallels of latitude as horizontal parallel lines.

Fig 6 A Mercator chart can be seen as the image that would be cast on a paper cylinder by an illuminated globe inside it.

From the coastal navigator's point of view, this meets the main requirement of making a straight course appear as a straight line on the chart. Its relatively minor disadvantage is that distances are distorted. On the real world the meridians converge towards the Poles, so making them parallel on the chart involves 'stretching' land masses near the Poles. Having stretched east–west distances to account for the distorted meridians, north–south distances have to be stretched as well, to preserve the shape of land masses, so the parallels of latitude are not evenly spaced, but are moved further apart towards the Poles. On a chart covering an area the size of the English Channel or the North Sea this change of scale is just large enough to be apparent with normal chartwork instruments, but for most coastal navigation it can be almost entirely ignored.

Gnomonic charts

You are quite likely to come across references to charts drawn on the gnomonic projection, because this was once widely used for harbour plans, ocean routeing charts and charts covering polar areas. Although harbour plans and polar charts are no longer drawn on the gnomonic projection, polar areas provide perhaps the most obvious example of why the Mercator projection is not always appropriate. On the real world, the meridians come together at the Poles, yet the parallel meridians of a Mercator chart, by definition, can never meet. This paradox can only be resolved by using another projection.

Going back to the globe and paper analogy, gnomonic projection can be seen as the image that would be cast by a translucent globe, with a point source of light at its centre, standing on a flat piece of paper (Figure 7). The globe and paper will be in contact with each other at only one point (called the tangent point). This could be anywhere, though for polar charts the obvious place to choose is the Pole itself. The result is a pattern of meridians and parallels

that looks rather like a spider's web, with meridians radiating outwards from the Pole, and the parallels forming a pattern of concentric rings. One obvious drawback of this arrangement is that north appears to be in a different direction on different parts of the chart: on a chart showing the North Pole, for instance, north would be straight upwards from the middle of the bottom edge, but straight downwards from the middle of the top edge. This, however, is inevitable on any chart that attempts to represent polar areas, and the main reason that gnomonic projection has fallen out of favour for polar charts is that the scale changes as you move away from the Pole in much the same way as the scale of a Mercator chart changes as you move away from the equator. This effect is minimized, though not completely eliminated, by the projection now used for polar charts called the Universal Polar Stereographic, for which the point source of light in our globe and paper analogy has been moved from the centre of the earth to the opposite pole.

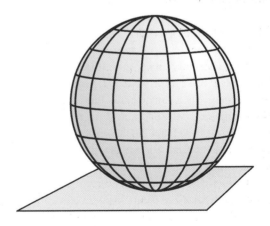

Fig 7 A gnomonic chart is the image that would be cast by an illuminated globe standing on a flat sheet of paper.

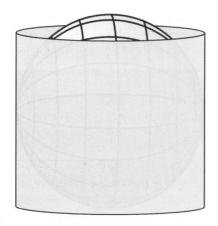

Fig 8 A transverse Mercator chart is rather like a Mercator chart, but with the globe's north/south axis running transversely.

Harbour plans

Until the 1970s, harbour plans were drawn on a projection that was usually (but wrongly) referred to as gnomonic. More recent harbour plans, however, are based on a transverse Mercator projection, which can be visualized as the image that would be cast on a roll of paper wrapped around the globe so that it touches both poles (see Figure 8).

The transverse Mercator projection is mathematically complicated, has curved meridians and parallels, and suffers distortions of scale in much the same way as a Mercator projection, but has technical advantages for surveyors and mathematicians specializing in precise positioning and the shape of the earth. So far as the practical navigator is concerned, charts drawn on the transverse Mercator projection cover such small areas that the distortions involved are negligible, and they can be treated as normal Mercator charts.

Rhumb lines and great circles

The only charts still being drawn on a true gnomonic projection are those used for planning ocean passages. To appreciate the

reason for this, imagine that you want to find the shortest distance from Falmouth to Bermuda. You might do it by sticking pins in a globe – one in Falmouth the other in Bermuda – and stretching an elastic band between them. The elastic band will naturally shorten itself until it lies along the shortest possible route. This is called a great circle route because it is part of a great circle whose centre coincides with the centre of the earth. It would not, however, cross every meridian at the same angle, so if you transfer a great circle route to a Mercator chart you find it forms a curve, bulging away from the equator (see Figures 9 and 10).

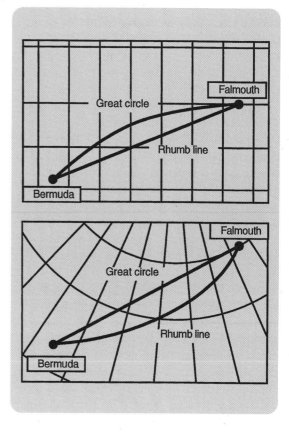

Figs 9 and 10 A Mercator chart (top) is most useful for navigation, except that the shortest distance between two points (a great circle) appears as a curve. On a gnomonic chart, the great circle route is straight.

The longer, constant-course route that appears as a straight line on a Mercator chart is called a rhumb line. For practical yacht navigation on passages less than about five or six hundred miles in length, the difference between the two is negligible, so coastal and offshore navigators can reasonably refer only to Mercator charts and rhumb line courses.

Scale

The representation of the earth's surface depicted on a chart is, of course, considerably smaller than the corresponding area on the earth itself. We are quite used to thinking of road maps being drawn to a scale of perhaps three miles to the inch, or of Ordnance Survey maps at one and a quarter inches to the mile, meaning that one and a quarter inches on the map represents one mile on the real world. Another way of expressing this is to say that distances on the map are one fifty-thousandth of the corresponding distance on the earth's surface, or that the map is drawn to a scale of 1:50 000.

All chart projections involve some degree of distortion; in particular the scale of a Mercator chart changes between its top and bottom edges, so the quoted scale of a chart is true only at a certain specified latitude.

Charts can be produced at any of a huge range of scales: the Admiralty chart catalogue includes a series of 19 charts which together cover the whole world at a scale of 1:10 000 000 (about 140 miles to the inch) but at the other extreme it also includes harbour plans at a scale of 1:2 500 (about 70 yards to the inch). $1/2500$ is considerably larger than $1/100 000 000$ so the harbour plan is described as 'a large scale chart'. The expressions 'large scale' and 'small scale' often seem to be a source of confusion, but it may help to remember that although a chart can cover a large geographical area or be drawn to a large scale, no one chart can ever be both. Alternatively you can think of charts as being divided into three main groups:

Harbour plans and port approach charts at scales ranging from 1:2 500 (about 30 inches to the mile) to 1:25 000 (about 3 inches to the mile).

Coastal or passage charts usually at scales between 1:75 000 (about 1 mile to the inch) and 1:150 000 (about 2 miles to the inch).

Planning charts at scales which may be as small as 1:3 500 000 (almost 50 miles to the inch), showing very large areas indeed but with so little detail that for pleasure craft they are only really of use in the very early planning stages of a major cruise.

The chart title panel

All charts are identified by a number and a name, such as *Channel Islands and Adjacent Coasts of France*, to give some indication of the area covered. The numbers are not in any logical geographical sequence, so when ordering charts it is a good idea to use name and number, to reduce the risk of being given a chart of the Persian Gulf for a cruise to Holland!

The name and number appear together on the back of the chart so that they can be seen when it is folded, and the number also appears in the margins on the business side. The title is also printed on the face side, but its position varies from chart to chart so as not to obscure important detail. Immediately underneath is a lot of small print including specifications of the chart itself, such as the units of measurement of depths and heights; the datum levels from which depths and heights are measured; the scale, geodetic datum, and projection used; and details of the surveys on which the chart is based. The survey information is included because it gives the navigator a useful clue about how much faith to have in the accuracy of the chart.

Finally, there may be several notices and warnings. Do not dismiss these as being irrelevant to yachts, because although most concern bigger vessels and commercial shipping, it is becoming increasingly common to find references to harbour regulations that affect small craft.

Chart symbols

There are numerous features in the real world which may be of navigational interest, but which are too small or complicated to be accurately represented at the same scale as the rest of the chart. Reduced to 1/75 000 of its real size to appear on a coastal chart, for instance, a prominent church would be barely a millimetre long, a lighthouse would be smaller than a full stop in this book, and a buoy reduced to a microscopic speck.

Symbols overcome this problem. The ones used on commercially-produced and foreign charts are very similar to those used by the Admiralty, but there are too many of them for any chart to include a comprehensive key such as you might find on an Ordnance Survey map or road atlas. Instead, the UK Hydrographic Office publishes a booklet called *Chart NP5011 Symbols and Abbreviations Used on Admiralty Charts*.

Chart corrections

The real world is constantly changing. On land, buildings are put up or knocked down, road layouts are changed, and new roads built, so most people have probably found themselves driving along a road that does not appear on their road map. Much the same happens at sea: the shape of the coastlines and seabeds can be changed by the action of wind and water, deep water channels can be dredged or harbours silt up, and buoys or navigation marks can be installed, moved, or taken away altogether. On land, where we often navigate mainly by signposts and where the consequences of getting lost are seldom disastrous, an out-of-date map is merely annoying, but at sea we are so much more dependent on charts that it is important to keep them up to date.

There are three ways of achieving this, of which the most drastic is for the Hydrographic Office to publish a new chart or a new edition of an existing chart. This may happen when an area has been re-surveyed, when it has been affected by several major changes or by a very large number of more minor ones. The vast majority of changes, however, are nothing like important enough to warrant the production of a new chart and can be written on to an existing chart by hand, in pen and ink.

Between these two extremes are changes which are too big or complicated for pen-and-ink corrections, but which affect only a relatively small area of the chart. In these cases the Hydrographic Office publishes a block correction – a new section that can be pasted on to the existing chart, to replace the affected area.

Details of all three methods of updating are given in *Notices to Mariners*, published at weekly intervals and available for a small charge from Admiralty chart agents (see Figure 11). Many, if not most, of the Notices included in the weekly editions are irrelevant to most British yachtsmen because they relate to far-flung corners of the world, so for most recreational navigators, it's much more convenient to use the searchable library of *Notices to Mariners* on the Admiralty website.

To correct a folio (set) of charts it is a good idea to begin by arranging the charts in numerical order, because the searchable database expects you to list the charts you have by number, rather than by name. It will then show you all the relevant notices affecting each chart. Each Notice gives simple but very specific instructions about the correction to apply to each chart: in most cases you are told to 'insert', 'move' or 'delete' a symbol at some specified position. Convention dictates that pen and ink corrections should be made in violet ink using a fine nib drawing pen, but in practice any waterproof ink – such as a fine red ballpoint – will do.

Block corrections are also included in the

Notices to Mariners and are simply cut out and pasted in place. It is worth rounding off the corners slightly to prevent them lifting when the chart is in use, and it is a good idea to mark the exact position of the block on the chart before applying any paste. 'Wet' paste is best applied to the chart, as this is less likely to distort than the block, but with modern 'dry' paste this precaution is unnecessary.

Finally, once the correction (pen-and-ink or block) has been applied, write the year, and the number of the *Notice to Mariners*, in the bottom left-hand margin of the chart. The virtue of this is that it will later provide a double-check that all the relevant corrections have been applied, because each *Notice to Mariners* includes a note of the last Notice affecting that chart. *Notices to Mariners* also include temporary notices giving details of short-lived changes, and preliminary Notices giving advance warning of changes that are about to occur or for which full details are not yet available. It would be pointless to mark these on the chart in indelible ink so they should be applied in pencil.

Other publications

Navigation can require a mass of other information that cannot be shown on a chart without cluttering it or confusing the picture, so a large, long-distance cruising yacht may well carry quite a library of reference books including:

- *Admiralty List of Lights and Fog Signals* in eleven volumes, each covering a particular geographical area and giving details of navigational lights and fog signals, including a description of the structure from which each light is shown.

- *Admiralty List of Radio Signals* giving details of various radio services, with each of its six volumes specializing in a particular application, such as coast radio stations, radio navigation aids, weather services and so on.

- *Admiralty Tide Tables* produced in three volumes, of which volume one covers Europe and the British Isles, giving complete

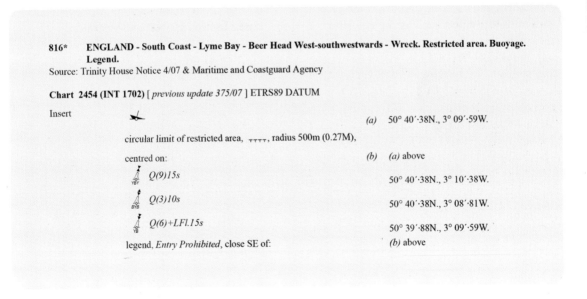

816*   **ENGLAND - South Coast - Lyme Bay - Beer Head West-southwestwards - Wreck. Restricted area. Buoyage.**
       Legend.
Source: Trinity House Notice 4/07 & Maritime and Coastguard Agency

Chart **2454 (INT 1702)** [*previous update 375/07*] ETRS89 DATUM

Insert

circular limit of restricted area, ⊤⊤⊤⊤, radius 500m (0.27M),

centred on:

Q(9)15s
YBY

Q(3)10s
BYB

Q(6)+LFl.15s
YB

legend, *Entry Prohibited*, close SE of:

(a)   50° 40'·38N., 3° 09'·59W.

(b)   (a) above

50° 40'·38N., 3° 10'·38W.

50° 40'·38N., 3° 08'·81W.

50° 39'·88N., 3° 09'·59W.

(b) above

Fig 11 *Notices to Mariners* give simple, detailed information about changes affecting Admiralty charts.

tidal height and time information for a number of major ports, with supplementary tables that allow similar information to be calculated for more minor harbours and anchorages.

■ *Tidal Stream Atlases* showing the direction and rate of tidal streams in the form of hourly chartlets.

■ *Yachtmen's Almanacs* Although much of the above information is almost indispensable, the format of the official publications – generally substantial books giving considerable detail and covering wide geographic areas – is inconvenient and expensive for most pleasure craft, so several commercial publishers produce yachtsmen's almanacs, dealing with smaller areas and in slightly less detail. Of these, the best known and most popular is the *Reeds Nautical Almanac* covering the United Kingdom and Ireland, and the Atlantic coast of Europe from Denmark to Gibraltar. As well as providing data about lights, fog signals, radio services and tides, most yachtsmen's almanacs offer a compendium of other useful information such as the collision regulations, notes on radio procedure and seamanship, and brief details of harbours.

■ *Pilot books* are produced by a number of specialist publishers and by some clubs and associations. They vary considerably in scope, content and style: some concentrate on hard factual information; some give detailed directions on routes in and out of harbours; while others are more like tourist guidebooks, so choosing a pilot is very much a matter of personal taste. When using them, however, it should be remembered that the commercial realities of publishing a specialist book are such that it may have taken a long time to research and be expected to have a long shelf life, so it is unlikely to be bang up to date.

■ *Admiralty pilots* are much more formal than yachtsmen's pilots, with descriptions of countries, coastlines and major ports that concentrate on details that may concern ships, but are of limited use to pleasure craft. Similarly, *Reeds Nautical Almanac* is very different from yachtsmen's almanacs in that it is solely concerned with the astronomical data required for astro-navigation.

2 Measuring Direction and Distance

Chapter 1 concentrated on the chart as a source of information, but it has an equally important role as a work sheet on which passages can be planned and the boat's position monitored. Both of these involve measuring direction and distance.

Measuring distance at sea

The old type of log that gave us the knot as a unit of speed (page 6) has long since given way to more sophisticated mechanical and electronic devices.

Walker log

One of the oldest is the Walker log. This uses a torpedo-shaped spinner a few inches long, towed behind the boat on a length of braided line. As it moves through the water, spiral fins on the torpedo make it spin, twisting the line. The on-board end of the line is hooked on to the back of the log instrument, where it turns a shaft connected to a reduction gearbox. This in turn moves the hands on a series of dials, rather like those of an old-fashioned gas meter, to give a direct reading of the distance the spinner has moved through the water.

Advantages of the Walker log are its rugged simplicity and the ease with which weed or debris can be cleared from the spinner. Its disadvantages are that its display has to be mounted right at the back of the boat; that the log line (usually 30 or 60 feet in length) has to be streamed before the log can be used, and recovered before entering harbour; it tends to under-read at very low speeds; and at speeds over about ten knots the spinner is inclined to jump out of the water and skitter along the surface.

There are definite techniques for streaming and recovering a mechanical trailing log, intended to reduce the risk of the line tangling. To stream the log, first attach the on-board end to the hook on the back of the display unit. Then, keeping the spinner in hand, feed out all the line to form a long U-shaped loop astern before dropping the spinner overboard, well off to one side of the loop. Some owners like to hold on to the line just astern of the display unit for a few seconds, just to absorb the snatch as the load comes on to the line.

When recovering the log, speed is essential, especially if the boat is moving fast. Unclip the inboard end from the hook on the back of the display, and drop it overboard, allowing it to trail out astern while you pull in the log line. Then holding the spinner, gather in the line, coiling it as you go. Trailing the line astern like this allows any kinks to unravel.

Electrical trailing log

The electrical trailing log is superficially similar to a Walker log, inasmuch as it uses a spinner towed astern of the boat on a long line. In this case, however, the spinner is in two parts, and the 'log line' is an electrical cable. The front part of the spinner is attached to the cable and only the rear part is free to rotate. As it does so, an electronic sensor in the front part makes and breaks an electrical circuit, so the on-board display unit receives a short pulse of electricity each time the spinner rotates. These pulses are counted electronically and are presented as a digital display of speed and distance run.

The advantages and disadvantages of this type of log are much the same as for the mechanical Walker log except that it is dependent on electrical power from internal dry batteries, which in return allows the display unit to be mounted almost anywhere on board, and that because the line itself is not twisting, it is rather easier to stream and recover.

Hull-mounted impeller logs

On cruising boats, hull-mounted logs are by far the most popular type, though in principle they are much the same as the electrical trailing log: a rotating impeller sends a stream of electrical impulses to a display unit mounted in the cockpit or near the chart table.

The impeller – which can be either a miniature version of the trailing log's spinner, or a paddle wheel an inch or so in diameter – is mounted in a fitting called a transducer, which either protrudes through the bottom of the boat or hangs down below the transom.

The disadvantages of this system are that an impeller so close to the hull can be affected by the water flow around the hull itself, and that it is difficult and potentially dangerous to withdraw the transducer to clear weed or debris from it at sea. The reason in-hull logs are so popular is primarily the convenience of not having to stream and recover 30 feet or more of log line at the beginning and end of each passage.

Other logs

At the top of the scale of price and sophistication are several alternative methods of measuring speed through the water:

Electromagnetic logs are based on the same principle as generators and electric motors: that electricity is created if you move a magnetic field past an electrical conductor. In this case the conductor is sea water and the magnetic field is created by the transducer. As the transducer moves through the water a small electric current is set up, measured by sensors on the transducer.

Sonic logs use accurate measurements of the speed of sound between two transducers mounted one ahead of the other. Each transducer emits a continuous stream of clicks, inaudible to the human ear, while listening for clicks transmitted from the other. When the boat is moving, the movement of the water past the hull slows down the clicks travelling forward whilst speeding up those travelling aft. The instrument accurately measures the time taken for each click to make the trip, compares them, converts the results into a display of speed through the water, and from this calculates the distance run. Another type of sonic log uses sophisticated echo sounder technology to measure the rate at which plankton and debris are moving past its transducer.

The big advantages of all three types are that they are much less susceptible to fouling than ordinary in-hull logs and that they can go on working at very high speeds or in rough sea conditions, when turbulence or air bubbles make impeller logs unreliable.

Calibrating logs

No log can be relied upon to be 100% accurate. This is particularly true of hull-mounted logs because – quite apart from any inherent inaccuracies in the instrument itself – the gradual build-up of fouling as the season progresses means that the boat is dragging an ever-thickening layer of water along with it, so the water flow past the impeller will be slower than the boat speed through the water. Conversely, around some parts of the hull, such as alongside a sailing boat's keel or near the propellers of a motorboat, the water flow may actually be accelerated, making the log over-read.

Errors can always be allowed for if you know about them, and most electronic logs have a calibration facility that allows them to be adjusted to take account of these variations. Finding, and if necessary correcting, log error is known as calibration. In principle it involves measuring the time taken to cover a known distance, using this to calculate true speed, and comparing this with the speed indicated by the log. Any accurately-known distance can be used, though the best are undoubtedly the 'measured distances' set up specially for the purpose. They consist of two (or sometimes three) pairs of transit posts, marking the start and finish of a precisely-measured distance, and shown on the appropriate chart. The course to steer to cover the measured distance is also shown.

Settle the boat on course and at a steady speed before crossing the first transit line; note the time at which you cross the start line and hold that course and speed without making any allowance for wind or tide until you cross the finish line, and note the time taken. Note the actual log reading at intervals of, say, 15 seconds so that you can work out the average log speed for the whole run.

The principle is that distance ÷ time = speed. The snag is that the distance is fixed, but the log is measuring speed through the water. If the water was perfectly still, it would be no problem, but still water is so rare that in practice it is important to repeat the process in the opposite direction. You can use the distance and time taken to work out the speed in each direction. From that, work out the average speed by adding the two speeds together and dividing by two, and compare the average with the averaged log speed.

A more accurate result can be obtained by making four or six runs, but this can be a very time-consuming process, especially as log errors are not necessarily the same at all speeds, so the calibration runs need to be carried out at a range of different speeds, and repeated as a double-check after the log has been adjusted.

A common mistake is to work out the average

time taken and divide the distance by this. The result invariably understates the boat's speed, because it must have been travelling in the 'slow' direction longer than in the 'fast' direction.

Example

Measured distance:	1 nautical mile (1852 m)
Time (First run):	2 min 36 sec
Time (Second run):	2 min 55 sec
Logspeed:	23.2 kts
First run:	36 sec ÷ 60 = 0.60 min 2.60 min ÷ 60 = 0.043 hrs 1 mile in 0.043 hrs = 1 ÷ 0.043 = 23.25 kts
Second run:	55 sec ÷ 60 = 0.92 min 2.92 min ÷ 60 = 0.049 hrs 1 mile in 0.049 hrs = 1 ÷ 0.049 = 20.41 kts
Average speed:	(23.25 + 20.41) ÷ 2 = 21.83 kts
Error:	23.2 − 21.8 = 1.4 over-read 1.4 ÷ 23.2 × 100 = 6% over-read

Measuring distance on the chart

Some large scale charts (harbour plans) have a clearly marked scale of distance – rather like the one you might find on a road atlas – usually printed somewhere near the bottom edge. But this is not always the case, and on

Fig 12 Bow dividers, which can be used with one hand, are ideal for measuring distances on a chart.

the smaller scale charts used for coastal and offshore navigation it would be impractical to provide such a scale because the scale of the chart varies slightly from top to bottom. One sea mile, however, is by definition one minute of latitude, so the latitude scales on each side of the chart constitute a scale of distance.

The slight difference between a sea mile and an international nautical mile is so small that for normal navigation it can be ignored: what is important, on small scale charts, is the distortion caused by the Mercator projection, which means that distance has to be measured at the latitude at which it is to be used. The longitude scale on the top and bottom edges of the chart is useless as a scale of distance.

It is relatively rare to find ourselves faced with the job of measuring distance in an exactly north–south line, so we need some means of transferring the distance between any two points on the chart to the latitude scale. **Dividers** are the tool for the job. For classroom navigation the kind of dividers used in technical drawing are perfectly adequate, and their sharp needle points give a reassuring sense of precision, but for practical navigation, traditional bow dividers have the big advantage that they can be opened and closed with one hand, by squeezing the bow to open them, and squeezing the legs to close them.

Sometimes it is necessary to draw arcs of measured radius on the chart, for which it is useful to have a drawing compass. Again, the type intended for technical drawing can be used so long as it is big enough, but it is generally better to use the larger and less sophisticated versions intended for marine navigation.

Measuring direction at sea

Direction at sea is measured using a compass – essentially an instrument which points north, and goes on pointing north regardless of the movement of the boat around it. In practice most yachts carry at least two compasses. One, the steering compass, is relatively large, fixed to the boat, and used to measure heading. The other is usually smaller, portable and is used to measure the direction of distant objects, so it is called a hand-bearing compass. Sometimes one compass can do both jobs: on many ships and a few large yachts an attachment called a pelorus allows the steering compass to be used for taking bearings, while on very small craft, a hand-bearing compass clipped into a bracket can serve as a steering compass.

There are many ways of making an instrument that will stay pointing in one direction, including gyroscopes, and what are called 'ring laser gyros', but although these have their advantages, they are much too sophisticated, and therefore expensive, to be of practical interest for yachts. The overwhelming majority of yacht compasses depend on magnetism, and in that respect can be seen as direct developments from instruments that were probably in use several thousand years ago. Compasses make use of the fact that the earth has a magnetic field, which is very much as though a huge bar magnet were embedded in its core and aligned with its north–south axis.

Any magnet that is free to swing tends to line itself up with the earth's magnetic field. This effect is particularly obvious in the small, flat compasses used for orienteering and rambling on land, in which a single straight needle-like magnet gives a direct indication of north. In marine compasses, several such magnets, or a single magnet in the shape of a ring, are mounted underneath a circular 'card', with a scale of degrees or compass points marked on it. The whole thing is suspended in a bowl filled with a mixture of water and alcohol, which slows down the movement of the card, to reduce the swinging that would otherwise be caused by the pitching and rolling of the boat.

Compasses intended for fast motorboats are much more heavily damped than those intended for sailing craft; the rapid slamming of a planing boat can be enough to make the card of a sailboat compass rotate continuously.

Steering compasses

On a steering compass the fore-and-aft line of the boat is marked by a line or pointer on the compass bowl, called the lubber line, against which the boat's current heading can be read from the card, so it is obviously important for the compass to be installed so that the lubber line is accurately aligned with, or parallel to, the centreline of the boat. Many compasses have supplementary lubber lines offset by 45° and 90° on each side, intended mainly for use in situations such as tiller-steered boats where the helmsman is likely to be looking at the compass from one side or the other.

Of course, there are variations intended to suit particular applications. On many small and medium sized sailing yachts, where cockpit space is at a premium, the compass is set into the aft bulkhead of the superstructure, so that the rear edge of the card is visible, rather than its upper surface. A compass intended for this type of mounting has an aft lubber line and a scale of degrees marked on the downturned rim of the card. An even more extreme variation is occasionally found in compasses intended for steel craft, whose structure effectively masks the compass from the earth's magnetic field. This problem can be reduced by mounting the compass as high above the hull as possible, so compasses have been produced that can be mounted on the wheelhouse roof, with mirrors or prisms arranged so that the helmsman effectively looks upwards at the bottom of the compass card.

Fig 13a A bulkhead-mounted steering compass on a sailing cruiser.

Grid compasses, intended primarily for aircraft navigation, enjoyed a surge of popularity after the Second World War, when many boats were fitted out from Army surplus stores! The claim that they were easier to steer by maintained their popularity for at least 20 years and several marinized versions were produced. A grid compass has a card with a particularly prominent north mark, set in a flat-topped bowl. On top of the bowl is a transparent cover, marked with a grid of parallel lines and with a scale of degrees around its edge. The required course is 'set' by rotating the cover, and the helmsman then steers so as to keep the north mark on the card lined up with the grid.

Hand-bearing compasses

A hand-bearing compass is basically a small, portable version of a steering compass, fitted with some form of sighting arrangement that allows it to be accurately lined up on a distant object (Figure 14). They can be subdivided into two groups: those intended to be used at arm's

length, which are usually fitted with a handle; and those intended to be held close to the eye, which are usually supplied with a neck strap. Which kind is best is very much a matter of personal preference, but anyone who uses spectacles or a hearing aid is well advised to go for an arm's-length compass because even small pieces of ferrous metal such as the hinges of spectacles can cause compass errors if they are only inches away.

Sighting arrangements vary. The classic Sestrel Radiant, for instance, has a prism mounted above the bowl, with a V-shaped notch on top. When the compass is held up at arm's length and eye level the lubber line and compass card can be seen in the prism. To take a bearing of a distant object, you line up the 'target' with the notch, rotate the compass until the lubber line appears in the prism immediately below the target, and then read off the bearing. Another common arrangement has two sights on top of the bowl, like the fore sight and back sight of a gun, and an edge-reading compass card.

Fig 13b A flush-mounted steering compass on a fast sportsboat.

Fig 14 A hand-bearing compass. On this type, the fore sight and back sight are inside the compass bowl.

Close-to-the-eye compasses do not have such obvious sighting arrangements: instead they have a small prism mounted on top, whose optics are arranged in such a way that when you look at a landmark across the top of the compass, its bearing appears in the prism immediately below.

Fluxgate compasses

A new type of compass is rapidly gaining in popularity. Unlike a conventional 'swinging card' compass, a fluxgate compass has no moving parts, but instead uses electronics to detect the earth's magnetic field and present that information on some kind of display. A fluxgate depends on the phenomenon of electromagnetic induction – as used in transformers and the ignition coil of a petrol engine. If you pass an electric current through a coil of wire wound around a suitable metal core, the core becomes a magnet. Which end is the north pole, and which the south, depends on the direction of the current flow in the wire, so if you apply an alternating current to the wire, the north and south poles of the core change places each time the current reverses. If you have a second coil of wire wound around this whole assembly the constantly-reversing magnetic field induces an electric current in the secondary winding (Figure 15).

In a fluxgate there are two cores side by side, with their primary windings receiving alternating current from the same source, but wound in opposite directions. This means that in a magnetically 'clean' environment (with no external magnetic influences) the induced magnetism in the two cores would be equal and opposite, so they would cancel each other out and produce no current at all in the secondary winding that surrounds both of

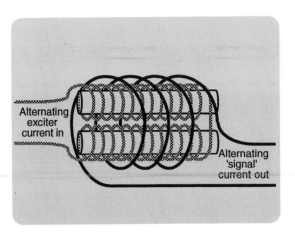

Alternating exciter current in

Alternating 'signal' current out

Fig 15 A fluxgate element – one of several at the heart of the most popular types of electronic compass.

them. The presence of an external magnetic field upsets the balance, causing a short surge of electricity in the secondary winding each time the primary current reverses. This effect is most pronounced if the two cores are parallel to the external magnetic field. In a practical fluxgate compass, several fluxgates are arranged in a circle. By comparing the voltages induced in the various secondary windings it is possible to deduce where north is relative to the ring of fluxgates.

At present, the most common use of this technology is to provide heading information for other electronic equipment such as autopilots or radars, but it can also be used to provide a steering display for the helmsman or as the heart of an electronic hand-bearing compass. Apart from the ease with which fluxgate compasses can be connected to other navigational electronics, their big advantages are that they can be fitted with an automatic correction facility to minimize the effect of deviation (see page 24); and that because the sensor and display are usually separate from each other, the sensor can be mounted anywhere on board and well away from distorting magnetic influences.

Their main disadvantage is that very large errors can occur if the fluxgate ring is not kept perfectly horizontal. There are electronic solutions to this problem, but the fact remains that 'the compass with no moving parts' actually requires more sophisticated gimbal arrangements than its swinging card counterparts.

Variation

All magnetic compasses – fluxgate or swinging card – measure direction relative to the earth's magnetic field. This is almost in line with the earth's north–south spin axis, but not quite. At present the north magnetic pole is amongst the islands of north Canada, some 600 miles from the true North Pole. This creates a discrepancy called variation between magnetic north (shown by a magnetic compass) and true north corresponding to the meridians on a chart. Variation varies from place to place, and from year to year: in the central Mediterranean and western Baltic, for instance, it is negligible, but on the west coast of Ireland and Scotland magnetic north is almost 10° W of true north.

Variation is always shown on the navigational chart, usually printed in the centre of the compass roses in the form '5° 10' W 2002 (10' E)'. This means that in 2002 magnetic north was 5° 10' west of true north. The figure in brackets means that it was moving east at ten minutes per year, so by 2010 it should have reduced to 3° 50'. For practical purposes this can be rounded off to the nearest degree – 4° W.

For various reasons it is impossible to predict the rate of change with any accuracy in advance, so the information given on charts more than five years old should be treated with some suspicion, even if the rest of the chart has been kept up to date. Isogonic charts showing variation and its annual change over very wide areas are published at five-yearly intervals, but a more practical approach is simply to take the variation from the most up-to-date chart of the area you have available, even if it is not the one you are navigating on at the time.

If you know about an error you can always allow for it – in this case by a simple arithmetical process.

> *To convert from Magnetic to True*, easterly variation should be added, or westerly variation subtracted.
>
> *Converting from True to Magnetic* is the reverse: westerly variation should be added and easterly variations subtracted.

So if the variation is 4° W and you want the helmsman to steer a course of 200° T (True), you should give him a course of 204° M (Magnetic):

200° (T) + 4° W = 204° (M)

Conversely, if you have taken a bearing of 150° with a magnetic compass, it should be plotted on a chart as 146° T (True):

150° (M) – 4° W = 146° (T)

There are various mnemonics (see page 28) to help remember whether to add or subtract variation, but one of the best ways of all is to lay a straight edge across the centre of a compass rose and see whether the numbers on the magnetic ring are higher or lower than the corresponding numbers on the true ring. If the variation has changed less than one degree since the chart was published, comparison of the true and magnetic rings can even be used to give a direct conversion, completely eliminating the risk of arithmetical errors.

Magnetic anomalies

In some areas, large naturally-occurring deposits of magnetic rock cause local distortions of the earth's magnetic field. Man-made features, including some power cables or large metal structures such as wrecks or pipelines, can have a similar effect. The man-made ones are usually so localized that you

would have to be extremely unlucky for them to have any real significance. The natural ones are less common but cover larger areas: they are marked on charts with a note giving any available information.

Deviation

Metal structures and electrical cables within the boat itself are much closer to the compass, and can therefore have a much greater distorting effect on it, giving rise to an error called **deviation**.

Beyond the simple statement that deviation is caused by electricity, magnetism and ferrous

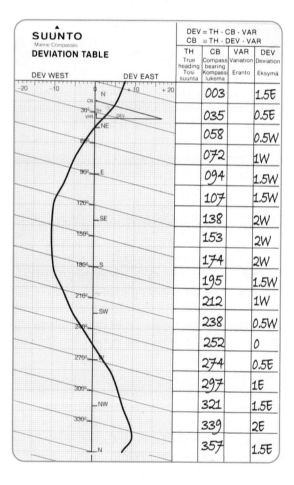

DEV = TH · CB · VAR			
CB = TH · DEV · VAR			
TH	CB	VAR	DEV
True heading	Compass bearing	Variation	Deviation
Tosi suunta	Kompassi lukema	Eranto	Eksymä
003			1.5E
035			0.5E
058			0.5W
072			1W
094			1.5W
107			1.5W
138			2W
153			2W
174			2W
195			1.5W
212			1W
238			0.5W
252			0
274			0.5E
297			1E
321			1.5E
339			2E
357			1.5E

Fig 16 A deviation card, like this, is drawn up by a compass adjuster, giving details of the deviation affecting a fixed compass.

metals on board the boat itself, a full explanation of it would be surprisingly complex: some idea of just how complex can be gained from the fact that although magnetic compasses have been in use for thousands of years, as late as the mid-nineteenth century the Admiralty felt it necessary to set up a committee to investigate what they described as this 'evil so pregnant with mischief'. Only 100 years before, Captain Cook had regarded the compass binnacle as a handy place to keep his iron keys! We can laugh at that now, but many modern yachtsmen and boatbuilders commit even worse magnetic blunders by surrounding their steering compasses with loudspeakers, electronic displays, power distribution boards and engine monitoring instruments, all of which can set up powerful magnetic fields.

Deviation can be minimized by taking care to site such equipment as far from the compass as possible. In the case of electronic instruments the equipment usually carries a label indicating its 'compass safe distance' – the distance at which that particular item will deviate the compass by less than one degree. Almost inevitably though, on a modern boat there will be some deviating components, such as engines and keels, that cannot be moved. These deviating influences can be counteracted, at least to some extent, by a compass adjuster, who places a combination of small needle-like magnets and soft iron rods around and inside the compass casing in an effort to cancel out the boat's own magnetism. He will then draw up a deviation card showing the remaining deviation.

Because deviation is caused by the boat's magnetic field, its direction and extent depend on which way the boat is pointing: it will be negligible when the boat's magnetic field is parallel to that of the earth and greatest when the two are at right angles to each other. For this reason the compass adjuster presents his results in the form of a table, showing the deviation on various headings.

Compass adjustment is a specialized job, and not one for the do-it-yourselfer. Measuring deviation, however, is a relatively straightforward task that should be done at least once a year, and after any repair or maintenance work that may have affected the magnetic characteristics of the boat.

Swinging for deviation

There are many possible ways of measuring deviation but they all involve comparing the direction indicated by the compass with the actual direction known by some other reliable means. This process is called **swinging the compass.**

Perhaps the most straightforward method is known as the 'swing by distant objects'. This involves taking the boat to an accurately-known position, then turning it round to point straight at each of several distant landmarks in turn. The true bearing of each mark can be found from the chart and converted to a magnetic bearing by applying variation. Comparing the known magnetic bearing with the corresponding compass heading gives the deviation. If the compass heading is less than the magnetic bearing the deviation is named east; if the compass bearing is the greater the deviation is named west.

Exactly how distant the 'distant objects' should be depends on the precision required and the accuracy of your known position. It is normal to aim for an accuracy of about one degree, in which case every 100 metres of possible error in position requires at least three miles distance between the boat and the landmarks.

Suitable position fixing methods include the intersection of two transits (see next section), circling very close to a charted wooden pile or around a navigational buoy. Buoys are much easier to find than suitable piles or transits, but they are not nearly as good for the purpose, partly because they are usually made of steel and can therefore induce their own local magnetic anomaly if you get too close to them, and partly because they can lie some distance downtide of their charted positions. If you have to use a buoy, stay at least 50–100 metres away from it to minimize the effect of deviation, and take care to use landmarks that are far enough away to minimize the effect of any possible position error.

Compass check by transits

Any two objects that appear to be in line with each other form a transit, and your line of sight along the transit can be drawn on a chart simply by ruling a straight line through the two landmarks concerned. Transits have many navigational uses, but in this context they are useful because it is easy to point a boat straight along a transit and it is equally simple to measure the true bearing of the transit on a chart. One drawback of this method is that it is not always easy to find enough transits in different directions to draw up a complete deviation card, though even a single transit can be useful as a quick check.

Swing by comparison

If you know the deviation on one compass, it can be used as a reference against which to measure the deviation on another. A common application of this is on flybridge motor cruisers. The upper steering position usually has excellent visibility and few sources of deviation, so producing a deviation card by distant objects or transits is a relatively straightforward matter. The deviation on the lower compass can then be found by comparing it with the indicated heading on the upper compass.

Deviation of hand-bearing compasses

A hand-bearing compass can be used anywhere on board, in positions which can have very different effects on its deviation. This makes it impractical to correct a hand bearing compass by fitting corrector magnets,

and equally impractical to draw up a deviation card for it. Because it is better to apply no correction than risk adding deviation when it should be subtracted, it is normal practice to assume that its deviation is nil.

It cannot be stressed too strongly, however, that this is only a convenient assumption: when using a hand-bearing compass it is important to be aware of possible sources of deviation in the vicinity including equipment such as anchors, gas bottles, galvanized rigging, radar scanners and other compasses, to name but a few. It also follows from this that a hand-bearing compass can only be used as a standard against which to measure the deviation of the steering compass if you can be absolutely certain that it is in a spot completely free of deviating influences.

Deviation and fluxgate compasses

Fluxgate compasses, too, are affected by deviation, though they have the advantage that the sensor can be located anywhere on board – even on top of a mast. Most also include an auto-correction facility. Different models have different correction procedures for which you should consult the manufacturer's manual.

Heeling error

Compasses are usually corrected and deviation cards drawn up with the boat upright, even though sailing boats in particular do not always operate in this position! When the boat heels, its magnetic geometry changes: the keel, for instance, may be vertically below the compass when the boat is upright, but moves out to port when the boat heels over on port tack. In some cases this can have a noticeable effect on the steering compass, known as heeling error. Heeling error can be measured and reduced, but it is a job for a professional compass adjuster.

Allowing for deviation

Once you know the deviation, it can be allowed for in exactly the same way as variation:

> *To convert from Compass to Magnetic,* easterly variation should be added, or westerly variation subtracted.
>
> *Converting from Magnetic to Compass is* the reverse: westerly variation should be added and easterly variations subtracted.

So if the deviation is 3° west and you want the helmsman to steer a course of 204°M (Magnetic), you should give him a course of 207°C (Compass).

$$204°(M) + 3°W = 207°(C)$$

SUUNTO Marine Compasses DEVIATION TABLE		DEV = TH - CB - VAR CB = TH - DEV - VAR		
		TH True heading Tosi suunta	CB Compass bearing Kompassi lukema	VAR Variation Eranto	DEV Deviation Eksymä
DEV WEST	DEV EAST				
		003			14W
		035			10W
		058			7W
		072			3W
		094			4E
		107			6E
		138			13E
		153			15E
		174			17E
		195			15E
		212			8E
		238			5E
		252			1E

Fig 17 An unadjusted compass, or one in a magnetically 'difficult' position, may have very large amounts of deviation, and calls for particular care (see text).

Despite the similarity, it is worth getting into the habit of regarding the conversion between compass and magnetic as quite separate from the conversion between magnetic and true, and carrying them out as two distinct processes, rather than adopting the 'short cut' of adding variation and deviation together and regarding them as a single error.

The reason for this becomes particularly apparent if you imagine yourself navigating a boat with an uncorrected compass in an area with a large variation (20°W).

Suppose you want to steer a course of 070° (T). From the deviation card in Figure 17, the deviation on a heading of 075° is 1°W, and on 060° it is 5°W – so on 070° one might expect the deviation to be about 2°W. Adding this to the variation of 20°W produces a 'total error' of 22°W – giving a compass course of 070° + 22° = 092° (C).

Applying variation and deviation separately gives a different – and more accurate – result, because 070° (T) + 20° = 090° (M). The deviation card shows that on a heading of 090° the deviation is 3°E, so the compass course required is: 090° – 3° = 087°.

Second error correction

When the deviation is also large, a further refinement is needed in order to achieve an accurate result. Suppose, for instance, the course required is 120° (T). Allowing for variation converts this to 120° + 20° = 140° (M). From the deviation card in Figure 17, the deviation for 140° is 13°E, suggesting a compass course of 140° – 13 = 127°(C).

On a course of 127°(C), however, the deviation is only 11° – giving a compass course of 140° – 11° = 129°(C). Checking, by converting it back to true, reveals that this is, indeed, the right answer. The reason this apparently tortuous process is required is that the deviation card is referred to compass heading: so a first, approximate, calculation is needed in order to find an approximate compass heading before the deviation card can

MNEMONICS

'True Virgins Make Dull Companions' gives the letters TVMDC, as a reminder that Variation (V) separates True (T) and Magnetic (M), and that Deviation (D) separates Magnetic and Compass (C).

'CAdET' is a reminder that to go from Compass (C) to True (T) you have to Add (Ad) Easterly (E) errors.

'Error east, Compass least; Error west, Compass best' is an alternative to the 'Cadet' rule that is particularly useful as a double check, or to work out deviation after a compass swing. It says that easterly errors make the compass heading smaller (least) than the true heading, while westerly errors make the compass heading bigger ('best').

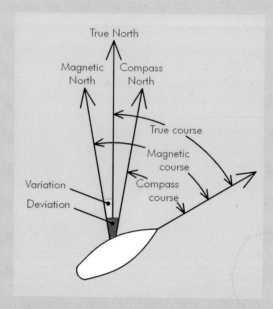

Fig 18 Variation is the difference between true and magnetic north: deviation is the difference between magnetic and compass north.

be used to find the appropriate figure for deviation.

Measuring direction on the chart

Direction is indicated in two ways: by the grid of intersecting north–south meridians at east–west parallels; and by compass roses each with a graduated ring of 360 marks at 1° intervals. Some, though not all, have a second, inner ring, slightly skewed from the outer ring, showing directions relative to magnetic north (see page 24).

Just as the distance you want to measure seldom runs north–south, so directions seldom run conveniently through the middle of a compass rose, making some means of transferring directions round the chart just as

important as dividers. There is quite a choice of devices available for the purpose.

Traditional parallel rulers

Traditional parallel rulers consist of two straight rulers, joined together by pivoting arms which allow the rulers to be moved apart while keeping their edges parallel, so that they can be 'walked' across the chart while preserving their alignment. Using them quickly and accurately takes practice and demands a flat unobstructed chart table but they are still the preferred choice of many experienced navigators.

Rolling parallel rulers

A rolling parallel ruler is a single wide ruler fitted with a pair of rollers fixed to a single shaft. This means that the ruler can be rolled from one place to another whilst preserving its

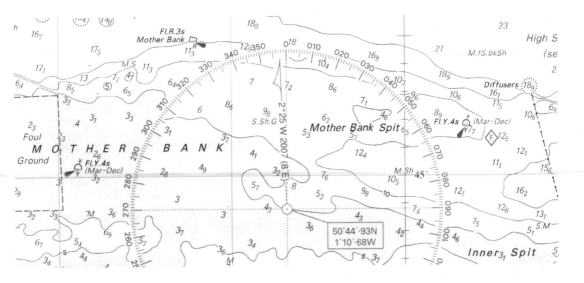

Fig 19 A compass rose shows direction on the chart: notice the arrow showing magnetic north and the note about variation.

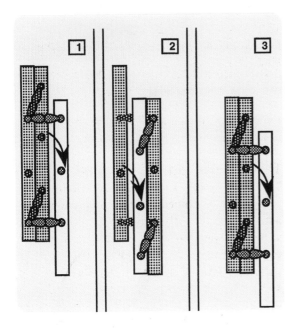

Fig 20 'Walking' parallel rulers are the traditional tool for transfering direction to and from the compass rose.

alignment. A rolling parallel is much quicker and easier to use than the traditional type, but in order to be effective it has to be bigger and

demands an even larger chart table, so they are really only of practical use on ships or very large pleasure craft.

Douglas protractor

An alternative way of measuring directions on the chart is by using one of many different types of protractor. These have their own scale of degrees so they do not rely on compass roses and do not, therefore, have to be moved around the chart. Using them calls for less manual dexterity than parallel rulers, but in most cases more mental dexterity.

The Douglas protractor has long been popular with air navigators, though it was originally devised for marine use. It consists of a square of stiff transparent plastic – five inches or ten inches for a genuine Douglas protractor, though other sizes are available from different manufacturers. Around its edge are two rows of markings from 0 to 360°, with an outer scale reading in a clockwise direction and an inner scale running anticlockwise. Inside these is a grid of equally-spaced lines, parallel to the edges of the protractor; and right in the centre is a small hole.

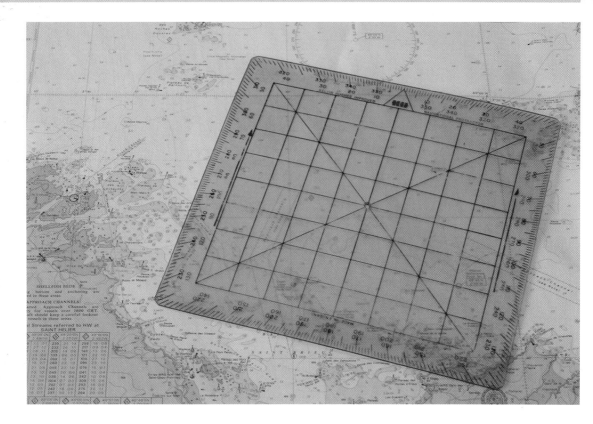

Fig 21 A Kelvin Hughes protractor – a larger and thicker variant of the Douglas protractor.

The most intuitive way of using a Douglas protractor to measure the direction of a line on the chart is simply to place it on the chart, with the central hole on the line and its grid aligned, by eye, with the nearest meridians and parallels. The direction of the line can then be read directly from the clockwise scale.

A similar technique can be used to draw a line in a particular direction: place the central hole of the protractor over the starting point of the line, ensure that the protractor's grid is lined up with the meridians and parallels, and make a light pencil mark on the chart alongside the required direction on the outer (clockwise) scale. Then move the protractor and use its edge to rule a straight line from the starting point through the pencil mark.

An alternative method makes use of the inner (anticlockwise) scale. This time the

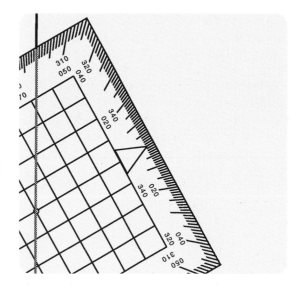

Fig 21a A Douglas protractor is a popular alternative to parallel rulers, especially on small boats.

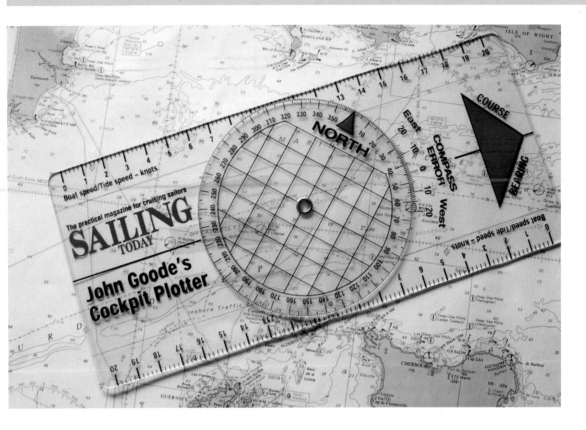

Fig 22 One of the many variations on the Breton-style plotter.

central hole is placed on the meridian and the protractor rotated until the mark corresponding to the required direction lies on the same meridian. Two edges of the protractor now lie in the required direction – the two parallel to the protractor's north–south line. Keeping this alignment, slide the protractor up or down the meridian until one of these edges passes through the starting point of the line you wish to draw, and then pencil it in. This method sounds tortuous, but with practice it often turns out to be quicker and slightly more accurate than the other.

Breton plotter

The Breton plotter and its several variants are a more recent development, but have gained enormous popularity amongst amateur navigators. It consists of a rectangular piece of

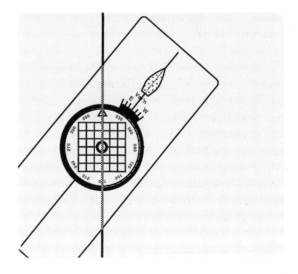

Fig 22a A Breton plotter incorporates a rotating protractor that can be aligned with the meridians and parallels to serve as a mobile compass rose.

transparent plastic with a circular protractor fixed to it, but free to rotate. In the centre of the protractor is a squared grid. Once the grid has been aligned with the meridians and parallels on the chart, the main body of the protractor can be rotated and the direction of its long edges read off directly from the protractor scale. In practice, when using the plotter to measure the direction of a pre-drawn line, it is easier to get the plotter base lined up with the line first and then rotate the protractor, and when drawing, to set the required direction on the instrument before placing it on the chart and sliding it around as necessary to get the grid aligned with the chart. One advantage of the Breton plotter is a supplementary scale on the base plate. Variation (see page 23) can be allowed for by aligning the rotating protractor with the appropriate mark on this scale, rather than with the plotter's centre-line.

Hurst plotter

The Hurst plotter (and its variants) is another type of protractor-based plotting instrument. This one has a square base-plate, on top of which is a 360° protractor that can be clamped firmly in place. Between the base-plate and the protractor is a pivoting arm. The protractor can either be lined up with the grid, to work in 'True' directions, or it can be deliberately offset to work in 'Magnetic' (see page 24), and then locked in place. A grid on the base-plate allows it to be aligned with the meridians or parallels on the chart, so the protractor then serves as a compass rose that can be positioned anywhere on the chart, while the arm forms a straight edge that can be swung around to point in any direction, but which always lines up with the centre of the protractor.

Captain Field's pattern parallel rulers

Most of the parallel rulers in use nowadays, whether of the 'walking' or rolling type, are of the 'Captain Field's pattern', marked with an

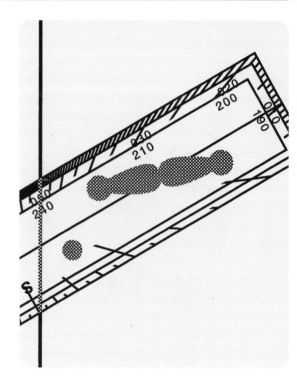

Fig 23 Captain Field's pattern parallel rulers combine some of the advantages of parallel rulers and protractors in one instrument.

anticlockwise scale of degrees. This combines many of the advantages of both parallel rulers and protractors, because when the rulers are in their closed position, they can be placed directly on the chart in much the same way as a Douglas protractor. The only difference is that the protractor's central hole is replaced by a mark on the middle of one of the rulers – usually identified by the letter S or an arrow. Keeping the S mark on any convenient meridian, rotate the rulers (keeping them closed) until the required direction on the scale crosses the same meridian. The rulers are now lined up and their precise position can be adjusted if necessary by opening or closing them.

Choosing a plotter

There is an enormous variety of plotting tools available, of which parallel rulers, Douglas

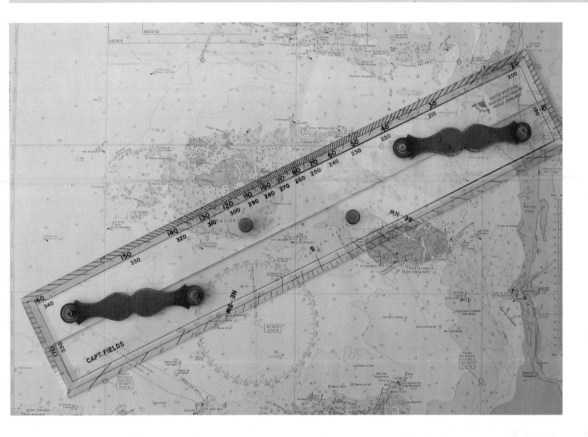

Fig 23a Captain Field's pattern parallel rulers.

protractors and Hurst and Breton plotters are only the most popular. It is worth mastering at least one or two of these common plotting tools, if only because they are the ones you are most likely to come across on friends' boats, charter craft, or deliveries, but it is also worth experimenting with others whenever the opportunity arises, because 'which one is best?' is very much a matter of personal opinion.

Chartwork

It almost goes without saying that chartwork should be as accurate as possible: the precision expected during Yachtmaster shore-based courses – 0.1 mile and 1° – may not always be practical at sea in a small boat, but it is a good target to aim for. Even this degree of precision can be achieved without resorting to the

engineering draughtsman's hard and super-sharp pencil: soft (2B) pencils leave a much clearer line, are less damaging to the chart, and much easier to rub out. On charts made of synthetic, plastic paper it can even be worth using a softer pencil still, up to 4B. Hard pencils and ballpoint pens have no place anywhere near a chart other than for chart correcting! In the interests of clarity it is also important to be able to remove superfluous lines so a rubber is essential, and in the interests of the chart this too should be as soft as possible.

The skipper who does all his own navigating can use any signs, symbols and abbreviations he likes on the chart. But on larger boats or longer passages, where there is the slightest possibility that more than one person may be involved, it is essential that all the members of the navigating team are able to understand each other's chartwork. So it is worth getting into the habit of using the standard chartwork symbols shown in Figure 24.

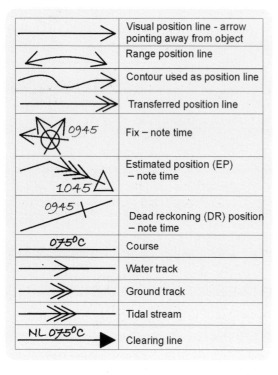

	Visual position line - arrow pointing away from object
	Range position line
	Contour used as position line
	Transferred position line
0945	Fix – note time
1045	Estimated position (EP) – note time
0945	Dead reckoning (DR) position – note time
075°C	Course
	Water track
	Ground track
	Tidal stream
NL 075°C	Clearing line

Fig 24 Standard chartwork symbols are always useful, and essential if there is more than one navigator on board.

The chart table

The size, shape and surroundings of a chart table are usually determined by the designer and builder of the boat, and sadly nowadays often seem to take second place to more superficially attractive features such as stereo systems and cocktail cabinets. But there is no doubt that a good chart table makes navigation considerably easier. Whether it faces fore-and-aft or athwartships does not seem to make much difference: what is important is that the navigator should be able to brace himself in position against the motion of the boat while leaving both hands free.

It should be flat, without hinges or joints to interrupt the movement of chartwork instruments, and as big as possible. A reasonable minimum size is 20½ in by 14 in (520 mm by 355 mm), because that is one quarter of an Admiralty chart. It needs something to stop the chart falling off, stowage for pencils, rubbers and instruments, reference books and other charts – and for night passages, a light. Traditionally chart table lights are red, as this was thought to have a less damaging effect on night vision than any other colour, but this is not, in fact, the case and a white or green light is perfectly acceptable so long as it is dim.

Electronic Navigation Equipment

Marine electronics have boomed over the last thirty years or so, with equipment becoming more sophisticated, more reliable and yet cheaper. Fifty years ago (about the time the first GRP boats were being built) an echo sounder weighed half a hundredweight and cost £300. For that price you could buy a new small car, so most yachtsmen relied on the lead and line for measuring depth. Now, you can buy a fish finder that will show the shape of the seabed as well as its depth for £100, while another £100 or so will buy you a satellite 'navigator' that can give you your position accurate to a matter of yards anywhere in the world by day or night.

So available and reliable are modern electronics, that it is tempting to wonder whether so called 'traditional' navigation is still

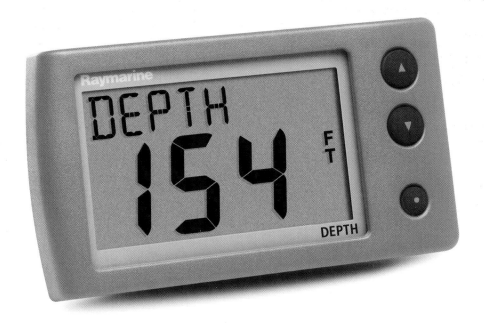

Fig 25 A compact and user-friendly digital echo sounder.

of any value. But while modern electronics very rarely 'fail' in the technical sense of the word, they are still vulnerable to broken or corroded wiring, to external influences such as radio interference and – perhaps most common of all – to human operators who either press the wrong buttons or misread the information on their displays.

A seamanlike approach to electronics is neither to ignore them altogether nor to be totally dependent on them, but to regard them as additional sources of information with their own strengths and weaknesses which – like those of a compass – need to be understood and kept in mind.

Echo sounders

An echo sounder, for measuring depth, is now virtually standard equipment on all but the smallest and simplest of boats. It works by transmitting pulses, or clicks, of ultrasonic sound from a transducer mounted on board, down to the seabed, and then receiving the returning echoes. Although the speed of sound in water varies slightly, it is always in the order of 1400 metres per second, so the time taken for each pulse to complete a down and back trip depends on the depth of water.

The most readily-understood timing system is that used in the 'rotating neon' type of sounder, in which the heart of the display unit is a fast-spinning rotor with a neon lamp or light-emitting diode at its end. Each time the rotor passes the upright position, the light flashes and the transducer is triggered to transmit its pulse. When the returning echo is detected by the transducer, the light flashes again, but by this time the rotor has moved on. How far it has moved depends on the time interval between transmission and reception, so the depth of water is indicated by the position of the second flash. It can be read directly off a scale marked on the face of the instrument around the window that covers the rotor.

For operation in deep water, the rotor speed can be slowed down, increasing the range of time intervals that can be measured and increasing the time between successive pulses, but reducing the accuracy and precision of the depth measurement.

With practice the appearance of the returning flash gives a clue to the nature of the seabed: a hard seabed such as rock produces a crisp echo which appears as a short flash; while a very soft bottom such as mud or weed gives a more drawn-out echo and produces a more diffuse or drawn-out flash. Sometimes, however, the echo sounder can be misleading.

Air bubbles are good reflectors of sound waves, so turbulence caused by the wash of passing ships can produce a mass of shallow flashes. The swim bladders of fish also contain air, so a single large fish can produce a brief flash, while a dense shoal of small fish produces a more consistent flash at a depth corresponding to the depth of the shoal. Fishermen find this useful and the echo sounder principle has been developed into fish finders, but for navigation purposes such echoes are simply a nuisance. Luckily, they are usually easy to identify because they are short-lived and erratic.

Another type of spurious flash can sometimes be seen in shallow waters over a hard bottom, and is caused by the returning echo reflecting back from the sea surface to make a second trip down to the seabed and back. If this second echo is strong enough to register on the echo sounder, it is called a reflection echo and appears as a relatively weak flash at twice the true depth.

A particularly worrying type of spurious echo can be produced by hard bottoms when the water is so deep that the echo does not return until after the rotor has completed one full revolution. The returning echo produces a flash on the display which is considerably shallower than the true depth: if, for instance, the echo sounder is set to an operating range of 0–25 metres and the true depth is 30 metres, the indicated depth will be 5 metres. Fortunately these second trace echoes can easily be identified by switching to a deeper operating scale which will indicate the true depth.

Recording paper sounders

Although they look very different and are much more expensive, recording paper echo sounders use much the same timing system as rotating neons, except that instead of a flashing light the timing display is a stylus or 'electric pen'. This is mechanically swept across a moving roll of special paper – similar to that used in fax machines – producing a mark each time a pulse is transmitted and each time an echo is received. Like the flashes of a rotating neon sounder, the distance between these two marks corresponds to the depth. Over a period of time as the recording paper unrolls, successive traces build up to produce a continuous permanent record. Although they have their uses for some commercial operations and for surveying, recording paper sounders have no particular merit for pleasure craft, especially as the need to keep them supplied with recording paper is an expensive nuisance.

Electronic displays

Electronics manufacturers are seldom keen on mechanical components, and whatever the merits of rotating neon echo sounders their dependence on fast moving mechanical parts makes them potentially unreliable and power hungry, while possible variations in motor speed can make them inaccurate. As technology developed and electronic timing devices became a practical proposition, most of the more upmarket manufacturers offered display units that indicated the depth by means of a moving pointer on a graduated dial. Some of these units have survived, but they have been almost completely superseded by all-electronic displays giving either a digital read-out or a graphical presentation similar to the trace of a recording paper sounder.

Added features

An echo sounder is basically a simple instrument measuring a single quantity – depth – so there are few added features that can usefully be incorporated. Most, however, include a shallow water alarm which can be set to sound a bleeper when the indicated depth is shallower than a chosen limit, and many have a deep alarm which bleeps or flashes when a preset depth is exceeded.

A carefully-set shallow alarm has an obvious value as a warning function when operating in shoal water, and a deep alarm can be useful when anchored, as a reminder to let more cable out to cope with the rising tide. Used together, they can play a part in pilotage or in fog navigation, when they can be used to guide you between two contour lines (see page 128).

Installation and calibration

For an echo sounder to work, the transducer has to be able to send its pulses down to the seabed. Wood is a very effective insulator of sound, so in wooden boats a through-hull installation is essential, with the transducer mounted in a watertight housing so that its transmitting face is in direct contact with the sea water below. A similar set-up can be used in GRP or metal boats, but it is not essential because these materials transmit sound. In-hull mountings can be used, so long as there is no air gap or bubbles between the transducer and the hull skin. The transducer can be bonded directly to the hull with a layer of epoxy glue or (better) mounted in a tube bonded to the hull and filled with vegetable oil to exclude the air.

The location of the transducer needs to be chosen with some care to avoid turbulence and air bubbles caused by the boat's own movement. Manufacturers' manuals invariably offer advice on this, but on sailing boats and low speed motorboats it generally boils down to 'about one third of the way back from the stem but not too close to the keel'.

On planing motorboats this would be the

Fig 26 A compact fish-finder showing the shape of the seabed, and with arch-shaped mid-water echoes probably representing fish.

worst possible position and may even be out of the water altogether, so the transducer should be further aft – at least two-thirds of the way back.

The sound from the transducer is not transmitted equally in all directions, but is concentrated into a funnel-shaped beam, about 30° across – part of which has to point straight down to the seabed. This is seldom a problem for motorboats so long as the transducer is vertical, rather than at right angles to the hull skin. It can be more difficult to achieve in a sailing boat, either because the keel gets in the way, or because the boat heels more than 15°. If these problems cannot be overcome by careful siting of a single transducer, the usual solution is to have two transducers, one on each side of the boat, with a manual or gravity-operated changeover switch to select the lower one of the two.

The speed of sound in sea water is not absolutely constant, so survey ships calibrate their echo sounders by lowering an iron bar to a measured depth below the transducer and

adjusting the display to show the correct depth. This is impractical and unnecessary for yacht navigation, but most yacht sounders include a simpler calibration facility or 'keel offset' to allow either for the depth of the transducer below the waterline or for its height above the keel. Both have their advantages: depth below the keel errs on the side of pessimism, and it is easy to remember that if the echo sounder reads zero you are aground; depth below the waterline is of more use for navigational purposes, which may require the true depth of water.

On boats that can safely go aground, the most direct way of setting the keel offset to show depth below the keel is to put the boat aground deliberately, and adjust the keel offset to give an indicated depth of zero. On other boats, or to set the echo sounder to show depth below the waterline, the true depth can be found by lowering any suitable weight to the bottom on a piece of string, and the keel offset adjusted accordingly so that the indicated depth matches the measured depth.

Satnav

The expression 'satnav', or satellite navigation, covers a number of electronic positioning systems. Of these systems, the only one that is currently relevant to yachtsmen is GPS. It is quite likely, however, that GPS may be joined by two similar systems (the Russian Glonass and the European Galileo) within a few years.

Fig 26a Economical hand-held GPS receivers have revolutionised navigation.

GPS

Development of the Global Positioning System (GPS) began in 1973 and by the time the system was officially operational in 1995 thousands of British yachts already carried GPS receivers.

In many respects GPS has solved the problems of position fixing at a stroke, giving continuous worldwide coverage with an accuracy of a few metres. The GPS constellation consists of about two dozen satellites – the actual number varies as old satellites break down and new ones are launched – in orbit at an altitude of almost 11 000 nautical miles. Each satellite continuously transmits a coded signal on two microwave frequencies – roughly ten times higher than marine VHF – including a message that says 'I am here' and 'the time is now'. The codes used on the two frequencies are different and only one, called the CA code (for Coarse Acquisition), is available to civilian receivers, but their messages are essentially the same.

The signal takes time to travel from the satellite to the receiver, so it is received slightly later than it was sent. Microwaves, like any other radio waves, travel at an almost constant speed of 162 000 nautical miles per second, so the difference between the time of transmission and the time of reception corresponds to the distance between the satellite and the receiver. If the signal arrives one-tenth of a second after it was sent, the receiver is 16 200 miles from the satellite – that is, it is on the surface of a sphere with a radius of 16 200 miles, centred on the satellite.

Doing the same with another satellite gives a second sphere intersecting with the first to produce a circle. The only place where the receiver can be on both spheres at once is somewhere on that circle. Repeating the process with a third satellite narrows the possible position down to two points, and a fourth satellite removes any possible ambiguity. That, at least, is what would happen if the receiver's internal clock was precisely synchronized with the atomic clocks in the satellites, but in practice that is not the case. When we are dealing with radio waves, timing errors of as little as a millionth of a second produce large errors of distance, so the position spheres do not initially intersect at a point, but form a three dimensional version of the traditional navigator's 'cocked hat' (see

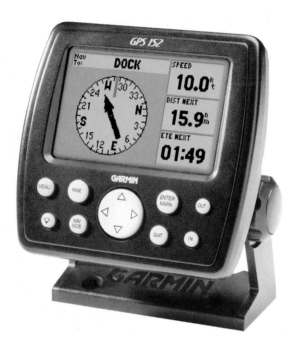

Fig 27 Stand-alone GPS sets have become relatively rare, but products such as this Garmin 152 are still available, and provide simple and cost-effective position fixing and basic navigation information.

page 51). The GPS receiver's computer is designed to recognize this problem, identify its most likely cause as clock error, and adjust its own clock accordingly until all the position spheres intersect as they should.

The geometry of GPS receivers

In order to produce a fix, a GPS receiver requires signals from four satellites. Most, however, can manage with only three, by using the surface of the earth as one of the position spheres. This is called a 2D (two-dimensional) fix, and whilst it may be acceptable for most navigational purposes, it is generally less accurate than a full 3D fix, because the earth is not such a neat geometric shape as the satellite range spheres.

There are a number of ways in which the GPS set's computer can be supplied with three or more satellite signals, of which the most obvious is to connect it to several separate microwave receivers. An alternative is to rely on a single receiver 'listening' to each of several satellites in turn – called multiplexing.

Accuracy and Selective Availability

The inherent accuracy of CA code GPS is about 15 metres (2σ). But it is owned and operated by the American Department of Defense, who did not want potential enemies to derive the full benefit of a system that had cost them over five billion dollars. Getting that five billion dollars out of their taxpayers, however, involved making a commitment to Congress that the system would be available to civilians. This posed a dilemma that was solved by a policy known as Selective Availability (SA). SA was not selective, nor did it have anything to do with availability: it involved the introduction of deliberate errors into the time and position information carried by the CA signal, to produce position errors of about 100 metres (2σ). SA was switched off in May 2000, with an assurance from the US Government

Fig 27a As the price of computing power and displays has fallen, chart plotters such as this Raymarine C70 have largely taken over from stand-alone GPS receivers.

that there was 'no intention' of reintroducing it. The fact remains however, that SA has only been switched off: the capability remains.

Differential GPS

All errors can be allowed for, as long as you know about them. The snag is that many of the errors afflicting GPS are apparently random and constantly changing, so calibration (as for logs) or correction tables (as for compasses) do not work. The solution is to use fixed shore-based reference stations to monitor the GPS signals and broadcast correction messages that can be received and automatically applied by any suitably-equipped GPS receiver.

This supplementary system is generically known as differential GPS (DGPS).

In theory, DGPS corrections can be broadcast by almost any means, but in practice, most DGPS reference stations are on the sites of old radio direction finding beacons,

and transmit on the same frequencies.

DGPS corrections can also be broadcast through communication satellites. At present (2008) an American system called WAAS (Wide Area Augmentation System) pools the data from a network of reference stations and broadcasts the corrections to most of the Atlantic, part of the Pacific, and the whole of the US mainland. Unfortunately, WAAS coverage doesn't quite reach most of Europe! A similar European system called EGNOS (European Geostationary Navigational Overlay System) began operating in 2005, and is expected to be fully operational in the next couple of years, improving the accuracy of GPS to about 2–3 metres.

Accuracy

In everyday language one might take 'an accuracy of 15 metres' to mean that 'all fixes are within 15 metres of the true position'. A more detailed look at a succession of fixes from a stationary 'navigator' shows that this could be misleading, because they are likely to be scattered (Figure 29). Sometimes different types of error cancel each other out, giving fixes very close to the true position. Sometimes errors add together to produce bad fixes, and occasionally a number of unusually large errors accumulate to produce a rogue.

It would be unreasonable to quote the accuracy of the system on the basis of the worst fix, because that ignores the vast majority that are very much better, but it would be equally unrealistic to refer only to the lucky fix that happens to be correct. For most purposes accuracies are quoted either in terms of percentage error circles or by means of a statistical measure called 'sigma' (σ).

The circular error probable (CEP) is the radius of a circle that contains 50% of all fixes. The CEP 95% is the radius of a circle containing 95% of fixes. σ is the standard deviation or 'root mean square error' (dRMS), and it can be found by measuring all the errors, squaring them, adding the squares together, dividing by the number of fixes to find a mean square error, and taking the square route of the mean.

For statisticians this is useful as a basis for further calculations, while for navigators it is a good indication of the practical value of a navigation system, because it tends to 'reward' a consistent performer with a lower error figure than an erratic one.

Doubling the standard deviation gives a

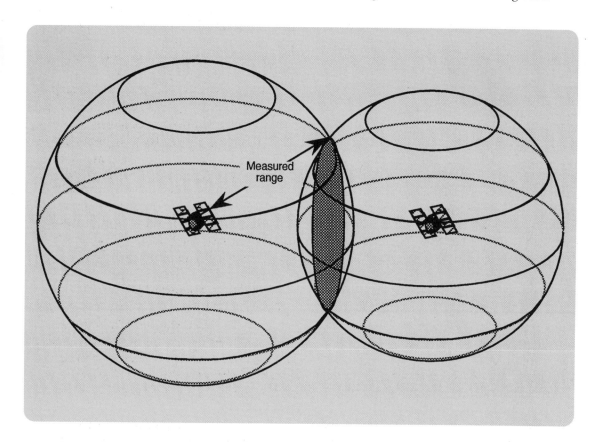

Fig 28 A GPS receiver uses precise time measurement to determine its distance from each of several satellites. One range fixes its position as being on the surface of an invisible sphere; two narrows the position down to the perimeter of a circle; four produces a 3-D 'fix'.

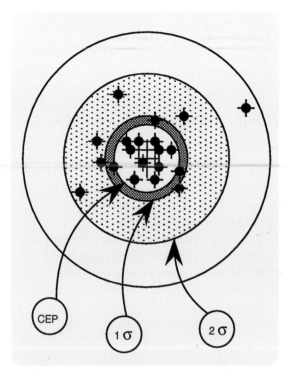

Fig 29 Random errors produce a scattering of fixes around the true position, so accuracy can be expressed at several different 'levels of confidence'.

measure called 2σ, which for a system with random errors, like those produced by SA in GPS, closely matches the CEP 95%. For navigation purposes, you can regard these as levels of confidence. GPS, for instance, may be described as being 'accurate to 15 metres (2σ)'. This means we have a 95% chance of being within 15 metres of where it says we are, or a one in twenty chance of being more than 15 metres away.

Three kinds of accuracy
As well as different measures of accuracy, there are also different kinds of accuracy.

■ *Absolute accuracy* is a measure of how your fix compares with your true position. It is what you need to find the entrance to an unfamiliar harbour.

■ *Relative accuracy* is an indication of consistency throughout an area, and is of more concern to surveyors than to navigators because it is what is required if, for instance, you want to measure the distance between two landmarks.

■ *Repeatable accuracy*, or repeatability, refers to a system's consistency over a period of time, and it is particularly useful to people like fishermen who have laid a string of crab pots and want to get back to precisely the same spot to collect them, but do not necessarily need to know the true position.

Waypoint navigation

For centuries navigators had to devote most of their time and effort to finding their position, even though this is seldom an end in itself. Navigation is much more concerned with where you are going than where you are.

For an instrument that is capable of working out where three spheres intersect on the surface of an approximately spherical earth, and almost instantaneously displaying the result in terms of latitude and longitude, many of the routine navigational tasks that follow on from knowing your position are extremely simple. Using this extra capability of electronic navigators has led to the development of a range of new techniques that are often collectively called waypoint navigation.

Entering waypoints
There is nothing magical about a waypoint: it is simply a position which has been stored ('entered') into the navigator's memory. Usually a waypoint is either your intended destination or some intermediate point that you want to pass through on the way there – hence the name 'waypoint'.

When entering waypoints it is important to be aware that many navigators require latitude and longitude to be given in a very rigidly defined format. It is quite common, for example, for a navigator to demand that the degrees of longitude be given as three figures. So if you enter 1°26'.10 W as '1 26 1', the navigator may store this as 126°10'.00 W. Alternatively, it may insist on the minutes being given to two (or three) places of decimals, in which case the same entry would be stored as 0°12'.61 W.

The third, and very common, pitfall is to neglect to enter the direction of latitude (N or S) or longitude (E or W). If you are on your way to Plymouth, for instance, you probably take it for granted that Plymouth is west of the prime meridian, but your electronic navigator does not. So it is quite likely to assume that a longitude of '4°11'.0' is 4°11'.0 East.

One or more waypoints that you intend to pass through in a particular order is called a route or sail plan. Some of the simplest navigators demand that you enter the waypoints in the correct order, but most allow you to pick, choose and rearrange. This is particularly useful for racing boats whose (human) navigator can store the lat and long of all the local race marks in his (electronic) navigator's memory at the start of the season, and quickly assemble the relevant ones into a route when the course is displayed at any time up to the five minute gun.

Pre-prepared waypoints

In planning a route for waypoint navigation it is easy to concentrate solely on the waypoints and to forget that the only reason they are there is because you are intending to travel from one to the other, and that – circumstances permitting – you will be doing so in a series of straight lines. Rather than putting a waypoint off each main headland along the way, and at a few buoys in between, it is much better to draw the route as a series of straight lines first, and then put a waypoint at each corner.

If you decide to start with the waypoints, either because they are already stored in the navigator's memory or because you have chosen to use waypoints from one of the many

published lists, it is important to draw the route in on the chart as well, to check that it does not pass dangerously close to any hazards.

Basic navigator functions

Six basic functions are common to almost all electronic navigators, though the terminology used to describe them, and the operating procedures required to achieve them, vary from one manufacturer to another.

The most fundamental of all is **position**, given in terms of latitude and longitude. If you plot your position on a chart it is a relatively straightforward matter to measure the **range**

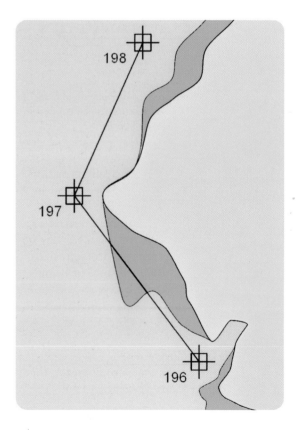

Fig 30 Let your route decide your waypoints, not vice versa! Pre-loaded waypoints, or those taken straight from a published list, should be used with care.

and **bearing** to a waypoint. An electronic navigator can do this too, except that it uses trigonometry, rather than geometry. Alternatively, by comparing your position now with your position a few minutes ago, you could work out the direction and distance you have travelled and, from that, work out your speed over the ground. These two are standard functions on electronic navigators and are usually called CoG (**course over ground**), and SoG (**speed over ground**). CMG and SMG for course made good and speed made good are common variations, as are TRK and VEL for track and velocity.

In practice, most GPS receivers use a rather more sophisticated technique for working out CoG and SoG, but both functions can be badly affected by positioning errors, and become increasingly suspect at low speeds. On a stationary boat, in particular, the CoG display is likely to fluctuate at random.

One way to improve the accuracy of CoG and SoG is to take an average over a period of time, and most of the better electronic navigators have a damping facility based on this principle. 'High' damping uses a long time interval and gives a steadier and generally more accurate reading, but is less responsive to genuine changes of CoG and SoG.

The final standard function is known as **cross track error**, usually abbreviated to XTE. XTE can only be used when the navigator has been given a route, consisting of two or more waypoints, because it is an indication of how far your present position lies from the straight-line track joining the two.

Other functions

Most electronic navigators offer a range of other functions, including a 'man overboard' facility, and 'time to go' – both of which have their limitations.

On all but a few particularly sophisticated instrument systems, the man overboard facility effectively 'freezes' the position at which the man overboard button is pressed, and stores it as a waypoint. It may be tempting to use this to guide the boat back to the spot at which the casualty fell overboard, but you should bear in mind that by the time you get back to that spot

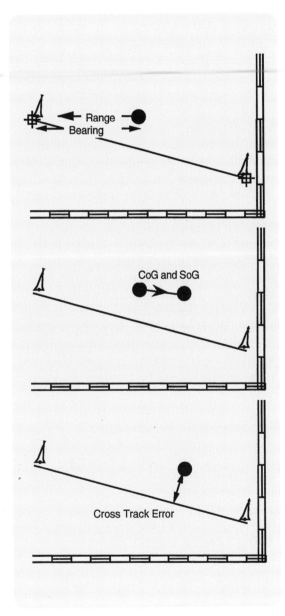

Fig 31 As well as position, most electronic navigators offer range and bearing to waypoint (top); course and speed over ground (middle); and cross track error (bottom).

45

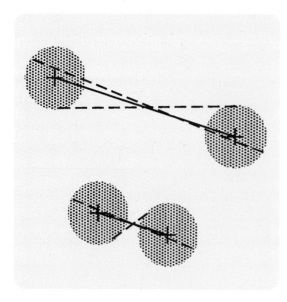

Fig 32 Small errors in successive position fixes (represented by the shaded circles) affect the accuracy of an electronic navigator's course and speed display. The effect is exaggerated at low speeds (bottom).

the person in the water will have drifted away from it with the tide. The real value of the man overboard facility is that it can allow you to give the Coastguard an accurate time and position, from which they can calculate the casualty's most likely movement.

The time to go facility is invariably based on the range and bearing of the waypoint, and the assumption that the boat's course and speed will be constant. For a motor cruiser, in good conditions, that may be a valid assumption, in which case the time to go should be reasonably accurate. Sailing yachts, by contrast, hardly ever maintain a constant course or speed, so the time to go is likely to fluctuate, and will hardly ever be more than a very rough estimate.

Quick plotting

No matter how seductive the display of an electronic navigator, its information is of very limited value until it can be related to the real world. The most obvious way to do this is to take the latitude and longitude readout, and plot them on a chart, but this involves manipulating parallel rulers, dividers and a pencil – and this, in itself, can be difficult in bad conditions. An alternative is to use some of the other functions 'backwards'.

Plotting by range and bearing

In your home waters it can be useful to draw a 'spider's web' of bearing lines and range rings on the chart, centred around some key feature, such as the harbour entrance. Draw the bearing lines at 5° or 10° intervals, and label them, and use a pair of compasses to draw concentric circles with radii of ½, 1, 1½ miles and so on (Figure 33).

When the chosen feature is the navigator's 'active' waypoint, it is easy to relate the displayed bearing to one of the pre-drawn bearing lines, and the displayed range to one of the range rings, so that a position can be plotted very quickly and with no chartwork instruments. The accuracy of a position plotted by this means depends largely on the distance between the boat and the waypoint: at 6 miles, an error of 1° represents about 200 metres, but at 60 miles you'd have to move at least a mile to change the bearing by 1°. On a short sea passage, one way to reduce the distances involved is to pick a reference position roughly halfway along the intended route.

Another variation is to store the centre of a compass rose as a waypoint, even if you have no intention of going there. The bearing can then be plotted quickly and easily, just by laying a straight edge across the rose.

Plotting by range and XTE

Rapid fixing by range and bearing gives flexibility to potter all over an area, but it is less useful on a passage from A to B, because its range limit is about 5–10 miles, and it requires a lot of preparation.

An alternative is to use range in conjunction with cross track error, by marking the chart at regular intervals (eg ½ mile or 1 mile) along

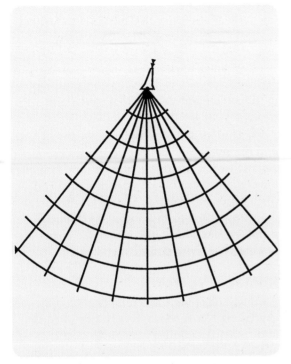

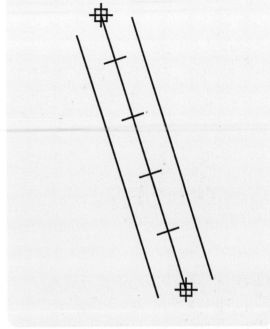

Fig 33 The range and bearing display can be used to plot positions quickly, by drawing a 'spider's web' on the chart around a chosen waypoint.

Fig 34 On long passages, range and cross track error can be used for quick plotting, so long as the chart has been marked up in advance.

the track, working backwards from each waypoint, and drawing lines parallel to the track at some convenient distance (such as 1 mile) each side of it (Figure 34). When the navigator shows that you are, for instance, 5 miles from the waypoint with an XTE of 0.7 mile to port, it should be easy to find the 5 mile mark, and measure or estimate 0.7 mile away from the track.

Chart plotters

For centuries navigators had to devote most of their time and effort to working out their position. Now, to a very large extent, GPS can be relied upon to take care of that. The snag is that even with quick plotting techniques, a human navigator working on a paper chart

can't hope to keep up with the flow of information available from the GPS receiver.

One solution is to use a chart plotter to display the boat's current position on an electronic chart. Of course, plotters have their drawbacks, but their great strengths are that they update the position continuously, without human intervention, and without introducing such very human errors as plotting 55°45'.6N instead of 55°46'.5N.

Even the simplest plotters, however, do more than this, allowing you to mark waypoints, plan routes, and measure directions and distances, while some can work out the course to steer to allow for tidal streams, or even plan the optimum route to follow to allow for forecast changes in wind strength and direction. They can then show how your actual position compares with your plan, give simple steering instructions to a human helmsman, or control an autopilot.

Any chart plotter is a combination of three main groups of components:

- the hardware
- the cartography
- the software

The **hardware** is the physical equipment (the casing, display, control panel, and so on) and the internal electronics, such as the power supply, processor and memory. It may be designed from the outset as a chart plotter; it may be combined with some other equipment such as a radar or autopilot; or it may be a desktop or laptop PC or even a PDA (Personal Digital Assistant).

The **cartography** refers to the electronic charts. They are available from various sources, in different formats and on different media, such as CD-ROMs, floppy discs, PCMCIA cards, flash memory cards, or custom-made cartridges of various shapes and sizes.

The **software** is the link between the two, converting the electronic cartography into a form which can be displayed on the screen, enabling us to carry out navigational tasks, and communicating with other electronic equipment such as a GPS receiver and autopilot.

Dedicated hardware v PC

In general terms, most dedicated hardware plotters are produced by specialist marine electronics companies, and are supplied with their own software already installed.

Dedicated hardware is good because it is rugged and waterproof (at least to some extent) and is designed to operate from an unreliable 12-volt supply. Its control panel and operating procedures are likely to have been designed specifically for use as a chart plotter, and although the choice of cartography is limited – usually to one particular supplier and one particular type of cartridge – the coverage is generally good and cartridges are readily available.

PC plotters consist of specialist plotting software that can be loaded into almost any personal computer, though laptops are the most popular for the job.

PC plotters are good because the initial outlay is relatively low (especially if you already own a suitable computer) and because the computer itself is very much more versatile than a dedicated plotter. Some PC software can use cartography from a variety of different suppliers, but additional or updated charts are not always easy to come by.

Raster v vector

Although there are many suppliers of electronic charts, the charts themselves can be divided into two main groups: raster and vector.

Raster charts can be regarded as electronic photocopies of paper charts, produced by scanning a master copy of a paper chart, in much the same way as a fax machine scans a document that is about to be sent. The chart is broken down into a vast number of tiny dots (pixels), and the position and colour of each pixel is recorded. Instead of sending this information down a telephone line, as a fax machine does, the chart scanner stores it on the cartographer's computer, from where it can be copied onto floppy discs or CD-ROMS, and supplied to customers.

Raster charts are relatively cheap and simple to make, but each chart uses up a lot of memory or disc space. Because they are electronically copied straight from the paper chart, they are familiar in appearance, and contain exactly the same information: nothing is added or taken away. The drawback of this is that they can only be used effectively at about the same scale as the original chart: if you zoom in, then letters and symbols become huge, but without any extra detail becoming visible; while if you zoom out, names and symbols become illegible.

Vector charts are produced by electronically tracing raster charts. The fundamental difference is that lines are not stored as strings of darkened pixels, but as lines. Vector charts originally became popular for small boat hardware plotters because although they are more expensive to produce, they occupy much less memory. The vector format also allows more flexibility in the way the chart is used: a vector chart can be zoomed in or out much further than a raster chart, but the letters and symbols always stay the same size.

Fig 35 A typical small boat chart plotter.

'Unfolding' electronic charts

At present, electronic charting is still in the process of rapid development; different manufacturers use different types of cartridges and discs, with different software and different keyboards and control panel layouts. Even so, there are a number of processes that are more or less common to all chart plotters –

analogous, in some ways, to the process of unfolding a paper chart ready for use.

Zoom in / zoom out are self-explanatory terms referring to the way in which the scale of the displayed image of the chart can be changed. From the user's point of view, zooming is usually a very simple process.

Scrolling and panning are ways of moving the screen image to make different areas visible: scrolling generally refers to a north–south movement and panning to an east–west movement. Many programmes also include different 'centring' options which allow you (for instance) to lock the centre of the display to your own position. Other options allow the user to choose whether to view the chart in the conventional 'north-up' mode, or to turn it round to 'course-up' mode.

Decluttering is only available on vector charts. In effect, each type of information is stored in a different database: contour lines in one; spot soundings in another; major lighthouses in another; buoys in another; and so on. The effect is rather as though a paper chart were built up using many different layers of tracing paper, each of which can be removed or replaced at will. Most software programmes add and remove some layers automatically as you zoom in and out, in order to stop the screen becoming cluttered. Many, however, allow you to choose 'more detail' or 'less detail', or to make your own selection of exactly what kind of information you want to see. It's important to appreciate, though, that the accuracy of information depends on the scale of the original chart, not on the zoom level you happen to have chosen, and to be aware that it is possible to inadvertently hide information which could turn out to be important.

Chart databases

On a raster chart, a feature such as a buoy is represented by a cluster of coloured pixels which together make up the shape of the buoy symbol exactly as it appears on the original paper chart. On a vector chart, however, the buoy's position is linked to a database of information about the buoy. The software can use this database in various ways. Some programmes, for instance, represent all navigation aids by means of the same diamond-shaped symbol. When you select one (by 'pointing at it' with the cursor) the data is revealed in a text panel somewhere on the screen. Other systems use the database information to display a symbol showing the shape and colour of the buoy itself.

More sophisticated versions of this are used on some electronic charts to provide graphic representations of the changing height of tide at particular places, to provide additional information such as lists of port facilities, or to superimpose arrows showing the tidal stream on top of the main chart.

Planning on a plotter

Almost all plotters include the same kind of facilities for creating and storing waypoints as are found in position fixers. They have an important advantage, though, in that you don't have to enter waypoint positions in terms of their latitude and longitude co-ordinates; there is a much simpler procedure for creating waypoints graphically, in effect by just pointing at the chart image and telling the plotter where you want to go.

Creating routes is usually almost as easy: it's just a matter of pointing at a succession of waypoints in turn. Most plotters now include a useful feature that is sometimes known as 'rubber banding', by which you can add a waypoint between two existing waypoints, and then move it, to 'stretch' the route like a rubber band to avoid obstacles. This allows you to take a broad-brush approach to passage planning, perhaps starting off with a straight line route from your departure waypoint to your destination, then adding extra waypoints to stretch your route around major headlands, before zooming in to look at each leg of the trip in more detail, and perhaps adding more intermediate waypoints to deal with minor hazards that didn't show up on the small-scale, large-area picture.

4 Position Fixing

Finding out where you are, or 'fixing' your position, is seldom an end in itself. It is, however, a vital first step in making a great many navigational decisions: you cannot decide which way to go until you know where you are starting from. There are many ways of 'getting a fix' other than by electronic means, of which one of the commonest and most useful is by compass bearings.

Compass bearings

If you take a bearing of a landmark by looking across the top of a hand-bearing compass towards it, your line of sight can be represented on the chart by a pencil line drawn along that bearing and passing through the symbol that represents the landmark. As that line represents your line of sight, your position must be somewhere along it, so it is called a position line. Doing the same with the bearing of another landmark produces a second position line. There is only one place where you can possibly be on both position lines at once, and that is where they cross.

If everything in a navigator's life were reliable, then two intersecting position lines would be enough for a fix, but in practice it is normal to take yet another bearing, of a third landmark. The third position line does not make a fix more accurate: its sole purpose is to guard against a gross error, such as a landmark wrongly identified or a bearing wrongly read or plotted.

In theory, one might expect all three position lines to cross at a single point – each one

confirming the accuracy of the other two. Such perfect fixes happen so rarely in real life that when an experienced navigator produces one he is more likely to ask himself what has gone wrong, than to pat himself on the back! More often the three lines intersect to form a triangle known as a 'cocked hat' (see Figure 36). Strictly speaking, it would not be true to say that a small cocked hat is more accurate or reliable than a large one, but you can generally

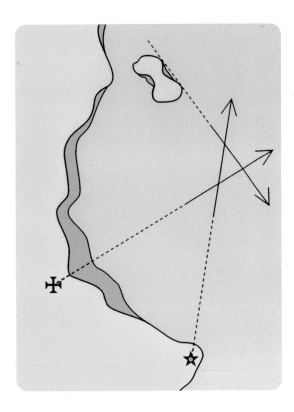

Fig 36 Three position lines rarely intersect at a single point, but form a triangle known as a 'cocked hat'.

be a lot more confident about a compact cocked hat. One that straggles around all over the chart shows that something is wrong. Rub out the lines and start again!

Improving the fix

There are a number of things you can do to minimize the size of the cocked hat. The most obvious of these is to make sure that the landmarks are correctly identified, ie that the features you have taken bearings of do indeed correspond with those on the chart. It is also a good idea to make sure the bearings are measured as accurately as is practical by, for example, trying to take bearings with the compass in a spot that is relatively free of

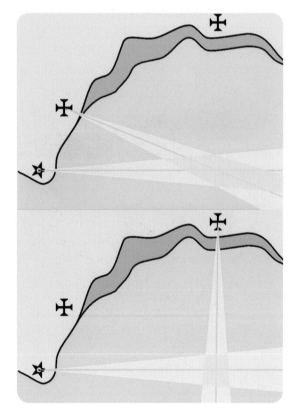

Fig 37 Small errors in bearing produce an exaggerated error in the fix if the position lines intersect at a shallow angle. So choose well-spaced landmarks for visual fixing.

deviating influences. No matter how carefully you take the bearings, though, some error is almost inevitable.

The effect of bearing errors can be minimized by a careful choice of landmarks. Ideally they should be spaced around the horizon, to give the largest possible angle of cut between the position lines. For a fix using two position lines, this means choosing objects which are as nearly as possible 90° apart. For a three-position-line fix the optimum angles are 60° or 120°.

The reason for this is shown in Figure 37: if two position lines cross at a shallow angle, a small bearing error creates a much larger position error than it would if the two position lines intersected at a larger angle.

Close objects are better than more distant ones, even if the distant ones are more conspicuous. As Figure 38 shows, the position error caused by a small bearing error is far greater when the landmark concerned is a long way away than if it is close at hand.

The order in which you take bearings can also make a difference, particularly on a fast moving boat or with landmarks at close range. Because the boat is moving while the fix is being taken, its position will be slightly different at the beginning of the fix than at the end. The bearing of objects directly ahead or astern will not change very much, but those which are abeam will appear to be moving aft. For this reason you should take bearings ahead or astern first, followed by those over the bow or quarter, and finish up with those which are almost abeam. Taking bearings in this order not only minimizes the effect of the boat's own movement on the size of the cocked hat, but also means that the final fix is as up to date as possible.

Accuracy v speed

Suggesting that bearings should be taken as accurately as is practical, and then that the boat's own movement affects the size of the cocked hat, begs the question, 'Which is

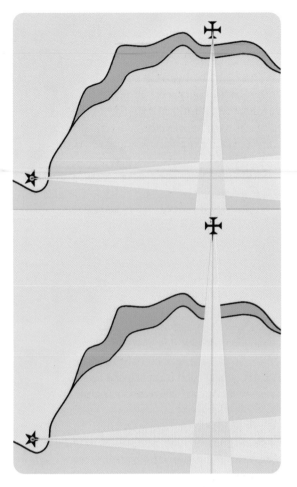

Fig 38 The effect of small bearing errors is exaggerated if the landmarks are far away. Choose near landmarks rather than distant ones.

about the distance a five-knot sailing boat would cover in one minute. If the landmark was 15 miles away, a bearing accurate to ±5° would produce a position uncertainty of 1.25 miles, equivalent to 15 minutes worth of movement for the same five-knot boat. So for distant landmarks it may be worth spending a minute or more on each bearing to take a more careful average of several swings of the compass card.

Choosing landmarks

Any charted feature can be used as a landmark for a fix by visual bearings. The best are compact, conspicuous and easily-identified, such as lighthouses, beacons, churches and water towers. But natural features such as headlands and rocks can also be used, and in many of the most attractive cruising areas are

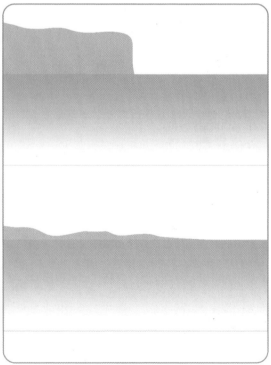

Fig 39 Steeply-sloping headlands are good landmarks. On shelving coastlines it can be difficult to decide where the edge of the land really is.

more important – accuracy or speed?'

The answer is that it depends on the distance of the landmark concerned. You should always wait until the compass card has stopped spinning, but for landmarks at very close range speed is much more important than precision and it may be sufficient to take a rough mental average of the bearing while the card is still swinging, to an accuracy of perhaps five or ten degrees. For a landmark one mile away, an accuracy of ±5° corresponds to a position accuracy of about 150 metres, or far more plentiful. The main requirement is the same as for man-made landmarks – that they should be positively identified. There is no point taking a bearing of a rock if you do not know which rock it is!

Headlands can be very useful landmarks indeed, because they are generally conspicuous and – so long as you know roughly where you are in the first place – are usually easy to identify. But there are a couple of pitfalls to be avoided. Gently-sloping headlands look as distinct on the chart as near vertical ones, but when it comes to taking a bearing of the real thing it can be very difficult to identify exactly where the headland really ends: at low water a considerable expanse of foreshore may be uncovered, extending the visible land further to seaward than it appears on the chart; conversely, at any distance more than about two miles or so, the edge of the land may be below the horizon, so that what appears to be the end of the headland is actually a point somewhere inland. Steeply-sloping headlands or cliffs give neither of these problems.

When plotting the bearing of a headland on a chart it can often be difficult to tell exactly which part of the headland you are seeing. The solution is to set the parallel rulers to the correct bearing, and then gradually move them in from seaward until one ruler just touches the coast. That first point of contact is the particular point you took a bearing of. Buoys also have their limitations as marks on which to base position lines, because they are not truly 'fixed' objects, but are free to drift downtide to the extent of their mooring chains, and have been known to drag their anchors or break adrift altogether. On the credit side, however, they are often easy to identify, and may well be much closer than any fixed landmark. These two advantages usually more than make up for their drawbacks: a position line based on a buoy a mile away is likely to be more accurate than one based on a distant headland or lighthouse, even if the buoy is 50 metres out of position.

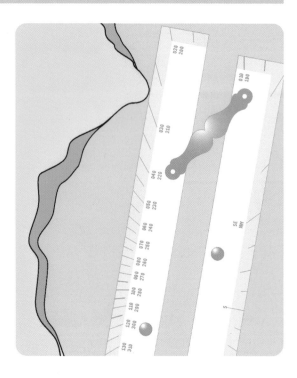

Fig 40 Having taken a bearing of a headland, move the parallel rulers in from seaward until they just touch the coastline.

Transits

The strict definition of a transit is 'two or more objects on the same bearing from an observer'. What that means in everyday language is that a transit occurs whenever two objects appear to be in line with each other. Transits make ideal position lines because:

- they are instant, because there is no need to wait for a compass card to settle;
- they are accurate, because they are independent of errors such as deviation or human error;
- they are quick to plot, because a transit can be drawn on the chart simply by ruling a straight line that passes through the two landmarks.

Transits are so useful that many have been set up deliberately, with conspicuous marks positioned to indicate a safe route through

Plotting direction-based fixes

You should very rarely find yourself in a situation in which you do not have at least a rough idea of where you are, so there is no need to draw the full length of every position line on the chart. For the first one, a couple of inches or so in the vicinity of where you expect the fix to be should be enough. And the second and third position lines can be even shorter – just enough to produce the cocked hat. By convention the ends of the position lines are marked with single arrows to show that they are derived from bearings, and the boat's assumed position within the cocked hat is marked by a spot surrounded by a circle (see Figure 24 on page 34). Finally, and perhaps most important of all, the fix should be labelled with the time at which it was taken.

Assessing the quality of a fix

Although one cannot say for certain that a fix given by a compact cocked hat is reliable, it is certainly true that a large cocked hat gives an unreliable fix. So as a general rule of thumb, it is fair to use the size of the cocked hat as a means of assessing the quality of the fix. In one particular situation, however, this rule fails: that is where the boat and all three landmarks lie on the perimeter of the same circle.

Although this sounds unlikely it can easily happen when crossing a bay (Figure 42). The geometry of this situation is such that if all the bearings are subject to the same error, such as deviation, they will still produce a good looking fix but in the wrong position.

Am I inside the cocked hat?

Any fix that produces a cocked hat begs the question 'where is the boat's true position?' Clearly it cannot be at all three intersections at once. It is usual to assume that the true position is in the centre of the cocked hat, equidistant from all three position lines.

All things being equal that is a reasonable 'best guess', but it is important to appreciate

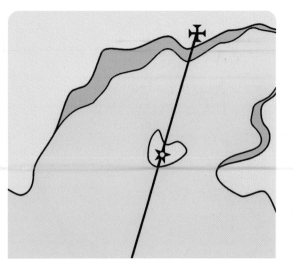

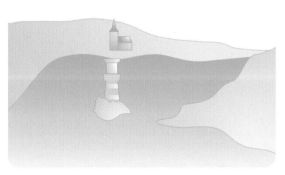

Fig 41 Two objects in line form a transit – and a charted transit is a very accurate, very simple position line.

narrow channels, or to mark the ends of a measured distance. These, and naturally-occurring transits, are often shown on charts or mentioned in pilot books. A transit does not have to be purpose-built to be of use for navigation, though: any two objects can be used so long as they can be positively identified and are shown on the chart. Their virtues make transits well worth looking out for, but it is most unlikely that you will find yourself on two or three transits at once. A transit can often be found that will provide one position line, but the other one or two position lines required for a fix will have to be derived by other means, such as compass bearings.

that the probability of your true position being inside the cocked hat is only 25%! In other words, there is a three-to-one chance that you are outside it. For this reason, if one corner of the cocked hat is a considerably more dangerous place to be than any of the others, it is as well to assume your position to be in the worst corner, and to bear in mind that there is a small but distinct possibility that even that is unduly optimistic.

Position lines by range

Visual bearings and transits both produce straight position lines because both are based on direction. Range measurements – your distance away from an object – produce equally valid position lines, but they are circular in shape. If, for instance, you know you are two miles from a lighthouse, then your position must lie somewhere on the circumference of a circle with a radius of two miles, centred on the lighthouse.

There are three reasonably common ways of measuring range from a yacht: radar, sextant and 'rising and dipping distances'.

Radar

The use of radar is covered more fully in Chapter 8, but essentially radar is an electronic device that measures the range of objects by measuring the time taken for a short pulse of microwave energy to make the there-and-back trip between its aerial and the object in question. By using a directional aerial it can also measure the object's bearing. So over the course of a couple of seconds, a radar set can build up a map-like picture of its surroundings on a screen. Regularly-spaced range rings can be superimposed on the picture to give a sense of scale and a quick way of estimating the distance of objects. Alternatively a variable range marker (VRM) – an adjustable range ring – can be used to give a more precise measurement of range.

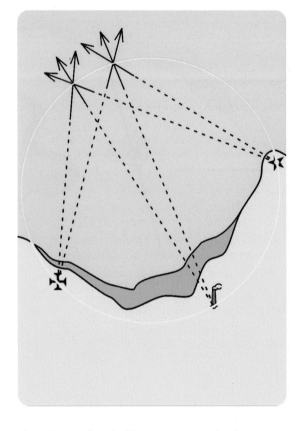

Fig 42 A small cocked hat can give a misleading impression of accuracy if you happen to be on or near the circle which passes through all three landmarks.

Sextant

Although it is usually associated with astro-navigation on ocean passages, a sextant can also be used for coastal navigation. Its use is limited, and for coastal navigation is unlikely to justify the fairly high price of a good-quality sextant. But if you have one on board already, or acquire a cheap plastic one, it is worth being familiar with the range-finding technique called 'vertical sextant angles'. The principle is simple, and is based on the everyday experience that any object appears to get bigger as you get closer to it. If you know the height of an object and can measure the angle between the top and bottom of it accurately, it is a matter of simple trigonometry to work out its range, and even easier to use pre-calculated 'distance off' tables published in yachtsmen's almanacs.

Using a sextant

A sextant is an instrument designed to measure angles very accurately – typically to about a tenth of a minute. It does this by using a system of mirrors. Light from a distant object, such as a star or lighthouse, is reflected by the index mirror, down to the horizon glass, and from there back to the telescope. Only half the horizon glass is silvered, so by looking through the telescope, the observer can also see straight through the unsilvered part, as well as seeing the reflected image in the silvered part. In other words, the sextant allows him to look in two directions at once. The angle between these

two directions can be changed by moving the index arm – on which the index mirror is mounted – and it can be read off from the scale. On most sextants the main index scale is marked in degrees: minutes are shown on the micrometer drum used for precise adjustment.

Like all navigational instruments, a sextant is subject to a number of errors. Only one of these, index error, is really significant for coastal navigation, and it is relatively easily corrected. Start by moving the index arm to set the sextant to zero, then look through the telescope at the horizon. Because there is 0° difference between the view through the horizon glass and the reflected view through the horizon and index mirrors, the horizon should appear as a single unbroken line. Usually, however, there will be a break or step between the two images. This can be reduced, and eventually eliminated, by adjusting the micrometer drum.

If this adjustment has moved the index arm forward, on to the main scale, the index error is described as being 'on the arc' and the amount of error can be read directly from the micrometer drum. It should never be more than a few minutes. If the adjustment involves moving the index arm backwards, the error is described as 'off the arc'. This is a little more complicated because the micrometer scale is designed for readings on the arc.

In Figure 44, for instance, the micrometer reading is 54', but the main scale is between zero and one degree off the arc. Because the main scale and micrometer are reading in different directions, it is the difference between the two that counts:

$$-1° + 54' = -6'$$

so in this case, the index error is 6' 'off the arc'.

It is a good idea to check the index error every time a sextant is used, because it can vary due to temperature changes or vibration.

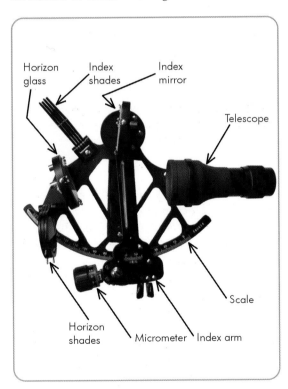

Horizon glass   Index shades   Index mirror

Telescope

Scale

Horizon shades   Micrometer   Index arm

Fig 43 Although it is mainly intended for astro-navigation, a sextant can also be useful in coastal navigation.

Fig 44 Before using a sextant, it must always be checked for index error – which makes the horizon look 'broken' when the sextant reads zero. Adjust the micrometer drum to make the horizon look straight, and read off the index error (see text).

Once the index error has been checked, the apparent height of the object can be measured by moving the index arm forwards until the top of the reflected image (or the centre of the lantern if it is a lighthouse) appears to be level with the direct image of the shoreline. This angle can then be read off from the index scale and micrometer.

The index error correction is applied arithmetically, following the rule that 'if the error is *off* the arc you add it *on* to the reading, and if it is *on* the arc you take it *off* the reading'.

The vertical sextant angle (VSA) tables are almost self-explanatory: the height of the object appears down the side, and the range is across the top. Find the row corresponding to the height of the object and move along it until you come to the measured angle, then move up to read off the range from the top of the page. For greater accuracy, especially when dealing with short objects, the height should first be corrected to allow for the height of tide (see Chapter 5): ignoring this produces a position line which is slightly nearer the object than it should be.

Vertical sextant angles should be used with care if the shoreline immediately below the target is obscured by the horizon because this has the opposite effect, making the object appear shorter than it really is and therefore exaggerating the range to produce a position line further offshore than it should be.

Dipping distances

A third method of measuring ranges requires no equipment whatsoever. It relies on the curvature of the earth, which makes distant objects dip below the horizon as you move away from them, or rise above it as you move towards them. Unfortunately, it can only be used at night, on brightly-lit objects such as lighthouses, and only over certain ranges. As you move towards a major lighthouse at night you will first see the 'loom' of its light, like a searchlight sweeping across the sky. As you get closer still, the loom appears more intense, but the beam looks shorter until, quite suddenly, the light itself appears as a bright pinpoint with no perceptible loom at all.

Going away from the light the reverse happens – the pinpoint flash gives way to the loom.

The distance at which that transition from flash to loom takes place is called the light's 'rising' or 'dipping' distance. The rising or dipping distance depends on two factors: the height of the light above sea level; and the height of the observer's eye above sea level. The height of the light can be found from the chart or from the list of lights.

Strictly speaking the quoted height (called the elevation) should be corrected to allow for the effect of tide (see Chapter 5), but except in the case of short lighthouses or very large tidal ranges this seldom makes much practical difference. Once you know the height of the

HEIGHT OF OBJECT		DISTANCE OF OBJECT (NAUTICAL MILES)															
ft	m	0·2	0·4	0·6	0·8	1·0	1·2	1·4	1·6	1·8	2·0	2·4	2·8	3·2	3·6	4·0	5·0
		° '	° '	° '	° '	° '	° '	° '	° '	° '	° '	° '	° '	° '	° '	° '	° '
33	10	1 33	0 46	0 31	0 23	0 19	0 15	0 13	0 12	0 10							
39	12	1 51	0 56	0 37	0 28	0 22	0 19	0 16	0 14	0 12	0 11	0 10					
46	14	2 10	1 05	0 43	0 32	0 26	0 22	0 19	0 16	0 14	0 13	0 11					
53	16	2 28	1 14	0 49	0 37	0 30	0 25	0 21	0 19	0 16	0 15	0 12	0 11				
59	18	2 47	1 24	0 56	0 42	0 33	0 28	0 24	0 21	0 19	0 17	0 14	0 12	0 10			
66	20	3 05	1 33	1 02	0 46	0 37	0 31	0 27	0 23	0 21	0 19	0 15	0 13	0 12	0 10		
72	22	3 24	1 42	1 08	0 51	0 41	0 34	0 29	0 26	0 23	0 20	0 17	0 15	0 13	0 11	0 10	
79	24	3 42	1 51	1 14	0 56	0 45	0 37	0 32	0 28	0 25	0 22	0 19	0 16	0 14	0 12	0 11	
85	26	4 01	2 01	1 20	1 00	0 48	0 40	0 34	0 30	0 27	0 24	0 20	0 17	0 15	0 13	0 12	
92	28	4 19	2 10	1 27	1 05	0 52	0 43	0 37	0 32	0 29	0 26	0 22	0 19	0 16	0 14	0 13	0 10
98	30	4 38	2 19	1 33	1 10	0 56	0 46	0 40	0 35	0 31	0 28	0 23	0 20	0 17	0 15	0 14	0 11
105	32	4 56	2 28	1 39	1 14	0 59	0 49	0 42	0 37	0 33	0 30	0 25	0 21	0 19	0 16	0 15	0 12
112	34	5 15	2 38	1 45	1 19	1 03	0 53	0 45	0 39	0 35	0 31	0 26	0 23	0 20	0 17	0 16	0 13
118	36	5 33	2 47	1 51	1 24	1 07	0 56	0 48	0 42	0 37	0 33	0 28	0 24	0 21	0 19	0 17	0 13
125	38	5 41	2 56	1 58	1 28	1 11	0 59	0 50	0 44	0 39	0 35	0 29	0 25	0 22	0 20	0 18	0 14
131	40	6 10	3 05	2 04	1 33	1 14	1 02	0 53	0 46	0 41	0 37	0 31	0 27	0 23	0 21	0 19	0 15
138	42	6 28	3 15	2 10	1 37	1 18	1 05	0 56	0 49	0 43	0 40	0 32	0 28	0 24	0 22	0 19	0 16
144	44	6 46	3 24	2 16	1 42	1 22	1 08	0 58	0 51	0 45	0 41	0 34	0 29	0 25	0 23	0 20	0 16
151	46	7 05	3 33	2 22	1 47	1 25	1 11	1 01	0 53	0 47	0 43	0 36	0 30	0 27	0 24	0 21	0 17
157	48	7 23	3 42	2 28	1 51	1 29	1 14	1 04	0 56	0 49	0 45	0 37	0 32	0 28	0 25	0 22	0 18
164	50	7 41	3 52	2 35	1 56	1 33	1 17	1 06	0 58	0 52	0 46	0 39	0 33	0 29	0 26	0 23	0 19
171	52	7 59	4 01	2 41	2 01	1 36	1 20	1 09	1 00	0 54	0 48	0 40	0 34	0 30	0 27	0 24	0 19

Fig 45 Vertical sextant angle tables convert the measured altitude of a tall object into a measured range. (Source: *Reeds Nautical Almanac*.)

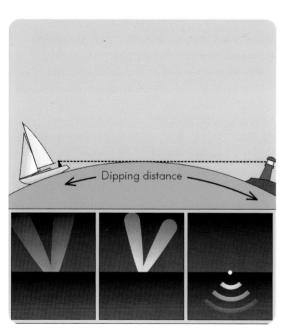

Fig 46 The dipping distance of a light is the range at which it first appears above the horizon or drops below it.

light and your own height of eye, the dipping distance can be found either from tables published in yachtsmen's almanacs, or by calculator using the formula:

Range in miles = $1.15 \times (\sqrt{Ht_{eye}} + \sqrt{Ht_{object}})$
where both heights are in feet
or
Range in miles = $2.08 \times (\sqrt{Ht_{eye}} + \sqrt{Ht_{object}})$
where both heights are in metres.

Using tables, find the row corresponding to the height of the light and the column corresponding to your height of eye. The rising or dipping distance is shown in the square where the row and column meet.

Plotting fixes based on range

Plotting any kind of range-based fix requires a pair of drawing compasses. These are set to the measured range and used to draw an arc, centred on the object from which the range

HEIGHT OF LIGHT			HEIGHT OF EYE									
		metres	1	2	3	4	5	6	7	8	9	10
metres	feet	feet	3	7	10	13	16	20	23	26	30	33
10	33		8·7	9·5	10·2	10·8	11·3	11·7	12·1	12·5	12·8	13·2
12	39		9·3	10·1	10·8	11·4	11·9	12·3	12·7	13·1	13·4	13·8
14	46		9·9	10·7	11·4	12·0	12·5	12·9	13·3	13·7	14·0	14·4
16	53		10·4	11·2	11·9	12·5	13·0	13·4	13·8	14·2	14·5	14·9
18	59		10·9	11·7	12·4	13·0	13·5	13·9	14·3	14·7	15·0	15·4
20	66		11·4	12·2	12·9	13·5	14·0	14·4	14·8	15·2	15·5	15·9
22	72		11·9	12·7	13·4	14·0	14·5	14·9	15·3	15·7	16·0	16·4
24	79		12·3	13·1	13·8	14·4	14·9	15·3	15·7	16·1	16·4	17·0
26	85		12·7	13·5	14·2	14·8	15·3	15·7	16·1	16·5	16·8	17·2
28	92		13·1	13·9	14·6	15·2	15·7	16·1	16·5	16·9	17·2	17·6
30	98		13·5	14·3	15·0	15·6	16·1	16·5	16·9	17·3	17·6	18·0
32	105		13·9	14·7	15·4	16·0	16·5	16·9	17·3	17·7	18·0	18·4
34	112		14·2	15·0	15·7	16·3	16·8	17·2	17·6	18·0	18·3	18·7
36	118		14·6	15·4	16·1	16·7	17·2	17·6	18·0	18·4	18·7	19·1
38	125		14·9	15·7	16·4	17·0	17·5	17·9	18·3	18·7	19·0	19·4
40	131		15·3	16·1	16·8	17·4	17·9	18·3	18·7	19·1	19·4	19·8
42	138		15·6	16·4	17·1	17·7	18·2	18·6	19·0	19·4	19·7	20·1
44	144		15·9	16·7	17·4	18·0	18·5	18·9	19·3	19·7	20·0	20·4
46	151		16·2	17·0	17·7	18·3	18·8	19·2	19·6	20·0	20·3	20·7
48	157		16·5	17·3	18·0	18·6	19·1	19·5	19·9	20·3	20·6	21·0
50	164		16·8	17·6	18·3	18·9	19·4	19·8	20·2	20·6	20·9	21·3
55	180		17·5	18·3	19·0	19·6	20·1	20·5	20·9	21·3	21·6	22·0
60	197		18·2	19·0	19·7	20·3	20·8	21·2	21·6	22·0	22·3	22·7
65	213		18·9	19·7	20·4	21·0	21·5	21·9	22·3	22·7	23·0	23·4

Fig 47 Dipping distance tables show the dipping distance of a light, based on its height and the observer's height of eye above sea level. (Source: *Reeds Nautical Almanac.*)

was measured. As with direction-based fixes there is no need to draw in the complete position line – an inch or two is enough.

Such short arcs can look very much like straight lines, so to differentiate a distance-based position line from a direction-based position line, it is usually marked by a single arrow at each end. Just like a fix by visual bearings, the boat's assumed position should be marked with a spot surrounded by a circle, and the whole fix labelled with the time at which it was taken. (See Figure 24 on page 34.)

Position lines by depth

For most of the time in coastal navigation the closest solid land is directly below you. It too can be used to give a position line based on a well-defined depth contour.

Like all fixing methods this has its limitations and its strengths: position lines based on depth are unreliable in very deep water, where the echo sounder's inaccuracies may be significant, or on soft or moving seabeds where the chart may not accurately represent the true depth, but on the other hand, in poor visibility the echo sounder may be the only source of information available on a boat without other electronic nav-aids.

The depths shown by spot soundings (numbers) or contours on a chart represent the depth when the tide is at its lowest, so they very rarely represent true depth of water, but have to be 'adjusted' to allow for the height of tide (see Chapter 5). If, for example, the height of tide is 3.4 metres then the depth of water over the 5 metre contour will be 8.4 metres. To put this another way, when the height of tide is 3.4 metres and the echo sounder shows a depth below the water line of 8.4 metres you must be on the 5 metre contour. This in turn means that the 5 metre contour itself is a position line – even though it may turn out to be a very wiggly one!

Line of soundings

An alternative way of using an echo sounder to find your position – though it is really almost a last resort, and can only be used effectively when you are crossing a number of well-defined contours – is known as a line of soundings. Again, being based on depth measurement it requires the height of tide to be taken into account.

Record the depth and log reading each time you cross a contour, remembering to subtract the height of tide from the depth shown by the echo sounder: if you are looking for the 10 metre contour, for instance, and the height of tide is 3 metres, you will be crossing the contour when the echo sounder displays a depth of 13 metres. It may help later if you also record a few intermediate depths at regular intervals.

Mark all these adjusted depths on the edge of a strip of paper, at intervals corresponding to the distance you have travelled between each reading. Then draw your approximate track on to the chart, and move the strip of paper around the area, keeping it parallel to the pencilled track, until the depths shown on the

paper correspond with the soundings shown on the chart. The position of the last sounding on the chart corresponds with the boat's position at the time.

Mixed fixes

Although it is tempting to think in terms of 'a visual fix' or 'a radar fix' it is worth remembering that most fixes are simply a combination of several position lines. There is no rule that says all the position lines have to come from the same source, so it is quite possible to combine two or three different types of position line in a single fix, so long as you stick to the principle that they should cross at as large an angle as possible.

A good example of the kind of situation where a mixed fix might be used is at night, after an offshore passage, ready to enter harbour in daylight later in the morning. The range and bearing of a single lighthouse – range based on its rising and dipping distance and bearing by hand bearing compass – with a check on the depth by echo sounder, gives a fix as much as 20 miles offshore.

Running fixes

A landfall fix using a range and bearing is one example of how you can fix your position when there is only a single landmark in sight, but there is an alternative, called a running fix. In Figure 49 the navigator has taken a bearing of the lighthouse, but for some reason or another has not been able to cross it with another position line in order to produce a fix. Sometime later the boat has moved on. If he had been starting with a fix instead of with a single position her navigator could work out her estimated position (see Chapter 7). But he did not: he knows only that he was somewhere along the position line A B C.

If he had been at A, his estimated position

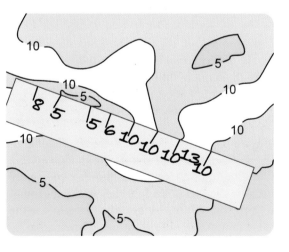

Fig 48 As a last resort, a position can sometimes be found by marking up a strip of paper with echo sounder readings corrected for height of tide, and moving it around until it matches up with the chart.

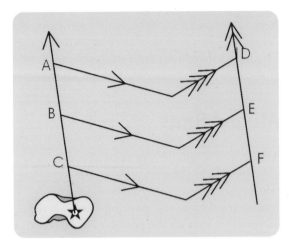

Fig 49 A position line can be 'transferred' to allow for the distance the boat has travelled since the bearing was taken.

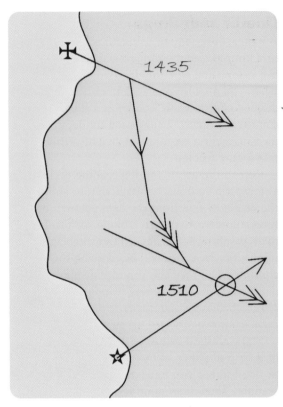

Fig 50 A running fix does not have to use only one landmark: a transferred position line can be particularly useful if you lose sight of one landmark before sighting the next.

would be D; if he had been at B, then his estimated position would be E; and if he had been at C, his estimated position would now be F. D E and F all lie on a straight line, parallel to the original position line but separated from it by the distance and direction the boat has moved since the original bearing was taken. The line D E F is called a 'transferred position line', and once it has been worked out it can be treated like any other position line and crossed with a new bearing of the same object (or a range) in order to produce a running fix.

You do not, in practice, have to work on three points along the original line of bearing: one is enough. It can be anywhere, though it is usual to choose the point nearest to where you believe yourself to be. From this point, plot an EP (see Chapter 7), then draw in the transferred position line parallel to the original line of bearing and passing through the EP.

A running fix is not only subject to all the usual errors that afflict any other fix based on visual bearings, but is also highly dependent on the accuracy of the estimated position used to transfer the position line. That, in turn, is dependent on the accuracy of the boat's log

and compass, on the tidetables, sea state, and on the ability of the helmsman and navigator.

With so many things that could go wrong a running fix is not to be relied on, but neither should it be dismissed as useless: even a rough position can be very useful in the middle of a longish passage. Besides, if there is only one thing in sight at a time, then the chances are that you do not need a high degree of accuracy because there is unlikely to be anything around to hit! You do not, incidentally, have to use the same landmark for both position lines, so a running fix can be equally useful when following a relatively featureless coastline, where the only recognizable landmarks are too far apart for more than one to be visible at once.

Doubling the angle on the bow

A special case of the running fix is known as 'doubling the angle on the bow'. If you note the log reading when a landmark is, say, 30° off the bow and then again when the yacht has sailed on far enough for the landmark to be 60° off the bow, then your distance off the landmark is the same as the distance travelled (see Figure 51).

This technique is really only a rule of thumb: it hardly justifies the name 'fix' because it completely ignores so many significant factors such as the effect of wind and tide. But for a boat on a steady course and in an area of weak tidal streams, it can be a useful quick check.

Four point fix

This special case occurs when the initial angle on the bow is 45° ('four points', in the old 'points' notation), because when this is doubled it becomes 90° – and the landmark is therefore abeam. Again the distance off corresponds to the distance travelled between the two bearings.

The simplest fix of all

The simplest fix of all is inherently more accurate than any of the others, yet it requires no measurement, no arithmetic, and no plotting apart from marking it on the chart and labelling it with the time. It is achieved simply by passing very close to some fixed and charted object.

Of course such a simple fix has its drawbacks – nothing can be quite that perfect. It depends on there being a suitable object

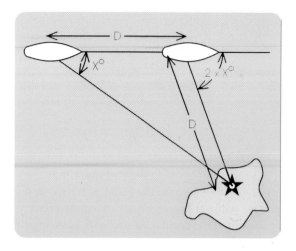

Fig 51 A special case of a running fix, known as doubling the angle on the bow, can be a useful rough check.

precisely positioned, surrounded by safe water and in a convenient location. Ideally this calls for a post or beacon driven into the seabed, in water deep enough for the yacht. Buoys and lightships are slightly less perfect objects because – like any anchored vessel – they usually drift a few yards away from their designated position, and can occasionally break loose altogether or drag off station.

The value of 'the simplest fix of all' should not be understated, though: its accuracy is generally on a par with that of the most sophisticated electronic position-fixing devices, and the ease and speed with which it can be plotted make it invaluable in rough weather or when sailing short-handed. For high speed craft, in particular, it is often worth making a slight detour to pass close to a buoy or beacon, rather than trying to obtain a fix by any other means.

5 | Tides

It is almost impossible to spend more than a few days anywhere on the coast of north-west Europe without becoming aware of the effect of the tide – the regular raising and lowering of sea level – so it must have been common knowledge even to prehistoric sailors in these areas.

Even land-locked waters, such as the Baltic and Mediterranean, are tidal to some extent, but their tides are so much smaller that they are easily masked by the effects of wind and barometric pressure. This is probably why tides failed to arouse the curiosity of the ancient Greek philosophers. Not until the Roman invasion of Britain were they the subject of any kind of scientific analysis. A proper explanation of them, however, had to wait until Newton 'invented' gravity.

The causes of tides

Tides are caused by the gravity of the sun and moon. Although the sun is much bigger and heavier than the moon, it is so much further away that its effect is less, so it is worth getting to grips with the moon's effect first.

The moon's tides
Imagine the world as a uniform ball of solid rock covered by a layer of water. Although it is usually said that the moon orbits around the earth with the earth's gravity stopping it from flying off into space, that is something of an over simplification; the two bodies really make up a single system held together by the mutual attraction of each other's gravity, and spinning

about a point somewhere between the two.

The effect of gravity decreases with distance, so the water closest to the moon is attracted towards it rather more strongly than is the solid mass of the earth itself. The water on the far side, being further from the moon, is attracted less strongly. The overall result is to produce two bulges, or tidal waves, one on each side of the earth, but both moving round it to follow the moon in its 28-day orbit.

Meanwhile, of course, the earth is still spinning on its own axis, so any given point on its surface will pass the crest of one tidal wave, then the trough, then the crest of the other and so on. The moon goes round the earth in the same direction as the earth's own rotation so it takes slightly longer than twelve hours for a fixed point to go from one high tide to the other, but even so, these tides are called half-daily or 'semi-diurnal'.

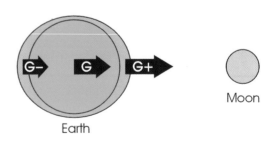

Fig 52 Tides are caused by the moon's gravity pulling on the water nearest to it more strongly than on the earth itself, whilst leaving the water on the other side of the earth behind.

Diurnal tides

This straightforward picture of two more-or-less equal semi-diurnal tides per day would hold true only if the moon's orbit were permanently lined up with the equator – which it is not. The earth's axis is at an angle to the moon's orbital plane, so the moon appears to wander from north to south and back again every month. This skews the picture of the earth with its two symmetrical tidal waves: a stationary observer anywhere north of the equator would see one hump as being much bigger than the other. In other words, he would see a major high tide roughly once every 25 hours. This is called a diurnal tide.

Tides in the real world

All this theory suggests that if the world were really completely covered with water, we would experience semi-diurnal tides twice a month (while the moon crosses the equator), and diurnal tides the rest of the time. The reason that this is not the case is because of the presence of land, which divides this huge body of water into separate seas and oceans, each of which behaves as if it were a huge bowl, with the water sloshing around inside it.

If you were to fill a washing-up bowl with water and gently rock it, you would find that the water would slosh backwards and forwards with a certain natural rhythm, and that if your

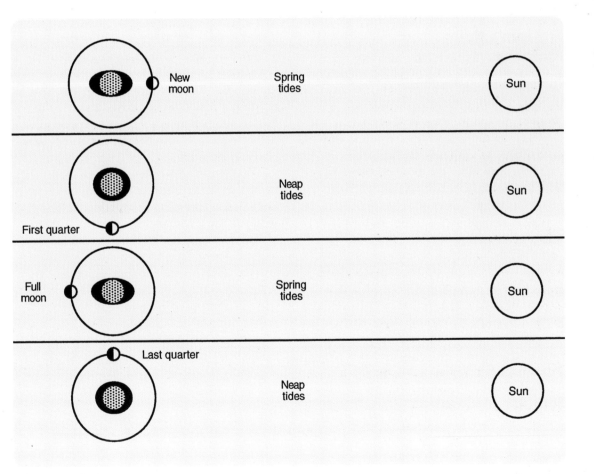

Fig 53 Big tides (springs) occur when the gravitational forces of the sun and moon are together or directly opposed. Small tides (neaps) occur in between.

rocking matched that rhythm, small but regular movements would be enough to build up an exaggerated surge of water in the bowl. Exactly how fast your rocking action would need to be depends on the size of the bowl: a small bowl needs faster movements than a big one.

Much the same thing applies to the world's oceans, though it is complicated by their irregular shapes. The Pacific, in general, reacts most strongly to diurnal tides. The Atlantic is roughly half the size, so it responds strongly to the semi-diurnal tides. This means that around Britain and northern Europe, the most obvious characteristic of tides is an alternating pattern of high and low water with about 12 hr 25 min between successive highs.

The sun's tides

The effect of the sun's gravity alone on a water-covered world would be very much the same as that of the moon, except that because it is so much further away the tides it produces would be about half the size.

When the sun and moon are in line with each other, the sun's tide-raising forces supplement those of the moon, causing bigger than average tides. A week later, when the moon has moved round 90°, so that the sun's gravity is at right angles to the moon's, the tide-raising forces of the sun and moon are opposing each other. The sun's gravity isn't enough to cancel out the lunar tide altogether, but it reduces it, producing a smaller high tide.

A week later still, at full moon, the sun and moon are in line again, and although they are on opposite sides of the earth their tide-raising forces are again supplementing each other to produce another period of big tides.

Springs and neaps

To sum up the story so far: the Atlantic Ocean is primarily affected by the moon's gravity, which produces a half-daily pattern of alternating high waters and low waters. On to this basic rhythm, the sun superimposes a half-monthly pattern of bigger-than-average tides

(with high highs and low lows), interspersed by smaller-than-average tides, with relatively low high waters and relatively high low waters. The big tides are called *springs* and the small ones are *neaps*.

It is worth noticing, incidentally, that at any given place, high water spring tides always occurs at about the same time of day – give or take an hour. In Plymouth, for example, HW springs are always at about breakfast and supper-time, while in Southampton they are always about midday and midnight.

Other factors

There are numerous other factors which superimpose even slower rhythms on to these half-daily and half-monthly patterns.

Although the sun and moon are in east-west alignment twice a month, to produce spring tides, they only come close to the three-dimensional alignment that is required to produce a really big tide twice a year – in March and September. This produces even higher highs and lower lows, sometimes called *equinoctial springs*.

A less noticeable effect is caused by variations in the distance between the earth and the sun and moon, strengthening or reducing the effect of their gravity.

On the very rare occasions when the sun, earth and moon are all perfectly lined up and at their closest points of approach to each other simultaneously, they are said to be 'in syzygy'. That word is more significant for Scrabble players than for navigators, but the event which it describes is important because the associated low water is the lowest level to which the tide is ever predicted to fall, and is called the lowest astronomical tide (LAT).

Tide levels and datums

Like most complex phenomena, tides have given rise to a glut of technical terms. Some of these, like 'high water full and change' have now become obsolete, but many others are still useful, and have survived with specific and distinct meanings (see Figure 54).

High Water The highest level reached by the sea during one tidal cycle.

Low Water The lowest level reached by the sea during one tidal cycle.

Chart Datum The level to which charted soundings and drying heights are referred. On charts of British and European waters, this corresponds to the lowest astronomical tide (LAT).

Lowest Astronomical Tide (LAT) The lowest level to which the tide is ever predicted to fall, without allowing for possible meteorological effects.

Highest Astronomical Tide The highest level to which the tide is ever expected to rise, without allowing for meteorological effects.

Height of Tide The actual level of the sea surface at any given moment measured from chart datum.

Range of Tide The height difference between low water and the following high water, or vice versa.

Spring Tides Tides with the greatest range in each fortnightly cycle.

Neap Tides Tides with the smallest range in each fortnightly cycle.

Equinoctial Springs Spring tides with an unusually large range occurring at the time of

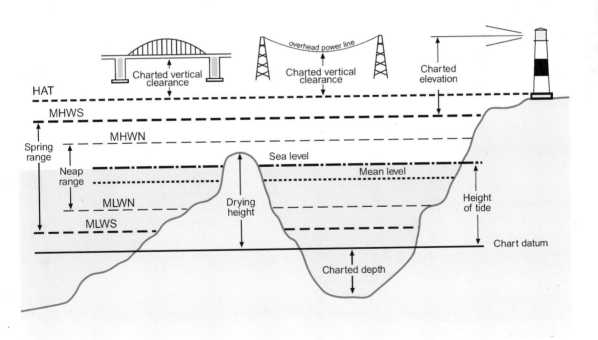

Fig 54 The rise and fall of the tide means that the marine navigator is concerned with several different sea levels, so it is important to know which is which. Charted depths and heights are generally based on the most pessimistic level!

the equinoxes (late March and late September).

Mean High Water Springs (MHWS) The average height of high water at spring tides throughout a whole year.

Mean Low Water Springs (MLWS) The average height of low water during spring tides throughout a whole year.

Mean High Water Neaps (MHWN) The average height of high water at neap tides, taken throughout the year.

Mean Low Water Neaps (MLWN) The average height of low water during neap tides, taken throughout the year.

Sounding The depth of the sea bed below chart datum, shown on charts either as spot soundings or contours.

Drying Height The height of a feature such as a rock or shoal, which is sometimes covered by the tide, measured above chart datum.

Charted Height The height of a feature such as an island, which is rarely or never covered by the sea, measured from mean high water springs (MHWS).

Elevation The height at which a light is displayed from a fixed structure measured above mean high water springs (MHWS) – or above sea level in the case of a lightship or light float.

Rise of Tide The height of sea level at any given moment, measured above the nearest low water.

Tidetables

Although the factors governing the tides are complicated, they can be predicted, and those predictions are published in the form of tide tables. These range from wallet-sized cards,

giving details of local tides, to the Admiralty Tidetables. The tidetables included in yachtsmen's almanacs are generally similar in content and layout to those produced by the Admiralty.

The height of tide can vary minute by minute and from place to place, so it is quite impractical to publish full predictions for every point around the coast and for every hour of the year. Instead, detailed predictions are given for a selection of major ports, called standard ports. These give the time and height of high and low water for each day, with a graph that allows the height at in-between times to be estimated with a fair degree of accuracy.

TIME ZONE –0100	ST MALO
Subtract 1 hour for UT	
For French Summer Time add	TIMES AND H
ONE hour in **non-shaded areas**	

MAY				JUNE		
Time	**m**	**Time**	**m**	**Time**	**m**	**Ti**
1 0312	9.3	**16** 0429	10.2	**1** 0425	10.6	**16** 0
0958	3.9	1118	3.3	1118	2.7	1
TH 1549	9.5	F 1659	10.4	SU 1655	10.9	M 1
2229	3.9	2338	3.2	2346	2.6	
2 0414	10.1	**17** 0516	10.5	**2** 0524	11.2	**17** 0
1102	3.1	1218	3.0	1218	2.2	0
F 1644	10.3	SA 1741	10.8	M 1749	11.5	TU 1
2327	3.0					1
3 0508	10.9	**18** 0023	2.9	**3** 0048	2.0	**18** 0
1159	2.3	0557	10.8	0619	11.7	0
SA 1734	11.2	SU 1244	2.8	TU 1313	1.8	W 1
		1818	11.1	● 1841	12.0	○ 1
4 0026	2.2	**19** 0102	2.7	**4** 0143	1.6	**19** 0
0557	11.7	0634	10.9	0712	12.0	0
SU 1252	1.7	M 1321	2.6	W 1406	1.6	TH 1
1820	11.9	1852	11.3	1931	12.3	1

Fig 55 Tide tables give the times and heights of high and low waters every day at a number of standard ports: this extract from *Reeds Nautical Almanac* is for St Malo, on the Channel coast of France.

Standard port – high and low water

To find the time of high and low water at a standard port is a simple matter: find the page of the tables that relates to that particular port, and look through it to find the relevant day.

Times are given using the 24-hour clock, based on the standard time of the country concerned – so for British ports, times are given in UT – which for all practical purposes is the same as GMT. When a daylight-saving scheme is in operation (BST), an hour has to be added to the time shown in order to convert it to clock time. The standard time of all our Continental neighbours is one hour ahead of GMT : the zone time is shown at the top of the relevant page. In the extract in Figure 55, for instance, the zone time is given as '– 0100' signifying that if one hour is subtracted from the time shown it will be converted back to GMT.

When cruising abroad most yachtsmen prefer to work in local clock time, rather than keep referring back to BST or GMT, so the convention of referring tidetables to local standard time is generally convenient. It is something to be careful of, though, when making a passage between two countries which have different standard times or daylight saving schemes.

Standard ports – intermediate heights and times

Unless you happen to be entering or leaving harbour at high or low water, you are likely to want to know the height of tide at some time other than those given in the tables, or to know the time at which the tide will reach some predetermined height in order to get out over a bar or a marina cill. This is easily done by using the graph or **tidal curve** that is printed with the tables for each standard port.

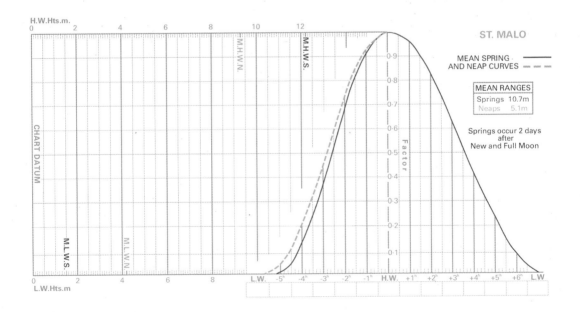

Fig 56 The tidal curve can be used to calculate the height of tide at a specific time, or the time at which the tide will reach a specific height (see text). (Source: *Reeds Nautical Almanac*.)

The 'graph' is really two graphs, representing the changing rise of tide over a complete tidal cycle at springs (solid line) and neaps (dotted line). Because tides vary in height, range and time there is no height scale as such, and times are given as hours before or after high water. Instead, a grid on one side of the main graph serves as a ready-reckoner, to adapt the general graph to suit the height of a particular tide. Before this can be used, it has to be prepared using the information provided by the main tide tables:

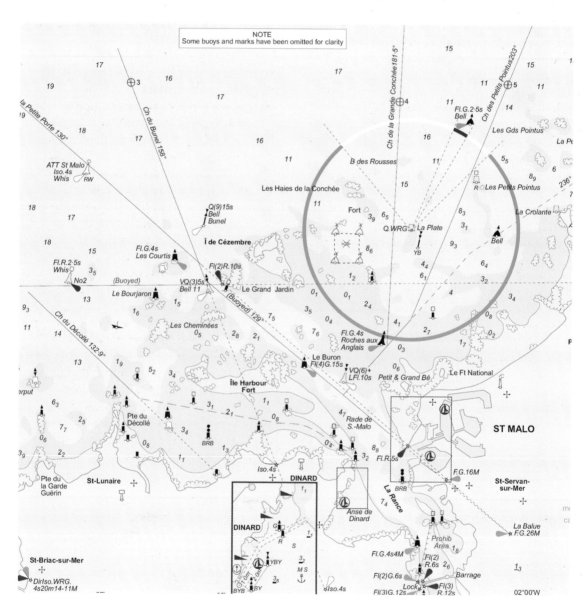

Fig 57 Extract from *Reeds Nautical Almanac* showing the approaches to St Malo.

1 Write the time of high water in the box provided under the graph.
2 Mark the height of low water on the horizontal scale at the bottom left hand corner of the ready-reckoner section, and the height of high water on the corresponding horizontal scale at the top of the ready-reckoner section.

3 Join the high and low water marks with a straight pencil line.
4 Subtract the height of low water from the height of high water and compare the result with the figures given in the 'mean ranges' box to decide whether this particular tide is a spring, a neap or in between.

To find height at a given time

5 Work out how the required time compares with high water and mark the corresponding point on the horizontal scale at the bottom of the graph.
6 From the required time draw a line straight upwards to meet the appropriate (spring or neap) curve.
7 From this intersection draw a horizontal line straight across and into the ready-reckoner to meet the diagonal line you drew in step 3.
8 From this point draw a straight vertical line to meet the height scale along the top or bottom edge of the ready-reckoner, and read off the height.

To find the time for a required height

This is effectively the same problem in reverse, so the preparation – steps 1 to 4 – is exactly the same.

5 Find the required height on the horizontal scale of the ready-reckoner.
6 Draw a straight vertical line to meet the sloping line you drew in step 3.
7 From this intersection draw a horizontal line, across into the graph.
8 Where this horizontal line meets the appropriate curve (springs or neaps) draw a vertical line downwards to meet the time scale at the bottom of the graph.
9 Read off the time in terms of hours before or after high water. Add or subtract this to the time of high water to convert this to standard time.
10 Add one hour if necessary to convert from standard time to summer time.

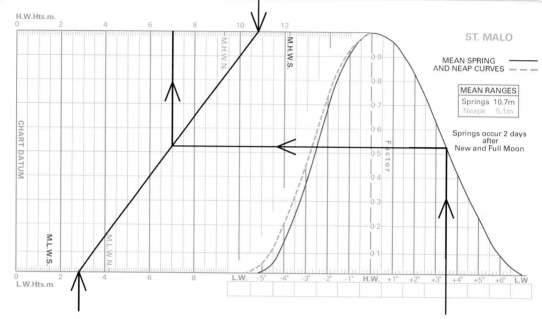

Fig 58 Example 1 for tidal heights. (Source: *Reeds Nautical Almanac.*)

Tidal heights – example 1

In one of the minor channels leading in to St Malo, the chart shows a least depth of 0.4 metres. What will be the actual depth of water at 0930 (BST) on 18 May?

From the tide tables (Figure 55):
High water St Malo is at 0557,10.8 metres
Low water St Malo is at 1244, 2.8 metres.

1 Subtract the height of low water from the height of high water to give the range:10.8 – 2.8 + 8.0. Comparing this with the 'Mean Ranges' panel on the tidal curve shows that this is nearly a spring tide.
2 Mark the height of low water on the scale at the bottom left of the tidal curve, and the height of high water on the corresponding scale across the top, and join these two marks with a straight line (see Figure 58).

The required time is 0930 BST. As BST is the same as French Standard Time, and the tidetables are in French Standard Time, no conversion is required. 0930 is 3 hours 33 minutes after high water.

3 Find 3 hours 33 minutes after high water on the time scale below the curve, and draw a vertical line up to meet the graph. As this is nearly a spring tide, the solid curve is most appropriate.
4 Where the vertical line meets the curve, draw a horizontal line into the ready reckoner on the left hand side, to meet the sloping line drawn in step 2.
5 Where the horizontal and sloping lines meet, draw a vertical line to meet the height scale along the top (or bottom) edge of the ready reckoner, and read off the height of tide. In this case it is 7.0 metres, so the depth in the channel will be 7.0 + 0.4 = 7.4 metres.

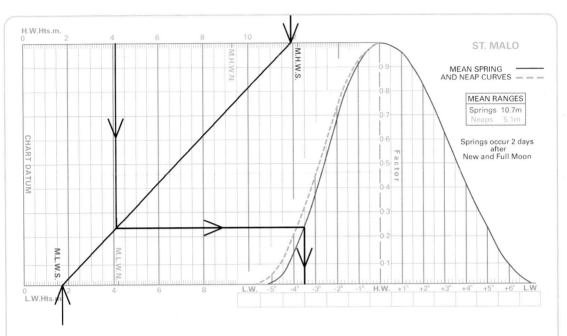

Fig 59 Example 2 for tidal heights. (Source: *Reeds Nautical Almanac.*)

Tidal heights – example 2

The Marina Les Bas Sablons at St Malo can only be entered by going over a cill, which is 2.0 metres above chart datum. What is the earliest time that a yacht drawing 1.6 metres can enter the marina, with a clearance of 0.5 metres, during the afternoon of 4 May?

The yacht draws 1.6 metres, and requires an extra 0.5 metres clearance, so the depth of water required is 1.6 + 0.5 = 2.1m.
The cill is 2.0 metres above chart datum, so the height of tide required is
2.1m + 2.0m = 4.1m above CD.

From the tide tables (Figure 55):
High water St Malo is at 1820, 11.9 metres
Low water St Malo is at 1252, 1.7 metres.

1 Subtract the height of low water from the height of high water to give the range:
11.9 – 1.7 = 10.2. Comparing this with the 'Mean Ranges' panel on the tidal curve

shows that this is nearly an average spring tide (see Figure 59).

2 Mark the height of low water on the scale at the bottom left of the tidal curve, and the height of high water on the corresponding scale across the top, and join these two marks with a straight line.

3 Find the required height on the upper scale, and drop a vertical line down to meet the sloping line.

4 From where these two meet, draw a horizontal line across to meet the graph. As this is a spring tide, the solid curve is the most appropriate.

5 Where the horizontal line meets the solid curve, drop a vertical line down to meet the time scale.
    In this case, the time indicated is –3 hrs 30 mins, ie 3 hrs 30 mins before high water, or 1450. As the tide tables were in French Standard Time, the answer is also in French Standard Time.

Secondary ports

Most harbours and anchorages, particularly the smaller more attractive places, are classed as secondary ports. They are generally of less commercial or military interest than standard ports, so they have not justified the long-term sequence of tidal observations required to produce full tidetables, nor would they justify the space required to publish a full set of predictions. Instead, it is up to the individual navigator to prepare his own tidetables, by applying published differences to the data which is given for a nearby standard port.

In *Reeds Nautical Almanac*, for instance, the entry for St Mary's (Figure 60) shows that it is referred to the standard port of Plymouth. The arrow indicates that tidetables for Plymouth can be found somewhere in the following pages.

Start by writing down the relevant data for Plymouth, exactly as it appears in the tidetables – do not add the hour for BST at this stage. The extract from the Plymouth tidetables (Figure 61) shows that on 16th May, low water was at 0918, 1.4 metres, and high water was at 1525, 4.7 metres.

The difference tables look complicated, but it will help to think of them divided into two halves – one dealing with times, and the other with height – and to sub-divide each half into four columns. The first time column tells us that when high water Plymouth is at 0000 or 1200 the difference for St Mary's is – 0035; and the second column says that when high water Plymouth is at 0600 or 1800, the difference for St Mary's is – 0100. Please note that this means 1 hour, not 100 minutes!

9.1.7   ST MARY'S

Isles of Scilly 49°55'·14N 06°18'·71W ⚓⚓⚓⚓⚓⚓

CHARTS AC 34, 883, 5603.10-11; Imray C7; Stanfords 2; OS 203

TIDES −0630 Dover; ML 3·2; Duration 0600

Standard Port PLYMOUTH (→)

Times				Height (metres)			
High Water		Low Water		MHWS	MHWN	MLWN	MLWS
0000	0600	0000	0600	5·5	4·4	2·2	0·8
1200	1800	1200	1800				
Differences ST MARY'S							
−0035	−0100	−0040	−0025	+0·2	−0·1	−0·2	−0·1

SHELTER Good in St Mary's Hbr, except in W/NW gales when ⚓ in Porth Cressa (9.1.6) may be more comfortable. Strictly no ⚓ in the apprs and Hbr limits (from Newman rock to Newford Is).

NAVIGATION WPT 49°53'·96N 06°18'·83W (abm Spanish Ledge ECM lt buoy) 307°/1·2M via St Mary's Sound to transit line B (040°). The 097·3° transit leads S of Bacon Ledge (0·3m) marked by PHM lt buoy. A charted 151° transit leads into the Pool between Bacon Ledge and the Cow and Calf (drying 0·6 and 1·8m). Pilotage is compulsory for yachts >30m LOA. Hbr speed limit 3kn. NB: Do not impede the ferry *Scillonian III* which arrives about 1200 and sails at 1630 Mon-Fri; Sat times vary with month. Also the blue-hulled cargo ship *Gry Maritha* thrice weekly.

LIGHTS AND MARKS See chartlet and 9.1.4. 097·3° ldg marks: W bcns; front, white △; rear, orange x; lts as chartlet. The R and G sectors of the Pierhd lt are not on the convential sides of the W sector. Buzza Hill twr and power stn chy (48m) are conspic.

TIME ZONE (UT)
For Summer Time add ONE hour in **non-shaded areas**

PLYMOUTH
TIMES AND HEIGI

MAY				JUNE		
Time	m	Time	m	Time	m	Tin
1 0122	4.5	**16** 0254	4.8	**1** 0252	4.9	**16** 03
TH 0757	1.7	F 0918	1.4	SU 0919	1.2	M 10
1418	4.5	1525	4.7	1527	5.0	16
2027	1.8	2139	1.5	2148	1.2	22
2 0236	4.8	**17** 0341	4.9	**2** 0354	5.1	**17** 04
F 0900	1.4	SA 1005	1.3	M 1016	1.0	TU 10
1515	4.8	1607	4.9	1623	5.2	16
2127	1.4	2224	1.3	2244	1.0	23
3 0334	5.0	**18** 0424	5.0	**3** 0451	5.2	**18** 05
SA 0955	1.0	SU 1046	1.2	TU 1110	0.9	W 11
1605	5.0	1645	5.0	1716	5.4	17
2220	1.0	2304	1.2	● 2337	0.8	○ 23
4 0425	5.3	**19** 0502	5.0	**4** 0546	5.3	**19** 05
SU 1046	0.8	M 1124	1.1	W 1201	0.8	TH 12
2310	0.7	1720	5.1	1807	5.5	18
		2341	1.1			
5 0515	5.4	**20** 0539	5.0	**5** 0028	0.7	**20** 00
M 1134	0.6	TU 1158	1.2	TH 0638	5.3	06
1739	5.5	1754	5.2	1251	0.8	F 12
● 2356	0.6	○		1856	5.5	18

Fig 60 Tidal difference tables give the difference between the tide at a minor (secondary) port compared with the tide at a nearby standard port.

Fig 61 The difference tables for St Mary's refer to these tidetables for Plymouth Devonport.

In this particular instance, high water Plymouth is between 1200 and 1800, but nearer to 1200. If the differences involved were small, it would be reasonable to take the nearest, but in this case it would be as well to interpolate – ie to estimate a suitable figure somewhere between the differences given in the table. In this case, as the time of high water is about ⁷/₁₂ of the way from 1200 to 1800 we need to pick a figure that is ⁷/₁₂ of the way between – 00h35m and – 01h00m: ie – 00h49m. Applying this difference to the time of high water Plymouth gives a time of high water at St Mary's of 1436 GMT. The next two columns of the difference table give the corresponding information for low water, so by the same process we can work out the time of low water at St Mary's to be 0845GMT.

As an alternative to the arithmetic, there are two graphical methods of interpolating. One of these involves drawing a sketch graph of the changing time differences plotted against time, as in Figure 62. Then draw a vertical line up from the time of high (or low) water on the horizontal axis to meet the graph, and from where they meet draw a horizontal line across to the vertical scale and read off the time difference.

The other involves drawing a horizontal scale to represent the time of day, and a sloping line marked off with the time differences. Make sure that the time difference where the two lines intersect corresponds with the appropriate time of day. Join the other ends of the two scales, corresponding to the other tabulated time and its time difference, so as to form a triangle as shown in Figure 63. Finally, draw another line, parallel to the third side of

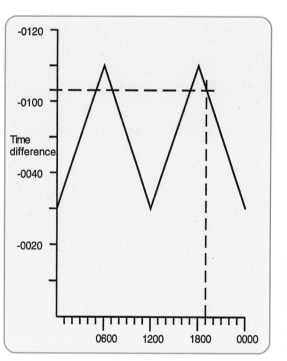

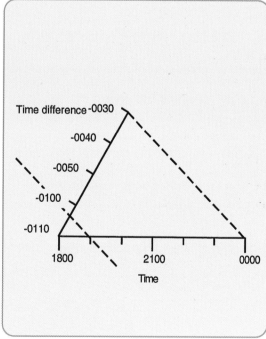

Fig 62 You may be able to interpolate tidal differences more easily by using the tabulated figures to draw a simple graph. Here, the time difference is – 0030 when high water is at midnight or midday, and – 0110 when high water is at 0600 and 1800.

Fig 63 An alternative diagrammatic method of interpolating tidal differences, which requires less drawing.

the triangle, from the time of high (or low) water on the time scale, and read off the time difference from where this last line cuts the time difference scale.

The height differences work in very much the same way, except that because the numbers involved are usually smaller, the need to interpolate arises less often, and is generally easier. In this case the height of high water Plymouth is 4.7 metres. The table shows a correction of 0.1 metres for a high water height of 4.4 metres, and + 0.2 for a high water height of 5.5 metres. 4.7 is about a quarter of the way from 4.4 to 5.5, so the appropriate correction is about a quarter of the way from – 0.1 to + 0.2 which works out to zero. So the height of high water St Mary's is also 4.7. The same procedure is used to derive the height of low water at St Mary's, before converting the times to BST by adding one hour.

Secondary ports – intermediate times and heights

The procedure for calculating the height of tide at secondary ports for times between high and low waters is exactly the same as for standard ports, except that the basic high and low water data first have to be derived from difference tables, and that as there are no graphs published for secondary ports, the graph for the relevant standard port has to be used instead.

Finding the height required

One of the great advantages of operating in tidal waters is that the rise of tide makes it possible to go to places that would otherwise be too shallow. St Mary's is a good example: one of its most convenient approach channels is partly blocked by a drying sandbank, on which the chart shows a drying height of 0.8 metres.

A very common navigational problem is to

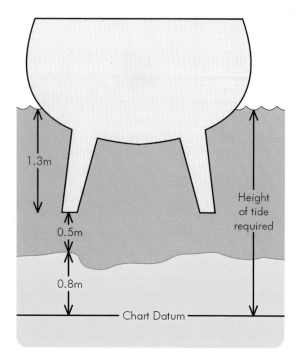

Fig 64 A simple sketch, like this, makes it easy to work out your under-keel clearance from the information given on the chart and in tide tables, and reduces the risk of making a mistake.

decide whether the height of tide is enough to allow a bar like this to be crossed in safety or, if not, the time at which the tide will have risen sufficiently. Although this is a fairly straightforward calculation, it is very easy to lose track of precisely what is going on, so it may help to draw a rough sketch like that shown in Figure 64.

This shows chart datum as a horizontal line, with the highest part of the bar standing at 0.8 metres above it. It is good seamanship to allow a safety margin – in this case a fairly minimal 0.5 metres, though if there were any sea running it would be sensible to allow considerably more. On top of this there is the boat itself, with a draught of 1.3 metres. With a picture like this it is immediately obvious that in this case the height of tide required is 0.8 m + 0.5 m + 1.3 m = 2.6 m.

The effect of weather

Tidal calculations, giving answers with a precision of minutes and tenths of a metre, *look* very accurate. The astronomical data on which the predictions are based is as reliable as sunrise and sunset, and the calculations which convert these into tidetables are the result of decades of painstaking observations so, barring mishaps in the production of the tables themselves, tidal predictions are inherently reliable. What cannot be allowed for, however, is the effect of weather.

Prolonged high barometric pressure over a large area can depress the sea level, or winds blowing the sea on to the coast can raise it, so tidetables have to be based on the assumption of average weather conditions. Every 11mb of pressure difference can make a change of 0.1 metres to the predicted height, and a prolonged force 5 blowing onshore can raise the sea level by 0.2 metres.

The combined effect of wind and barometric pressure typically produces variations of about ±0.2 metres in height and ±10 minutes in time, but in extreme conditions the differences can be very much greater. Northerly winds blowing into the funnel-shaped North Sea, for instance, have been known to raise the sea level at its southern end by 2 metres or more. More local effects can be caused by the passage of an intense, fast-moving depression, causing relatively rapid changes in sea level lasting for an hour or so, and usually of a few tenths of a metre.

The cumulative effect of meteorological factors on tidal heights and times is very difficult to predict with any accuracy, so although tidal calculations should usually be carried out as precisely as possible, their accuracy should not be relied on.

Tidal anomalies

The Rule of Twelfths is a good approximation to the typical tidal curve of places such as Plymouth, which is exposed almost directly to the Atlantic tide. There are many places, however, where the presence of shallow water

RULE OF TWELFTHS

For some purposes a very approximate calculation is all that is required, and the use of full tables and graphs is not warranted. One cannot, however, assume that the tide rises and falls at a constant rate. The bell-shaped graph in Figure 56 on page 69 is typical. From low water the tide rises slowly at first, then increasingly quickly, before slowing down again towards high water and then reversing the slow-fast-slow pattern as it falls towards low water again. A good approximation to this typical curve is given by a simple arithmetical process called 'the Rule of Twelfths', which says that:

in the first hour the tide rises one twelfth of its range

in the second hour it rises two twelfths of its range

in the third hour it rises three twelfths of its range

in the fourth hour it rises three twelfths of its range

in the fifth hour it rises two twelfths of its range

in the sixth hour it rises one twelfth of its range.

Notice that this calculation is based on the range of the tide, so the result will be the rise of tide not the height of tide. Low water must be added to the rise of tide in order to get the height above chart datum.

or islands close offshore causes distortions in the shape of the tidal wave, in much the same way as a shelving beach distorts incoming swell into surf.

Much of the central south coast of England is affected by such so-called 'tidal anomalies', as are parts of the North Sea. The tidal curve for the Hook of Holland, for example, shows two roughly equal low waters, followed by a rapid rise to high water, and a 'stand' – during which the tide stays high for about one and a half hours before falling again to its next low water.

At Southampton (Figure 65) the stand at high water is so pronounced that it is difficult to determine exactly when high water occurs, so the tidal graph uses low water as its reference point instead. This makes the graph look unusual, but makes hardly any difference to the way it is used. Such strangely shaped graphs as these do, however, demonstrate that the Rule of Twelfths has to be used with some

care, and may have to be abandoned altogether in areas where there are pronounced tidal anomalies.

Tidal streams

Raising sea level by several metres across a huge area takes an enormous volume of water. That water obviously has to come from somewhere, so one side effect of tides – **vertical** movements of the sea's surface – is the **horizontal** movement of large quantities of water from place to place. These horizontal movements are called tidal streams.

Tidal streams can be subdivided into two main groups: 'rectilinear' and 'rotary'. Rectilinear tidal streams are found in reasonably well-defined channels, where the water can only flow in two main directions. In the case of a river estuary, a tidal stream can quite clearly be seen to be moving 'in' or 'out'.

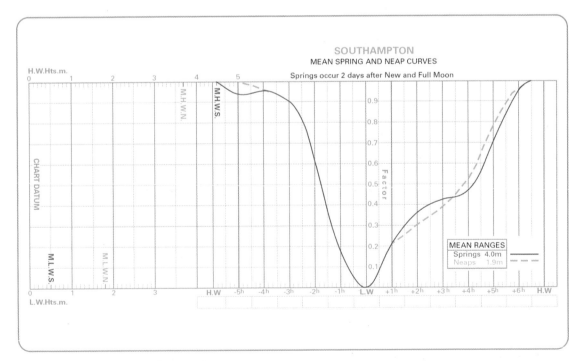

Fig 65 In some areas, such as the Solent, the bell-shaped tidal curve is seriously distorted. At Southampton, 'High Water' is so drawn out that the curve has to be centred around low water instead. (Source: *Reeds Nautical Almanac.*)

These two directions are often referred to as 'flood' and 'ebb': the flood tide corresponds to the rising sea level and the ebb to the falling sea level.

In many cases, though, the expressions 'flood' and 'ebb' are confusing or even misleading, so it is generally better to refer to the compass direction of the water flow. Where the water movement is not constrained by a definite channel the tidal streams are continually changing in direction, and turn through 360° in each tidal cycle. This gives rise to the name 'rotary' tidal streams – even though the flow is considerably stronger in approximately opposite directions than in any others.

Tidal stream information

The waters around the British Isles include some of the world's strongest tidal streams. Rates of three knots or more are quite common, so a sailing yacht's speed over the ground can easily be halved or doubled by the tidal stream. Their effect on motor boats may be less obvious, but strong tidal streams can have a definite effect on the sea state, so for any British yachtsman the tidal streams are a force to be reckoned with.

There are two main sources of tidal stream information: tidal diamonds printed on charts; and tidal stream atlases (see page 80), available either as separate books or reduced in size and included in yachtsmen's almanacs. Both types of presentation depend on the fact that tidal streams are closely related to the tides, because instead of using clock times, they refer to hours before or after high water at a particular port.

Tidal diamonds

On an Admiralty chart, tidal diamonds are diamond-shaped symbols printed in magenta ink – hence the name tidal diamonds, even though other publishers use alternative symbols. Each diamond is marked with a letter that corresponds to a particular part of a table of information printed elsewhere on the chart

which presents the tidal stream data in numerical form.

Like the tidal stream atlases, the table uses the time of high water at a specified standard port as a reference rather than clock time. Each broad column within the table corresponds to a particular tidal diamond, and each row to a time before or after high water at the standard port. Having found the column corresponding to the appropriate tidal diamond, and the row corresponding to the appropriate time, the spring and neap rates are given in knots and the direction of flow in degrees True.

Tidal diamonds have the advantage of precision, particularly in terms of direction – which can be difficult to measure on the

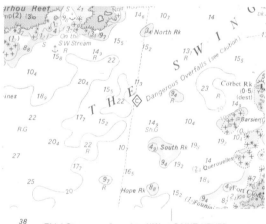

Hours	Geographical Position	A 49°44'6N 2 11·8W			B 49°44'2N 2 18·7W			C 49°43'3N 2 14·9W			D 49°41'3N 2 14·5W		
Before High Water 6		267	3 4	1 5	218	5 0	2 0	227	6 5	2 6	234	2 8	1 1
5		275	3 1	1 4	210	5 1	2 1	222	6 8	2 7	186	1 4	0 6
4		269	2 4	1 1	207	3 9	1 6	223	4 8	1 9	100	1 4	0 6
3		271	1 1	0 5	202	2 2	0 9	170	1 2	0 5	078	1 5	0 6
2		067	0 9	0 4	072	1 1	0 4	051	2 6	1 0	062	1 6	0 6
1		075	3 3	1 5	051	2 8	1 1	041	4 6	1 8	054	1 6	0 6
High Water		091	3 1	1 4	024	5 5	2 3	047	5 5	2 2	047	1 7	0 7
After High Water 1		267	0 3	0 2	018	4 8	2 0	038	5 1	2 0	020	1 2	0 5
2		287	1 9	0 8	018	3 4	1 4	037	3 9	1 6	354	0 5	0 2
3		285	2 3	1 0	014	1 9	0 8	041	1 9	0 8	278	0 5	0 2
4		273	3 3	1 5	186	0 6	0 2	164	0 5	0 2	252	1 7	0 7
5		259	3 1	1 4	201	2 8	1 1	231	5 1	2 1	250	3 1	1 2
6		264	3 2	1 4	214	4 3	1 7	229	6 2	2 5	239	2 9	1 2

Tidal Streams referred to HW at SAINT HELIER

(Column sub-headings: Directions of streams (degrees) · Rates at spring tides (knots) · Rates at neap tides (knots))

Fig 66 Tidal diamonds on charts mark a specific position, for which tidal stream data is given in tabular form elsewhere on the chart.

TIDAL STREAM ATLASES

Tidal stream atlases present information pictorially in the form of 12 or 13 chartlets, each of which is a 'snapshot' of the situation at a particular time in the tidal cycle. Arrows indicate the direction of the tidal stream, and their length and thickness give an impression of its rate. A more accurate indication of the speed of the tidal stream is given by the numbers, arranged in pairs, which show the rate in tenths of a knot at neap and spring tides: 13, 25 for instance, means the neap rate is 1.3 knots increasing to 2.5 knots at springs. The comma indicates the geographical position to which the figures refer.

For tides which are between springs and neaps, or those that are bigger than average springs or smaller than average neaps, it may be necessary to interpolate. So long as the figures involved are small a fairly rough and ready interpolation is usually enough, but very strong tidal streams call for more accuracy. For this reason,

Admiralty Tidal Stream Atlases include an interpolation chart (Figure 68).

1 Mark the spring rate on the upper of the two dotted lines that run across the chart and the neap rate on the lower dotted line.

2 Join these two marks with a pencil line.

3 From the tide tables find the height of high and low water at the relevant standard port for that day, and subtract one from the other to find the range.

4 Find this range on the vertical scale on the left hand side of the diagram and follow the horizontal line across to meet the sloping pencil line.

5 From where they meet move vertically upwards or downwards to read off the rate from the horizontal scale printed at the top or bottom of the chart.

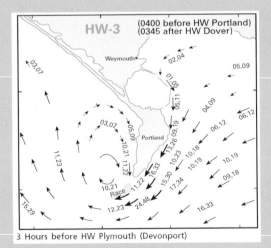

Fig 67 Tidal stream atlases represent the tidal streams pictorially, on a series of chartlets – one for each hour of the tidal cycle.
(Source: *Reeds Nautical Almanac.*)

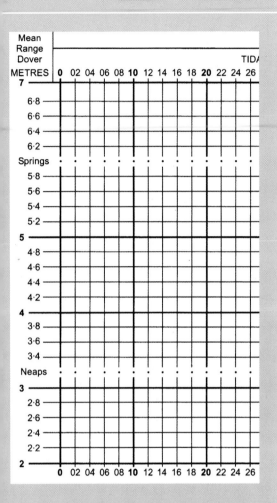

Fig 68 An interpolation chart, like this one from the *Admiralty Tidal Stream Atlas*, can help work out accurate tidal stream information for tides that are neither springs nor neaps.

chartlets of a tidal stream atlas. Their downside is that it is less easy to get an overall view of the changing patterns of the tidal streams for strategic planning, and if the position you are interested in is not very close to a tidal diamond it can be difficult to decide which is the most appropriate.

Interpolating for time

Whether it is derived from tidal stream atlases or tidal diamonds, tidal stream data is like a company's balance sheet or a car's MOT: it is a report on conditions at a particular moment. So if high water at the standard port is at 1353, the data given for 'two hours after high water' is a prediction for 1553 – not for 1600 or 1545.

In practical navigation, however, we are usually concerned with tidal streams over a period, so it is normal to work on the convenient assumption that tidal stream data is valid for a complete hour – half an hour on each side of the precise time to which it relates. In other words, the 1553 prediction would be taken to cover the period from 1523 to 1623. If, for some reason, you want to find the tidal stream over a period that does not fit neatly within one of these one-hour blocks, the most correct way is by a process of 'vector addition', which involves drawing lines on the chart. Suppose, for the sake of argument, that the published tidal stream data predicts that at 1050 the tidal stream will be 070°(T) 1.5 kts, and that at 1150 it will be 110°(T) 0.9 kts (see Figure 69), but that we require the tidal stream from 11.00 to 12.00. With this information we assume that the tidal stream from 10.20 to 11.20 is 070° 1.5 kt and that from 11.20 to 12.20 it is 110° 0.9 kt.

If this were true, then for the first 20 minutes of the hour (from 11.00 to 11.20) a drifting object would move in a 070° direction at 1.5 kts, so it would travel 0.5 mile (Figure 69). At that point it would be subject to the next hour's tidal stream, so it would 'alter course' to 110° and slow down to 0.9 kts – at

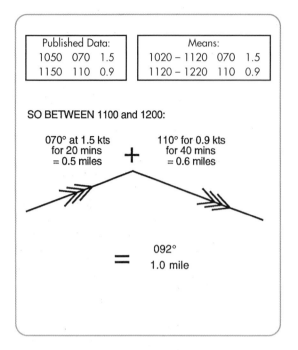

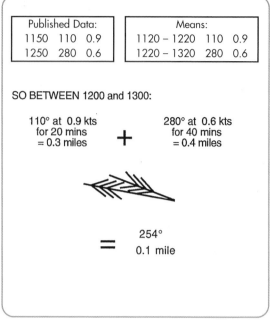

Fig 69 When you are interested in a time interval that spans two tidal stream atlas chartlets or two sets of tabulated data, it may be possible to estimate an 'average' tidal stream ... BUT

Fig 70 ...mental averaging must be done carefully and treated with caution: in this case it would have given a very wrong answer.

which speed it would cover 0.6 mile in the remaining forty minutes.

As Figure 69 shows, over the complete hour it would have moved in a 092° direction and covered a distance of just over 1 mile. One might have arrived at a very similar answer by mental interpolation, and with care and experience that may be a perfectly satisfactory technique. It needs to be treated with caution though, as Figure 70 shows.

Here, the raw data gives a tidal stream at 1150 of 110° 0.9 kt, and 280° 0.6 kt at 1250. Interpolating for direction would suggest that between 1200 and 1300 the tidal stream is flowing in a direction of about 195° and interpolating for rate suggests a speed of about 0.75 kts, but the vector addition method highlights the fact that the tide has turned during this hour, so its overall effect is movement in a 254° direction at 0.1 kt.

Interpolating for position

Each tidal stream prediction is valid for only one particular position – either the tidal diamond or the comma on a tidal stream atlas chartlet. At locations between these points, the tidal stream may be doing something different. In this case interpolation between two or more sets of published predictions is generally quite reasonable, unless there is a very large discrepancy between them. If, for instance, the tidal stream at one diamond is 110° 0.9 kt and at another is 120° 0.7 kt, then it is quite reasonable to assume that midway between them it will be about 115° 0.8 kt. Where there is a large discrepancy one has to accept that you simply do not have the necessary information and you must use your skill and judgement to make an informed guess. Navigation is still an art!

Tidal streams – example

The available tidal stream information (tidal diamond or tidal stream atlas) suggests that the spring rate at a particular spot in the Dover Straits is 2.4 knots, and that the neap rate is 1.4 knots. If high water Dover is 5.9 metres and low water is 1.5 metres, what will be the actual rate?

The tide tables for Dover show that a spring tide has a range of 6.0 metres, and a neap has a range of 3.1 metres. On the day in question, however, the tide is neither a spring nor a neap: its range is 5.9 – 1.5 = 4.4 metres.

1 On the interpolation chart (see Figure 71), mark the spring rate (2.4 knots) on the dotted line labelled 'Springs', and the neap rate (1.4 knots) on the dotted line labelled 'Neaps'.
2 Join these two marks with a straight line.
3 Find the actual range (4.4 metres) on the scale on the side of the table, and draw a horizontal line across the table to meet the sloping line.
4 From where these two lines cross, draw a vertical line to meet the rate scale on the top or bottom of the table, and read off the actual rate.

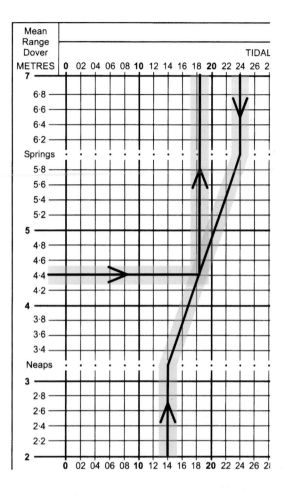

Fig 71 Using the tidal stream interpolation chart to work out the actual rate.

Estimating tidal streams

Tidal streams are nothing more than moving water – something of which we all have everyday experience. If you watch rainwater flowing down a gutter, it is obvious from the leaves and twigs on its surface that the water in the deepest part of the gutter is flowing faster than the water in the shallower parts. It is the same with tides: tidal streams are generally strongest in deep water and weaker in the shallows, where they are slowed down by contact with the seabed. It is the depth of water that is important – not the proximity of the shore.

Tidal streams flow faster around headlands, or where a channel narrows, than they do in bays or wider sections of the channel. This could be compared to water flowing through a funnel: the water flows faster through the narrow section than it does through the less constricted part immediately upstream.

If you stir a pan of water, swirling eddies develop around the back of the spoon. The same thing would happen if you held the spoon stationary and the water flowed round it, and – on a much larger scale – where a prominent headland juts out into a strong tidal stream. This can set up quite strong 'back-eddies' or 'counter-currents'. A good example of this is around Portland Bill, where the tidal stream on both sides flows south for about ten hours out of every twelve hour tidal cycle. The presence of eddies can sometimes be seen either by turbulence where opposing tidal streams meet, or by a collection of scum and debris in the 'dead' area in the middle of the eddy.

Direct personal observation of the effects of tidal streams can also provide useful information to supplement or confirm the data given in almanacs, charts and tidal stream atlases. Moored boats, or the 'wake' that develops when the tide flows past navigation marks or crab pot buoys, give a good indication of the direction of the tidal stream, and an impression of its strength. Over a period of time, the boat's movement over the ground, derived from a succession of fixes, can be compared with its course and distance travelled; any discrepancy may be due to the tidal stream, though it can be difficult to separate this from other factors such as compass or helmsman error and leeway.

Tidal streams and sea state

Tidal streams can have a marked effect on the sea state – which can be especially significant for high-speed motorboats.

Overfalls, sometimes called tide rips, are relatively localized effects, caused where a strong tidal stream is deflected upwards or broken into turbulence by obstructions on the sea bed, producing particularly steep and irregular waves close downtide of the obstruction. Although overfalls are made worse by strong winds, the fact that they are not created by the wind means that they can produce rough water even in otherwise calm conditions. On the other hand, this makes

them easily predictable, so areas prone to overfalls are often marked on the chart.

Most of the waves one encounters at sea are generated by the wind, but their size and shape can be modified by the tidal stream. If the tidal stream is flowing in the same direction as the wind that created the waves, the relative wind speed over the surface of the moving water is reduced, so the waves it creates are smaller. As well as this, the tidal stream has the effect of 'stretching' the length of each wave, reducing its slope and making its crest less likely to break. When the wind and tide are in opposition, the opposite happens; the wind speed relative to the surface of the water is increased, making the waves larger while, at the same time, the tidal stream shortens their wavelength to produce higher and steeper waves that are more likely to have breaking crests.

This can mean that a passage that would be uncomfortable in wind against tide conditions becomes pleasant when wind and tide are together, or that a passage that seemed perfectly reasonable when wind and tide were together becomes unpleasant or even dangerous when the tide turns.

It can also have a major effect on passage-planning strategy. Sailing boat navigators, whose boat speed may be little more than that of the tidal stream, will usually plan a passage so that the tide is in their favour – so they are likely to choose wind-against-tide conditions to make progress upwind.

A planing motor cruiser, on the other hand, can easily overcome a contrary tide – even one of five knots or more – but might be forced to throttle back to displacement speeds by wind-against-tide sea conditions. Its navigator might well accept a foul tide, in order to make progress upwind in flatter water.

6 Lights, Buoys and Fog Signals

Lighthouses have been used to guide – and sometimes mislead – navigators, for centuries. The Pharos of Alexandria was built over 2250 years ago and was regarded as one of the wonders of the ancient world, with a wood-burning fire that could be seen over 20 miles away. In two millennia, of course, lighthouses have become considerably more sophisticated, and even in an age increasingly dependent on electronic navigation aids, they are still of major importance in coastal navigation.

Their range has not increased dramatically: the big developments – apart from improving reliability – have been to give them distinctive characteristics that make it possible to distinguish one light from another. These characteristics can be divided into three groups: rhythm, period and colour.

Rhythm

The simplest possible rhythm for a light is **fixed** – showing continuously and steadily. Unfortunately, a great many lights that have nothing to do with marine navigation also show continuously and steadily, so fixed lights are mostly used in minor roles, such as marking the ends of jetties. More important lights usually have more sophisticated rhythms. A **flashing** light, in everyday language, simply means one that is going on and off, but its navigational meaning is more specific: it means that the total duration of light is shorter than the total duration of darkness.

If this situation is reversed, so that the light is visible for longer than the intervals of darkness, it is described as an **occulting** light. A fourth possibility is for the duration of light and darkness to be equal, in which case the light is described as **isophase**. There is nothing that can be done to vary the rhythm of a fixed or isophase light, but flashing or occulting rhythms are open to many variations.

A straightforward flashing light involves a regular flash and an occulting light a regular eclipse ('flash of darkness'). The flashes can, however, come in groups, with each group separated from the next by a longer interval of darkness, to produce a **group flashing** light.

As a further, but rarely used, variation, one group may be different from the next – such as a group of three flashes followed by a group of two flashes before the pattern repeats itself – in a rhythm known as **composite group flashing**.

Flashing, group flashing and composite group flashing all have their occulting equivalents.

For a flashing light, another possibility is to extend the flash to as much as two seconds to produce a **long flashing** (LFl) light. Alternatively, if the flashes are speeded up to between 50 and 80 per minute (about the same rate as a car's direction indicators) the light moves into a different classification known as **quick** (Q), while if they are faster still – 100–120 per minute – the light is classed as **very quick** (VQ). These, too, lend themselves to variations such as **group quick** in which a group of a specified number of quick flashes is regularly repeated.

Period

The 'period' of a light refers to how quickly its rhythm is repeated. For a flashing light, it simply means the time between the start of one

CLASSIFICATION	ABBREVIATION	EXAMPLE
Fixed	F	
Flashing	Fl	
Group flashing	Fl (3)	
Composite group flashing	Fl (2+1)	
Long flashing	LFl	
Quick	Q	
Group quick	Q(3)	
Very quick	VQ	
Interrupted very quick	IVQ	
Isophase	Iso	
Occulting	Oc	
Group occulting	Oc (3)	
Composite group occulting	Oc (2+1)	

Period

Fig 72 The rhythm of a light can be classified into one of four main groups, but the variations are almost infinite: this chart gives examples of some of the most common.

flash and the start of the next, while for a composite group flashing light it means the time from the start of the first flash of one group to the start of the first flash when that group is repeated.

Colour

Colour is one of the most obvious of all light characteristics – except perhaps to those who are red-green colour blind – but it is seldom used to distinguish major lighthouses for the simple reason that a coloured light is not visible over as great a range as a white light.

It really comes into its own for the short and mid-range lights set up in the approaches to harbours, where there may be large numbers of lights that the navigator has to identify quickly but positively. White, red and green are the most common colours, but yellow, orange, violet and blue are used occasionally. Any one of these colours may be used on its own, or they can be **alternated**.

Sectored lights

Another possible use of colour is of enormous value in night pilotage. A light can be arranged so that it shows a different colour when seen from one direction than from another. A common application of this is to indicate the line of a deep channel flanked by shallower water, where a light at one end of the channel is often arranged to show a white light over the deep water, a red light over the shallows on the port side, and a green light over the shallows on the starboard side.

On harbour plans and approach charts the sectors are clearly shown, but they are often omitted from coastal charts. This makes it easy to forget that you will see only one colour at a time – depending on which sector you happen to be in – rather than all the colours alternately. The key difference is that the abbreviation for an alternating light is preceded by the letters Al.

The range of a light

The distance at which a light can be seen depends on a number of factors, quite apart from the observer's eyesight. Its height above sea level and the observer's height of eye determine its **geographical** range – whether or not it can be seen above the horizon. The intensity of the light and the prevailing atmospheric conditions determine its **luminous** range – how far it could be seen if there were no horizon in the way.

The ranges quoted on charts and in lists of lights cannot possibly take account of all these variables: they have to cater for the officer of the watch on a container ship 80 feet above the sea on a crisp clear winter's night, as well as for a yachtsman in the small hours of a misty spring morning, so they quote **nominal** ranges, which assume an atmospheric visibility of ten miles and an observer's height of eye sufficient to ensure that the light is above the horizon. The practical effect of this is that you cannot necessarily expect to see a light at the nominal range given on the chart: it will appear at whichever is the lesser of the geographical and luminous ranges.

The *Admiralty List of Lights* includes a table

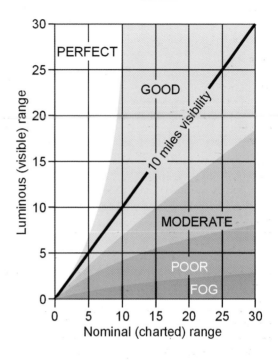

Fig 73 The range at which a light can be seen depends on atmospheric conditions, as well as on its brightness. In fog, a 20 mile light may only be visible for 2 miles. In very good visibility it might be visible for 30 miles or more.

for finding the geographical range, based on the elevation of the light and the height of eye of the observer. This table is not included as such in yachtsmen's almanacs: it is unnecessary because it is exactly the same as the rising and dipping distance table mentioned in Chapter 4 (see page 60).

The *Admiralty List of Lights* also includes a chart for estimating luminous range from the nominal range and prevailing visibility. This, too, is usually omitted from yachtsmen's almanacs, but a simplified version of it is given in Figure 73.

Sources of information

The chart is the most immediate source of information about lighthouses, buoys and the various other kinds of lit navigation aids, and large scale charts can be expected to provide almost everything you might need to know.

Coastal charts cannot provide as much information or they would be impossibly cluttered, so minor lights and buoys are omitted and the amount of detail given of those that remain is reduced. How much is left depends on the scale of the chart and the importance of the light, but in general, elevation is the first detail to be edited out, followed by period, and finally range. The light's colour and rhythm are usually retained.

The *Admiralty List of Lights and Fog Signals* includes considerably more detail, including a much fuller specification of the light's rhythm, a description of the light structure itself, and its height above the surrounding ground. This is particularly useful by day, when it can be handy to know whether you are looking for a high tower or a relatively squat building on top of a cliff. Yachtsmen's almanacs generally provide a little more information than can be found on a chart, but go into less detail than the *Admiralty List of Lights*.

Buoys and beacons

Major lighthouses are vastly outnumbered by a huge array of more minor visual aids to navigation – buoys and beacons – used to mark channels or specific hazards. They come in a wide range of shapes and sizes: buoys can be no bigger than a football or they can be substantial metal structures bigger and considerably heavier than most boats. Beacons range from tree branches stuck into the bed of little-used creeks, to large stone-built beacon towers that may be bigger than some lighthouses. Most large buoys and beacons have lights, but many smaller ones do not.

The IALA system

Until the early 1970s, each country had its own 'convention of buoyage' – the code by which the shape and colour of a mark conveyed information about what it was marking and where the best water was to be found.

Different codes for different countries was obviously a potential source of confusion, so over the following ten years most countries adopted a standardized system which brought together the best features of all those in use. It was known as the IALA system, named after the International Association of Lighthouse Authorities.

One irreconcilable difference was between the British and American systems, in which a red buoy meant opposite things on opposite sides of the Atlantic. That could only be resolved by having two IALA systems designated 'A' and 'B'.

IALA A is used throughout Europe and Scandinavia, and most of the rest of the world, but it has not completely ousted the older local systems. Around Scandinavia, for instance, many minor channels are still marked with 'finger posts' which look very much like the signposts used on country roads. IALA B is used around the USA and Pacific rim.

The IALA systems include three main groups of buoys and beacons:

- cardinal marks used mainly to mark hazards;
- lateral marks used to mark the sides of a clearly-defined channel;
- a miscellaneous group.

Cardinal marks

Cardinal marks are named after the four cardinal points of the compass. A north cardinal lies to the north of a hazard with clear water to the north of it; a south cardinal marks the southern edge and so on, although in practice very few hazards are marked on all four sides. All cardinal marks are black and yellow in colour and have a top mark consisting of two black cones: it is the orientation of the cones and the layout of the colours that differentiates one cardinal buoy from another.

A **north cardinal** has both cones pointing upwards, while the buoy or beacon itself has a yellow base and a black top. This is easy to remember if you think of the cones pointing to the top of the chart (north), and also pointing towards the black part of the buoy.

A **south cardinal** mark has cones which point downwards, pointing to the bottom of the chart. Like the cones on the north cardinal they also point towards the black part of the buoy or beacon, so a south cardinal mark has a black base and a yellow top.

A **west cardinal** mark has its cones points together. There are several ways to remember this: 'wasp waisted west'; 'west winds wool' (from its bobbin-like shape); or visualize the silhouette of the two cones as a letter W turned on its side. As with the other two the cones point towards the black part of the mark, so a west cardinal is yellow at the top and bottom, with a black band around the middle.

An **east cardinal** has the only remaining combination of cones and colours: its cones are points apart, pointing towards a black top and bottom, separated by a yellow band around the middle.

Not all cardinal buoys or beacons have lights, but those that do always have white lights, which are quick flashing or very quick flashing. The number of flashes identifies the type of buoy according to a pattern based on the numbers on a clock face, with north, corresponding to '12 o'clock', at the top. Each group of 12 flashes, however, merges into the one before and the one following, so a north cardinal shows a continuous flashing light. An east cardinal, at 'three o'clock', flashes in groups of three; and a west cardinal, at 'nine o'clock', flashes in groups of nine. Following this logic, the south cardinal, at 'six o'clock', should flash groups of six – as indeed it does –

but as this could be confused with the west cardinal, it is further identified by a long flash following each group of six.

IALA A lateral marks

Lateral marks are used to mark the sides of a channel. Going into a river estuary, for example, you would expect to find red, can-shaped (flat topped) buoys on your port side, and green conical buoys on your starboard side. If they have top marks then the top mark is simply a smaller representation of a can or cone shape in the appropriate colour.

Leaving the river, of course, you would be heading in the opposite direction, so the red can-shaped port-hand marks would be on your starboard side and the green conical starboard-hand marks would be on your port side. This means that it is vitally important to know the direction of buoyage for the area in which you are operating. In rivers and estuaries the direction of buoyage is always 'inward', and in open water it is clockwise around continents. Mainland Britain, incidentally, is not a continent, so the directions of buoyage in the North Sea and Irish Sea are both from south-west to north-east – following the rule by running clockwise around Europe.

In some places even these two rules can lead to ambiguity. A good example is in the Menai Straits between north Wales and Anglesey, with a harbour at each end and a marina in the middle. Approaching Bangor, at the north-eastern end of the Straits, the 'clockwise' rule and the 'inbound' rule give different answers. In such cases, the direction of buoyage is indicated on the chart.

Lateral buoys and beacons may or may not be lit. Those that are can show a light of the same colour as the buoy or beacon itself. Unlike cardinal marks, there is no standard rhythm, but it is quite common to find port-hand marks showing an even number of flashes in each group and starboard-hand marks an odd number. It may help to remember that 'port' has an even number of letters while 'starboard' has an odd number.

FOG SIGNALS

Most lighthouses, and some major buoys and beacons, are fitted with fog signals, making a noise which can be used to identify them, and as a rough guide to their direction, in fog. The most powerful – now being phased-out in the UK – is a **Diaphone** (Dia), which uses compressed air to produce a long, low note that finishes with a distinct 'grunt'.

Horns (Horn) can be of various types, using air or electricity to vibrate a diaphragm – as in a car's horn, but much more powerful. Just as with car horns, fog horns are often installed in groups, sounding a chord rather than a single note. They can be at any pitch, or even vary in pitch, but they never have the diaphone's grunt.

Sirens (Siren) are generally higher in pitch than horns or diaphones, but are very variable in tone and power. **Reeds** (Reed) are weak, high-pitched fog signals, often used at harbour entrances, and **Explosive** (Explos) signals are self-explanatory.

Bells, Gongs and **Whistles** are used mainly on buoys, where they may be operated either by the rocking or heaving motion of the sea, or by machinery. Bells and gongs are self-explanatory, but whistles are often much lower in pitch than one might expect if you have not heard one before.

Mechanically operated fog signals can have distinctive characteristics, much as lights do: the famous Fastnet Rock lighthouse, for instance, is 'Horn (4) 60s' – meaning that it sounds four blasts on its horn in quick succession, repeated at 60 second intervals. It is important to appreciate, though, that the way sound travels through waterlogged air can be erratic – it can seem to be reflected by some patches of fog, or be absorbed or muffled by others. This means that bearings of fog signals should be used with extreme caution, and with no attempt at any greater precision than 'ahead', 'astern' or 'to port' or 'starboard'. The distance at which a fog signal can be heard is equally erratic, so 'audible distances' are never quoted.

Preferred channel marks

Preferred channel marks are a variation on the normal lateral marks, used where a channel divides. They are rarely used in the UK, but are common in some other countries such as the Netherlands.

If the preferred channel is to starboard, the mark where the channel forks could be seen as the first port-hand mark of the main channel, so its predominant characteristics are those of a port-hand buoy: it is can-shaped, and red. It could also be seen as the first starboard-hand buoy of the minor channel, so it also has some of the characteristics of a starboard-hand buoy, in the form of a green band around the middle. Its light

is red, composite group flashing 2+1.

If the preferred channel is to port, the opposite applies: the mark at the fork has characteristics which are predominantly those of a starboard-hand buoy (green, conical), but with a red band, and a green composite group flashing 2+1 light.

Miscellaneous IALA marks

Safe water marks might seem a strange concept, rather at odds with the idea of marking specific hazards or the sides of a channel, but they are useful as 'landfall' buoys, marking the seaward end of a long harbour approach channel. Very much less common than lateral or cardinal marks, their role means that they are usually quite big buoys, and often, though not invariably, with lights. They may be spherical, or of the pillar shape associated with cardinal buoys, but their top mark is always a red sphere, and their colour scheme a distinctive pattern of vertical red and white stripes. Their lights are equally distinctive, being white, and either isophase, occulting or long flashing, or – very occasionally – Morse 'A' (a short flash followed by a long one).

Isolated danger marks are used to draw attention to hazards which are entirely surrounded by navigable water and which are sufficiently small in extent that they do not warrant two or more cardinal marks. Their colour scheme is a pattern of black and red horizontal bands, and their top marks consist of two black spheres. This could be taken as a reminder that those fitted with lights show white flashes in groups of two.

Special marks can be used for all sorts of other purposes. Very small ones are often seen off beaches, cordoning off areas reserved for swimmers or water-skiers, while slightly larger ones are often laid as the marks for yacht racing. Bigger ones still may be used to mark military exercise areas, the centre lines of traffic separation schemes or even the deepest part of a wide channel. All special marks are yellow and they may show a yellow light and have a yellow cross-shaped top mark (called a 'saltire'). They can be of any shape, except that where they are intended to be passed on a particular side, such as those marking a prohibited zone or a recommended channel, they are made the same shape as the corresponding lateral mark – can or cone.

Estimating Position and Shaping a Course

It is always nice to know where you are, but there may be times when fixing is impossible – such as on a boat without electronic position fixing devices and with no land or sea marks in sight. Even in these situations all is not lost, so long as you know the direction you have been steering (from a compass) and the distance you have travelled (from the log). If there were no wind or tide it is easy to see how these two could be used to deduce a position:

1 Starting from your last known position, draw a line on the chart representing your course steered.
2 Find the distance you have travelled from your last known position, by subtracting your log reading at the time from your log reading now.
3 Again starting from your last known position, measure that distance along the line representing your course.

A position derived only from the course steered and distance travelled, like this, is called a **Dead Reckoning** or DR position.

The time interval between successive DRs can be anything from a few minutes to several hours: the only requirement is that you have to know how far you have travelled and on what course. So long as your speed and course are reasonably constant a DR can even be plotted in advance to give a rough idea of how the navigational situation is likely to develop.

Because it ignores the on-going effects of wind and tide, the accuracy of a DR deteriorates with the passage of time: a DR based on an hour-old fix will be much less

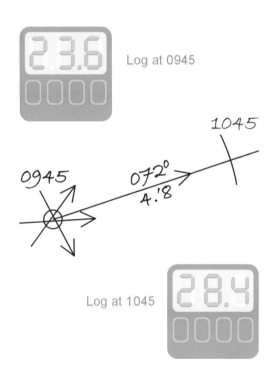

Log at 0945

Log at 1045

Fig 74 A dead reckoning position is based on course steered and distance travelled alone: it takes no account of leeway or tidal stream. In this example, the log reading at the time of the 0945 fix was 23.6, and an hour later it was 28.4, so the distance covered was 4.8 miles. The boat had been steering 072°, so the 1045 DR is found by measuring 4.8 miles from the 0945 position, along the line representing the course steered.

accurate than one originating from a fix taken in the past six minutes. So whether it is wise to depend on a DR for very long depends on how quickly you are approaching a potential hazard, and on how much your boat is affected by external factors such as wind and tide.

Chartwork – example 1

At 1540, a yacht passes very close to Ruytingen NW buoy, and immediately alters course to 165° (Magnetic). Variation is 3° West. Her log, at that time, reads 74.3. At 1640, her log reads 80.1. What is her 1640 DR position?

Passing close to Ruytingen NW buoy gives a good fix, so it is marked on the chart by a circle, and labelled with the time (see Figure 75).

The course steered is 165° (M). The 'Cadet' rule says that when converting from compass to true, easterly variation and deviation must be added, but in this case the variation is westerly, so it must be subtracted: 165° (M) − 3°(W) = 162° (T).

The course, of 162° (T), is drawn on to the chart, from the fix, and labelled. It is a matter of personal preference whether to use True or Magnetic for labels, but it must be specified!

From 1540 to 1640, the log reading has advanced from 74.3 to 80.1, indicating that the yacht has travelled 5.8 miles through the water. Using the latitude scale on the side of the chart (one minute of latitude = one nautical mile), a pair of dividers are set to 5.8 miles, and used to measure 5.8 miles along the course line, from the 1640 fix. That point represents the 1640 DR position, so it is marked with a cross and labelled with the time.

If a latitude and longitude are required, they can be read off from the scales on the side and top of the chart respectively: in this case 51° 03.'6N 02° 00.'1E.

Fig 75 Chartwork – example 1.

Allowing for wind

As well as providing the motive power for sailing yachts, the wind can make all boats – sail or power – slide sideways, so that they are not actually moving through the water in the direction they are pointing. This effect is called **leeway**.

A boat's propensity for making leeway depends on the balance between the windage offered by its rig, superstructure and topsides, and the lateral resistance offered by the underwater parts of the hull, keel, sterngear and rudder. This means that the amount of leeway made by a sailing boat is to some extent determined by its design: a boat with a high-windage rig and shoal draught is likely to make more leeway than one with a low-resistance rig and deep keel. Design is not the whole story however: the skipper and crew play their part too. Reefing or bad sail shape increase the amount of windage compared with the forward drive developed by the sails, so they tend to increase leeway. Excessive heeling also tends to increase leeway by reducing the lateral resistance of the keel.

Leeway is generally greatest when close-hauled, and reduces to nothing on a dead run – when, of course, it is in the same direction as the boat's forward movement anyway. 'Pinching' when close-hauled tends to increase leeway even more.

Many helmsmen luff up in gusts, either because they have a background in dinghy racing or because the 'weather helm' of many cruising boats increases the load on the steering in gusts. It is an efficient way of sailing, because it takes advantage of the shift in the apparent wind that occurs as a gust strikes. Navigationally, however, the effect is that the average heading may be several degrees closer to the wind than the course the helmsman thinks he is steering. This is often enough to cancel out leeway altogether, or even to produce 'apparent leeway' upwind.

Motorboats may make more leeway than a modern sailing boat because they often have high topsides and superstructures, without the advantage of a keel to increase their lateral resistance. They also have a tendency to heel to windward when underway in a fresh breeze, which can be counteracted by the helmsman steering downwind: this means that helmsman's errors are more likely to add to a motorboat's leeway than to reduce it.

Leeway is difficult to measure with any accuracy, particularly in the rough conditions in which it is likely to be greatest. When there is no tidal stream it can be measured by passing close to a mark such as a buoy, and then – after several minutes – comparing the bearing of the buoy with the course steered. Add or subtract 180° from the bearing of the buoy to find the direction actually travelled through the water. The difference between this and the course steered is the leeway in degrees. In tidal waters much the same can be achieved by taking bearings of a free floating mark such as a danbuoy.

A third option is to estimate leeway, based on experience after a number of longish

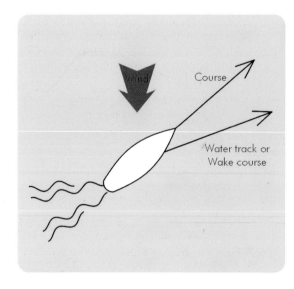

Fig 76 Leeway is caused by wind pushing the boat sideways, so that it follows a track through the water that is slightly downwind of the course steered.

passages. If there is a consistent error between your estimated position and your fix, which cannot be ascribed to tide, deviation or anything else, this may well be taken as an indication of your leeway.

Having measured or estimated your leeway, it can be allowed for when plotting the DR on the chart by adding or subtracting the angle of leeway to or from the course before drawing the course line on to the chart. To differentiate this 'course adjusted for leeway' from the

course actually steered, it is often called the **water track** or **wake course** (Figure 76).

Whether leeway should be added or subtracted depends on the relative wind direction: if you are on starboard tack (ie with the wind blowing from the starboard side) it should be subtracted. One simple way to make sure you apply leeway in the right direction is to pencil a large arrow on to the chart representing the wind direction, and then make sure that the water track drawn on the chart is downwind of the course (Figure 77). As an alternative, it may help to remember that 'subtract' and 'starboard' both begin with an S, and 'port' and 'plus' both begin with a P.

Allowing for tidal streams

The effect of the tidal stream can be considerably greater than leeway. This is particularly true for sailing boats, whose speed through the water may be little more – or even possibly less – than the speed of the tidal stream, but even planing motorboats can seldom ignore it altogether. The principle of accounting for the effect of the tidal stream can be explained by a simple, if rather far-fetched, example:

Imagine two boats starting off from the same place and both heading eastwards. One is capable of infinite speed, so it covers six miles in no time at all, then stops and drifts while it waits for the other to catch up. The other boat, meanwhile, is making six knots through the water, so after one hour the two are together again. During that hour, both have been affected by a tidal stream setting southwards at a rate of one knot, so in the one hour that it was waiting the first boat has drifted one mile southwards. Its actual movement could be plotted on a chart as a DR based on an easterly course and a distance run of six miles, followed by a southerly 'course' for a distance of one mile, to give an estimated position that takes account of the tide.

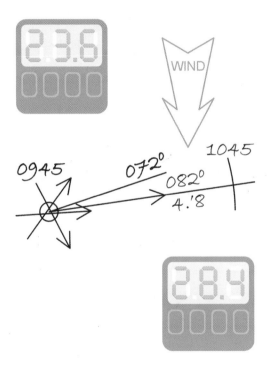

Fig 77 A more accurate and useful variant of a DR position takes account of leeway. The procedure is exactly the same as that used to find a DR in Figure 74, except that the wake course (water track) is plotted instead of the course steered. In this case, with a northerly wind and leeway estimated at 10°, the wake course is 082°. A single arrow is used to mark the wake course/water track, to differentiate it from the course.

The other boat has covered the same distance on the same course, and has been affected by the same tidal stream to end up in the same place, so the chartwork required to find its position is exactly the same, even though the route it took to reach that position was different. This means that in order to find an estimated position you should:

1 Draw a line on the chart representing the boat's movement through the water (its water track).

2 Measure along the water track a distance corresponding to the distance covered through the water, to give a dead reckoning position allowing for leeway.

3 From the DR position draw a line corresponding to the direction of the tidal stream.

4 Measure along this line a distance corresponding to the distance you would have drifted in the same time.

5 Mark this position – your estimated position – with a triangle and the time.

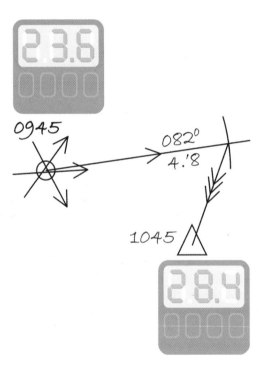

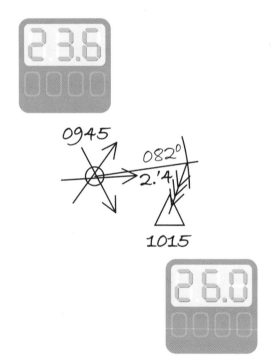

Fig 78 An estimated position (EP) is derived from the DR by allowing for the effect of tidal streams. In this case, the tidal stream is setting approximately 200° at 2.7 knots. From the DR position found in Figure 77, a line drawn in a 200° direction for 2.7 miles represents the tidal stream's effect between 0945 and 1045, and the EP is indicated as a triangle.

Fig 79 An EP does not have to be run over a full hour – but make sure you use the tidal stream that would be experienced in the same time, not a full hour's worth. Compare this with Figure 78: here, in the half hour from 0945 to 1015, the log reading has increased from 23.6 to 26.0, indicating a distance run of 2.4 miles. This has been used to work up the 1015 DR. In half an hour, the 2.7 knot tidal stream will have made the boat drift 1.35 miles, so the EP is 1.35 miles from the DR.

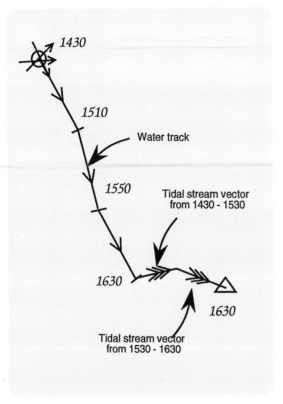

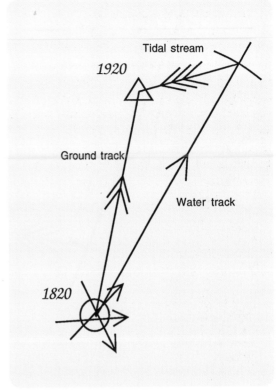

Fig 80 The same principle can be used to work up an EP over several hours. Again, it is important to use the right amount of tidal stream, by drawing in each hour's tidal stream vector, nose to tail from the latest DR. Here, a fix was taken at 1430, and DRs plotted at 1510 and 1550 (when the boat altered course) and again at 1630. The DRs took no account of tidal streams, so converting the 1630 DR into an EP requires two hours' worth of tide to be applied.

Fig 81 The direction and distance between two successive positions can be used to work out the boat's ground track and ground speed (course and speed made good).

Course and speed over the ground

Once you have two positions which relate to different times, it is possible to work out your course and speed over the ground. The **ground track** – sometimes known as the course over the ground or course made good – is the direction from the earlier position to the later one, and the distance made good is the distance between the two. From the distance made good, the speed made good can be found by dividing by the time taken.

On a longish passage it is usually convenient to work out an estimated position at hourly intervals, because this is an easily-remembered routine that fits neatly with the way tidal stream information is presented. This is not, however, essential, and an EP can be run over any convenient time interval. The important thing to remember is that the allowance made for tide must always cover the same time interval as the distance run (see Figures 78, 79 and 80).

The course and speed calculated by this method are only as accurate and reliable as the positions on which they are based, so if either of the positions is estimated, then the course and speed will also be estimates.

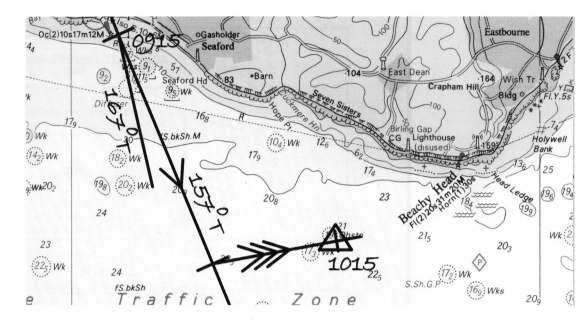

Fig 82 Chartwork – example 2.

Chartwork – example 2

A yacht leaves Newhaven, passing the outer breakwater light at 0915, and steers 170° (Magnetic). Variation is 3° West. Her log, at that time, reads 0.6. At 1015, it reads 5.4. Her skipper estimates that in the south-westerly wind, she is making 10° of leeway, and from the tidal stream atlas assesses the tidal stream to be 080° (True), 2.5 knots.

What is her estimated position at 1015?

Passing close to the breakwater light gives a good fix, so the 0915 position can be marked on the chart with a circle (to signify a fix) and labelled with the time (see Figure 82).

The course steered is 170° (Magnetic). Using the 'Cadet' rule, this corresponds to 167° (True). As the wind is on the starboard side, leeway has to be subtracted, giving a water track or wake course of 157° (True). Drawing the wind arrow on to the chart makes it easy to see whether leeway should be added or subtracted, because the water track will always be downwind of the course.

Comparing the two log readings shows that at 1015, the yacht has travelled 4.8 miles through the water. The latitude scale on the side of the chart is used as a scale of distance, and dividers are used to mark off a distance of 4.8 miles from the 0915 fix, to produce the 1015 position corrected for leeway.

From this position, the direction of the tidal stream is drawn on to the chart in an 080°(T) direction. The boat has been subject to a tidal stream of 2.5 knots for one hour, so the latitude scale is used to set the dividers to 2.5 miles, in order to mark off an hour's worth of tidal stream along the tidal stream vector.

This mark represents the boat's 1015 EP, so it is identified by a triangle, and labelled with the time.

Chartwork – example 3

At 2010, a yacht obtains a fix by visual bearing and radar range of Greenwich LANBY, 260° (M), 2.2 miles. The log reading is 103.2.

She steers 340° (M) until 2205 she alters course to 020° (M) to avoid a fishing boat: the log reading is 110.7. At 2225, with the log reading 112.1, she alters course to 340° (M) once more, and stays on that course until 2310, when the log reads 115.4. She makes negligible leeway, but the tidal stream data is:

2040 082° (T) 2.1 knots
2140 074° (T) 1.5 knots
2240 066° (T) 0.8 knots

Variation is 3°W

What is her estimated position at 2310?

There is no leeway to contend with, so once the fix has been plotted, finding the 2205 DR position is a matter of drawing in the course of 340° (M) = 337° (T) and measuring off the distance run: 110.7 – 103.2 = 7.5 miles (see Figure 83).

The 2225 DR is again based on the course steered and the distance run from the 2205 DR: 017°(T) for 1.4 miles. The 2310 DR is plotted in the same way: 337°(T) for 3.3 miles.

The last known position was at 2010, so the DR has been running for three hours: so three hours' worth of tide have to be applied to it to convert it to an EP. The tidal stream data for 2040 can be assumed to be valid from 2010 to 2110, and so on, so there is no interpolation required, and the three tidal stream vectors can be applied – nose to tail – starting from the 2310 DR, to produce the EP for 2310.

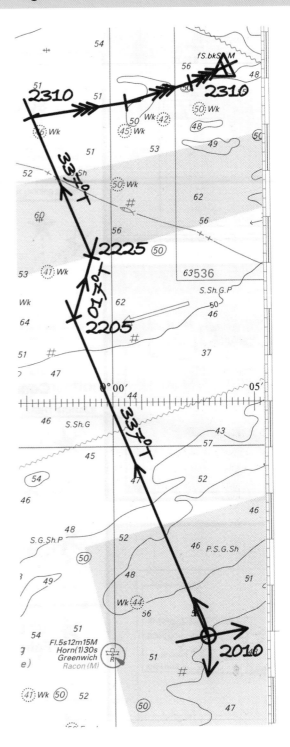

Fig 83 Chartwork – example 3.

Shaping a course

The process of estimating a position allows you to work out the direction and distance you have actually travelled – variously known as ground track, course made good or course over the ground – but it is a retrospective view, based on events that have already happened.

If you have set off by simply pointing the boat towards where you want to go, the effects of wind and tide mean that the chances of your ground track actually heading straight to your destination are slim. There are obvious advantages in being able to calculate a course to steer that will give you the ground track you really want. This is known as shaping a course: a

forward-looking process that in some ways can be seen as an EP worked out in reverse.

1 Draw your intended track on to the chart as a straight line, from where you are, and passing through your destination.
2 Estimate your likely speed, and from this work out roughly how long the passage is likely to take.
3 From tidal stream atlases or tidal diamonds, find the tidal stream you expect to experience.
4 From your starting point draw in the tidal stream vector, to represent the direction and distance the boat would move if it were stationary in the water and drifting with the tide.

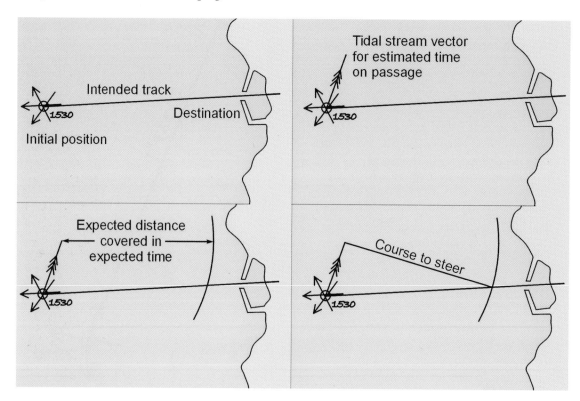

Fig 84 Allowing for the effect of the tidal stream in advance allows you to 'shape a course' so that your ground track (course over ground) corresponds with the direction you want to go. The intended track is drawn in first, from the present position to the intended destination, then the tidal stream from the present position. Then, from the end of the tidal stream vector, the expected distance run in the same time is marked off with a pair of dividers or a drawing compass. A line joining the end of the tidal stream vector to where the compass arc cuts the intended track indicates the course to steer.

5 Use your estimated speed to work out how far you would expect to travel through the water in the time interval covered by your tidal stream prediction.

6 Set a drawing compass or pair of dividers to this distance, and with one point at the end of the tidal stream vector, use the other to make a mark on your intended track (drawn in step 1).

7 Join the end of the tidal stream vector to the mark made in step 6. This represents the water track that is required in order to achieve your intended ground track. In other words, it is the course to steer with no allowance for leeway.

8 Add or subtract the expected angle of leeway to or from the direction of the water track to give a course to steer which is slightly more upwind.

Do not be concerned if some of the chart work in this process passes very close to (or even over) potential hazards: it often happens that shaping a course involves drawing on the yellow (land) part of the chart! Shaping a course is a purely geometric process that could be carried out almost as effectively on a blank sheet of paper because none of the lines drawn on the chart has any direct relationship to the boat's actual progress over the ground.

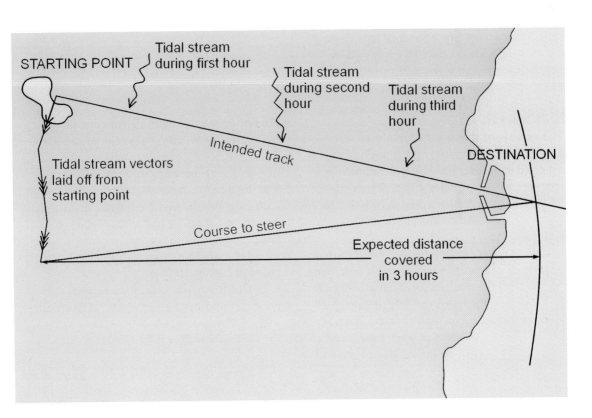

Fig 85 A course can be shaped for several hours. As with an EP run over several hours, it is important to allow for the same number of hours' worth of tide as the time taken to travel the distance, adding the tide vectors together.

Shaping a course for several hours

Much the same process can be used for passages likely to take several hours, though it requires a slight modification to take account of the fact that the tidal stream varies from time to time and from place to place.

At stage three of the process, use a tidal stream atlas or tidal diamonds to find the tidal stream for each hour of the intended passage. Remember that the tidal stream diamond which is relevant to the end of your passage may not be the same as the one that relates to its start. Then, from your starting point draw in these tidal stream vectors nose-to-tail, to represent the cumulative effect of tide over the whole passage – the direction and distance the boat would move if it were stationary in the water and drifting with the tide. From this point, mark off the distance you will travel, to cut the required track line to give the course to steer.

Is it worth it?

The process of shaping a course may seem long-winded, particularly for a passage that is expected to last several hours, so it may be tempting to ask whether it is really worth the effort. For boats whose speed is low compared to that of the tidal stream, the answer is almost invariably 'Yes'.

If you take the extreme – but not impossible – situation of a boat whose speed is less than the speed of the tidal stream then it is only by shaping a course that it can hope to reach its destination at all. For slightly faster boats, course shaping shortens passage times, and can often do away with an uptide slog at the end of a passage.

In general, the benefits of course shaping reduce as the boat's speed increases. Whether the benefits are worth the time involved is a decision entirely up to the skipper/navigator, but as a very rough guide it is a decision worth thinking about if the tidal stream setting across your intended track is more than about 5% of your boat's speed.

The classic geometrical method of working out a course to steer can be very accurate, but for many purposes a method based on mental arithmetic is just as good. It is called the 'one in sixty rule', because it relies on the fact that if you are one degree off course for 60 miles, then you will end up one mile off track. It is only an approximation, but it is surprisingly accurate, and holds true for angles very much larger than 1°: if, for instance, you are 10° off course, then you will be 10 miles off track after 60 miles or one mile off course after six.

The converse also holds true: if you are experiencing a tide which would push you one mile off track in an hour, then in a six knot boat you would have to steer 10° up-tide to counteract it. In more general terms:

$$\frac{\text{tide speed} \times 60}{\text{boat speed}} = \text{course correction required}$$

Do not be put off by the arithmetic involved: high levels of precision are seldom required, because it is impossible to steer to an accuracy of one degree anyway. So, rather than risk making a big mistake with a tricky calculation such as would be involved if you had a tidal stream of 1.4 knots and a boat speed of 22 knots, it is better to use approximations such as 'a bit more than a knot of tide' and a boat speed of 'about 20 knots'.

In this particular case, for instance, most people would need a calculator to work out

$$1.4 \times 60 \div 22 = 3.8.$$

'A bit more than one' × 60 ÷ 20 = 'three times one and a bit' = 'about four' seems easy by comparison, yet is still within ¼° of the right answer.

When the tidal stream is setting along the intended track there is no need to adjust your course to compensate, but it can be important to be aware of the tide's effect on the boat's speed over the ground. The arithmetic, in this case, is a matter of simple addition or subtraction. If the tide is with you, then:

Speed Over Ground
= Boat Speed + Tide Speed

If the tide is against you, then:

Speed Over Ground
= Boat Speed – Tide Speed

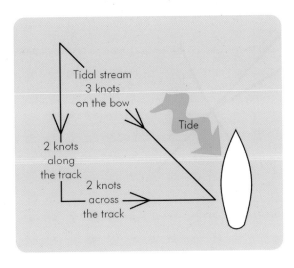

Fig 86 A rough estimate of the effect of a tidal stream at an angle to the boat's course can be made by thinking of it acting two-thirds along the track, and two-thirds across the track.

Tidal streams at an angle to the track can be treated as though they are made up of two components, one across the track and one along it. Again, it is better to use a reliable approximation than to try for great accuracy and run the risk of a major arithmetical blunder: you will not go far wrong by assuming that two-thirds of the tide's speed is acting across your track, while another two-thirds is acting along your track.

Suppose, for example, we are making 25 knots through the water, with a 3 knot tidal stream on the port bow (Figure 86).

The 3 knot tidal stream can be resolved into 2 knots across track, and 2 knots along track. 25 knots is an awkward number to deal with in the course to steer calculation; 24 knots is not very different and makes the arithmetic much easier:

$$2 \times 60 \div 24 = 60 \div 12 = 5° \text{ course}$$
$$\text{correction}$$

The boat speed calculation is simply:

$$25 - 2 = 23 \text{ knots}$$

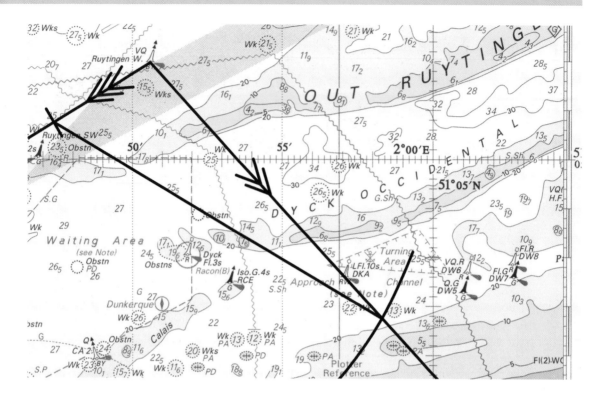

Fig 87 Chartwork – example 4.

Chartwork – example 4

From Ruytingen W buoy, what is the most direct course to steer for DKA buoy? The boat speed is estimated to be 8 knots, with negligible leeway, but there is a tidal stream of 2.4 knots, setting in a 239° (T) direction. Variation is 3°W.

From Ruytingen W buoy, draw in the intended ground track – a straight line passing through the destination. In practice, it is often useful to continue this line well beyond the intended destination (see Figure 87).

The distance to be covered is approximately 6 miles, so – at 8 knots – it should take less than an hour, so it is sufficient to consider one hour's worth of tidal stream. This is drawn in, from the starting

point, as a line in a 239° (T) direction, and 2.4 miles long.

Having allowed a full hour's worth of tide, it is important to allow an hour's worth of boat-speed, so the dividers or drawing compasses must be set to 8 miles. Then, with one point of the dividers in the end of the tidal stream vector, the other point is used to draw an arc across the intended track.

Joining the end of the tidal stream vector to the spot where the arc cuts the intended track gives the course to steer – in this case, 120° (T) or 123° (M). In practice, there is no real need to draw in the 'course' line, so long as you can measure its direction: it does not represent the boat's actual route, and it will probably have to be rubbed out anyway.

Chartwork – example 5

At 0815 a racing yacht's position is fixed by GPS at 50° 35.'8N 0° 04.'6E. Find the optimum course to steer to reach the yellow buoy just west of Newhaven, if the boat's speed is expected to be 4 knots, and the tidal streams are:

0845	263°	0.8
0945	266°	1.3
1045	254°	2.0

Leeway is negligible, and variation is 3°W.

From the fix, draw in the intended ground track as a straight line passing through the destination, and continuing beyond it (see Figure 88).

In this case, the distance to be covered is just over 11 miles, so at 4 knots it can be expected to take about three hours. The three hours of tidal stream is plotted on the chart as a series of three vectors – as though plotting the boat's position if she drifted with the tide.

In the same three hours, the boat will cover 12 miles through the water, so the dividers or drawing compasses are set to 12 miles. With one point of the dividers in the end of the cumulative tidal stream vector, the other point is used to draw an arc across the intended track.

The line joining the end of the tidal stream vector to the spot where the arc cuts the intended track, gives the course to steer – in this case, 358° (T) or 001° (M).

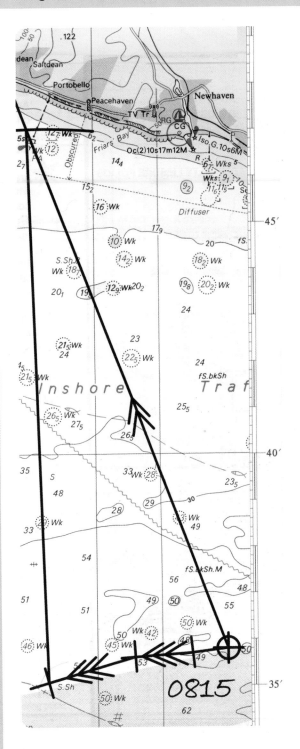

Fig 88 Chartwork – example 5.

8 Radar

Radar is quite unlike any of the other electronic navigation aids covered so far in this book. Not only is it more expensive to buy and more demanding of electrical power, but it also requires more skill on the part of the operator to set it up and adjust it to suit prevailing conditions and to interpret the picture on its screen. In return it is the most versatile of all electronic aids.

How radar works

The basic principle of radar is similar to that of an echo sounder: it transmits pulses of energy and measures the time that elapses before the echo of each one returns. One major difference is that instead of using ultrasonic sound, radar uses extremely high frequency radio waves, called microwaves – in the order of 9.5 GHz (9500 MHz) and with a wavelength of about 3 cm. The other big difference is that instead of being transmitted downwards, like the ultrasonic clicks of an echo sounder, a radar's microwave pulses are focused into a beam by a rotating aerial and transmitted horizontally through 360° around the boat.

So a radar is able to measure the range of a target from the time it takes a microwave pulse to make the out and back trip, and measures

Fig 89 A flush-mounted multi-function display in radar mode, at the helm position of a new motor cruiser.

Fig 90 Small, lightweight scanners and compact liquid crystal displays have brought radar within reach of all but the smallest cruising boats.

the target's bearing from the direction that the scanner is pointing. This information is used to build up a picture on the display – sometimes called a PPI or 'plan position indicator', because the overall effect is rather like a plan, or bird's-eye view, of the boat's surroundings.

Basic operation

All radars have seven main controls, though these may be combined with each other, automated, or buried in a system of menus or soft keys along with other controls.

On/standby/transmit

The on/standby/transmit control is used to turn the set on. It will have to be left in its standby mode for at least a minute or two

while the magnetron – the component that actually generates the microwaves – warms up, so on most modern sets this warm-up period is indicated by a count-down timer on the screen. Once the warm-up is completed, switching to transmit mode turns the transmitter on. This should produce a picture on the screen, though it may leave scope for considerable improvement by means of the other controls.

Brilliance

The brilliance control determines the brightness of the picture exactly like the corresponding control on a domestic television set, and should be adjusted to give a clear but not dazzling image. On radars with a liquid crystal display, the brilliance control may have to be used in conjunction with the contrast setting; the two are interdependent, and their adjustment depends on the angle from which you are looking at the screen.

Gain

Gain refers to the amount of amplification applied to the returning echo. In some ways it is easy to confuse the effect of the gain control with that of brilliance, because turning it up makes weak contacts look bigger, brighter and more consistent. The two are not interchangeable, however: brilliance is adjusted to make the picture clearer or more comfortable to look at; whereas the setting of the gain control can determine whether some contacts appear at all. As a rule, the gain should be turned up until the screen is filled with a background speckle, then turned down until the speckle just disappears, but it may need to be readjusted each time the radar's operating range is changed.

Range

The range control, as its name suggests, is used to adjust the operating range of the set, typically in about eight steps from one eighth or one quarter of a mile, to between 16 and 48 miles. The range to use depends on the job in hand: short ranges (between half a mile and 4 miles) are generally of most use for pilotage; medium ranges (4, 6 or 8 miles) for collision avoidance and long ranges (8 to 24 miles) for coastal and offshore navigation. Ranges in excess of 24 miles are of very little practical use for small boat radars.

Tuning

The tuning control, like its counterpart on a domestic radio, is used to adjust the receiver to give the best possible reception of incoming signals. As the radar is listening for echoes of its own transmissions, it may come as a surprise to find that any adjustment is required, but it should be borne in mind the returning echoes are very weak indeed, so a precise match between the transmitter and receiver is of paramount importance. The radar's tuning control offers very fine adjustment, to allow for small variations in the transmitting frequency caused mainly by variations of temperature. To tune a radar, start by setting the brilliance to a comfortable level, adjusting the gain until the background speckle just disappears, and selecting a medium range. Choose a weak contact somewhere near the edge of the screen and concentrate on that, while adjusting the gain control in small steps – allowing at least two seconds between each step – until the chosen contact is as big, bright and consistent as possible.

The adjustment of these first five controls is aimed at giving 'targets' (the physical objects that reflect radar waves) the best possible chance of appearing on the screen as 'contacts'. Two more controls are used to refine or clarify the picture, by removing unwanted contacts or clutter.

Sea clutter control

This is sometimes called STC or swept gain, and is used to remove the clutter caused by echoes from waves, that can otherwise form a bright circle or starburst pattern in the centre of the screen.

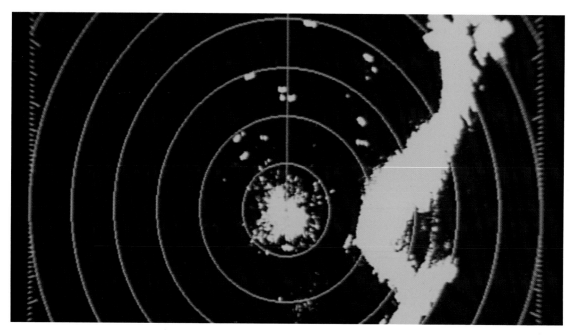

Fig 91 Sea clutter forms a bright 'sunburst' effect around the centre of the radar display, which can obscure important contacts.

Under normal conditions – with the sea clutter control turned right down – the radar may be receiving echoes from targets at a variety of different ranges, but with much weaker echoes from very distant targets than from targets close at hand. This means that the echoes which return very soon after each pulse has been transmitted need much less amplification than those which are received later.

The sea clutter control works by reducing the amplification of early returns even more, while leaving the later levels of amplification intact. On the screen this has the effect of obliterating weak contacts close to the boat, allowing stronger contacts to show up more clearly. If it is overdone, however, the sea clutter control is quite capable of suppressing the amplification to such an extent that even the strongest contacts – such as land – are obliterated at ranges up to several miles from the boat, so it should be used with considerable caution and always as little as is necessary.

Rain clutter

This control is sometimes known as FTC or differentiation and, as its name suggests, is used to remove the clutter caused by meteorological effects such as rain, snow or hail. A heavy rain shower can be quite an effective reflector of radar pulses, but it does not reflect them in the same way as a solid object. Instead of returning an echo which is a crisp copy of the transmitted pulse, rain echoes are weaker but more drawn out. On the screen this produces a large but relatively diffuse contact, often described as looking like a smudge or 'cotton wool'.

The rain clutter control acts by ignoring all but the leading edge of each returning echo. This effectively reduces the energy received from rain echoes to such an extent that they do not appear as a contact at all. Almost inevitably though, it reduces the energy received from real targets. The drawn out echoes produced by gently sloping coastlines such as beaches or mudflats are particularly

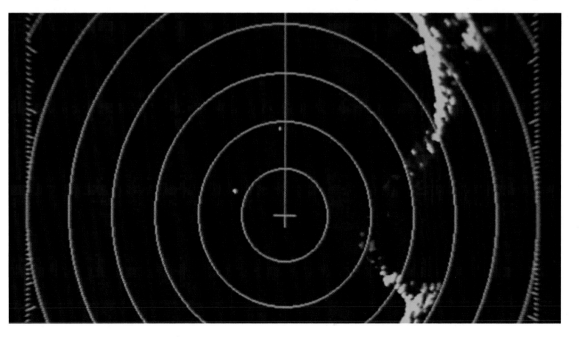

Fig 92 Sea clutter can be reduced with the sea clutter control, but it must be used with care: notice how excessive use of the sea clutter control has removed several genuine contacts that appeared in the previous picture, and is starting to make even the land disappear!

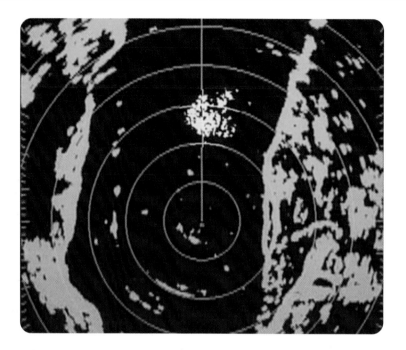

Fig 93 Rain clutter (the speckled patch just above the centre of this radar picture) can obscure contacts.

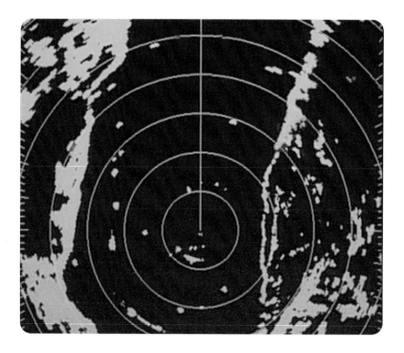

Fig 94 The rain clutter controls reduce rain clutter, but can weaken other contacts – notice how the coastline to starboard appears to be breaking up.

badly affected, so the rain clutter control, like the sea clutter control, should only be used when necessary.

Interpreting the picture

The first time one looks at a radar screen, it often comes as something of a disappointment: the picture may look crude and blobby, and bits of the coastline may be missing, making it difficult to relate what appears on the screen to the chart of the same area. A radar is definitely not 'an all-seeing eye' and interpreting the picture calls for practice, and a slightly deeper understanding of how the radar works.

To begin with, it may help to visualize the stream of microwave pulses leaving the radar scanner as being like the beam of a searchlight. In order to produce an echo, a target has to be 'illuminated' by the radar beam. Some materials, such as GRP, which are opaque to light are transparent to radar waves. But something such as a steel funnel in the way of the radar beam can block radar waves just as effectively as it blocks light, to cause a shadow zone which can never be illuminated.

The obvious solution to this problem is to make sure that the radar scanner is mounted higher than any large metal objects on the boat. Land has a very similar effect, though without the easy cure. Bays or river entrances will be hidden from the radar by surrounding headlands just as they are hidden from the naked eye. This is the main reason why there are gaps in the radar picture of the coastline.

The biggest obstruction of all is the earth itself. There is nothing unfamiliar about the idea of things being invisible because they are

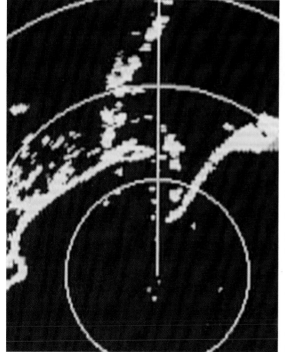

Fig 95 Comparing the radar picture (left) with a satellite photograph shows that radar is not an all-seeing eye; in particular, its view can be blocked by headlands and islands, creating gaps in its picture of a coastline.

111

'below the horizon', nor that hills can be seen at longer ranges than low-lying ground or the shoreline itself because they are tall enough to be 'above the horizon'. The same effect appears on radar: at long ranges hills may appear to be isolated islands and the true coastline may not show up at all. Microwaves bend very slightly to follow the curvature of the earth, so the radar horizon is about five% more distant than the visual one. Its distance can be found from the formula:

$$R = 2.2 \times \sqrt{H_a}$$

where R is the horizon range, and H_a is the antenna height in metres. So for an antenna nine metres above sea level, the radar horizon would be about six and a half miles away.

Once a target has been illuminated by the radar beam, its ability to produce an echo depends on its material, size, shape and to some extent on its surface texture. Some materials (such as GRP) are almost transparent to the microwaves. Others (such as wood) absorb microwaves. This is why yachtsmen should never assume that their GRP or wooden vessels will be 'seen' by a ship's radar. Some materials, most significantly metal, rock and water, are good reflectors of microwaves.

The effect of size is fairly obvious: in general a large target can reflect more of the radar energy than a small one, so it stands a better chance of appearing as a contact on the radar screen. The effect of size, however, is masked to some extent by the effect of shape. Spherical or cylindrical objects are poor reflectors because they scatter radar energy, instead of reflecting it back the way it came. Flat surfaces, on the other hand, can be very good reflectors indeed, because if they happen to be positioned exactly at right angles to the approaching radar beam the effect is very much like a mirror, directing the radar energy straight back to the antenna. At any other angle, however, a flat surface is likely to send

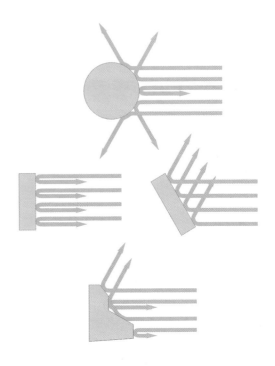

Fig 96 The strength of a radar echo is partly determined by the shape of the target: round objects scatter radar waves, while flat ones reflect them but possibly in the wrong direction.

the echo off in the wrong direction. The most reliable all-round reflectors tend to be those with uneven surfaces, because although some of the radar energy may be scattered the rough surface almost guarantees that at least some of it will be returned.

Pulse length and beamwidth

A radar scanner does not produce a perfectly parallel-sided beam, nor are its pulses of microwave energy instantaneous. The **beamwidth** of a radar set is expressed as an angle – implying that the edges of the beam diverge as the distance from the scanner increases. For most small boat radars the horizontal beamwidth is between 2° and 6°

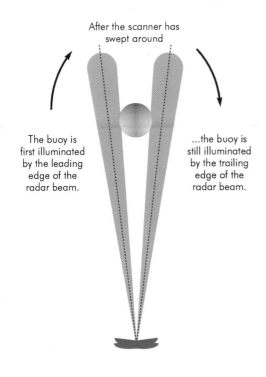

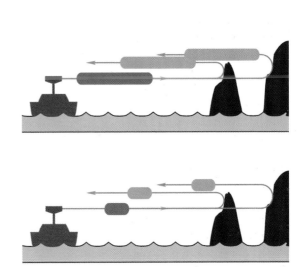

Fig 98 If a long pulse length is used, the echoes from two closely-spaced objects merge together, so the two objects appear as a single contact on the screen.

Fig 97 A small target may produce an echo whenever it is in the radar beam, so a large beamwidth makes small targets look much bigger than they really are.

– the larger the scanner the smaller the beamwidth.

The vertical beamwidth is invariably much greater, usually in the order of 25–30°. This is a good thing as it ensures that at least some part of the radar beam will be pointing horizontally even when the boat pitches and rolls.

A large horizontal beamwidth, by contrast, is a disadvantage because a good reflector will go on producing an echo for as long as it is 'illuminated' by the radar beam, so on a radar set with a 6° beamwidth even a small target such as a buoy can be expected to produce a contact 6° across. If you have two targets less than 6° apart, and both are expanded in this

way, then they will merge together to form a single large contact; the radar will be unable to discriminate between them. The effect of poor bearing discrimination is most obvious when you are looking for a narrow harbour entrance, because until you are close enough for the entrance to be wider than the radar beam, the gap will not show up on the screen.

The pulse length is specified in microseconds (μs) and is usually somewhere in the range between 0.05 μs and 1 μs. This means that the end of the pulse may be leaving the scanner when the start of the pulse has already been travelling for one millionth of a second – enough, at a speed of 162 000 nautical miles per second, for it to have covered some 300 metres. Just as horizontal beamwidth has the effect of making targets look wider than they really are, pulse length makes them look longer. This in turn affects the radar's ability to discriminate between two targets which are on the same bearing but at different ranges: if the two targets are less than half the pulse length apart they will appear on the screen as a single contact.

Most radars are capable of operating with two or three different pulse lengths. In general long pulse lengths are used for long ranges, because by transmitting for longer the radar is able to pack more energy into each pulse so it stands a better chance of receiving a discernible echo over great distances. Short pulse lengths are usually associated with short-range operation where the need for particularly strong echoes is less and the need for good range discrimination is likely to be greater.

On small boat radars the pulse length is one of many internal settings that are altered by the range control, though some offer a manual override.

Display modes

On the most basic radar display your own position is always at the centre of the picture with a bright line stretching upwards from it representing the boat's heading. For this reason it is known as a **relative motion head-up display**: 'relative motion' because the boat appears to be stationary at the centre of the picture whilst fixed objects, such as land, move past it; and 'head-up' because the boat's heading is always straight up the screen.

The head-up display is good because it is relatively easy to relate the radar picture with what you see by looking around the boat, especially if the radar display is mounted so that you face forward when looking at it, but it also has its drawbacks. The orientation of the picture depends on the boat's heading at that particular moment so, as the boat yaws, the entire picture, with the exception of the heading mark, rotates around the centre of the screen. This can make it very difficult to measure bearings as accurately as might otherwise be possible.

A more noticeable, but generally less significant, characteristic of a head-up display is that the orientation of the picture will only correspond with the north-up orientation of the chart when the boat is steering north: on southerly headings the radar picture will look 'upside down' when compared with the chart.

Most of the current generation of small boat radars can be connected to an electronic compass, using the heading information it provides to rotate the entire picture into a north-up mode. This goes a long way towards solving both problems: the radar picture is stabilized, and it should conform with the chart. This makes **north-up** presentation particularly useful for navigation but at the same time makes it rather more difficult to relate the screen image to the real world outside the boat: on southerly headings, for instance, an object on the starboard beam will appear as a contact on the left hand side of the display.

An alternative presentation is known as **course-up**. As the name suggests, this means that the boat's 'course' – usually whatever the heading happened to be at the moment 'course up' was selected – is towards the top of the screen. The general effect is very much like a head-up display in that objects ahead of the boat appear at the top of the screen and objects astern appear at the bottom. The big difference is that the heading marker is no longer fixed: as the boat yaws the heading marker yaws with it but the rest of the picture remains stable. Having a stable picture that is easy to relate to the real world makes the course-up mode particularly useful for collision avoidance.

A fourth display mode – called **true motion** – is now offered on some of the most up-market small boat radars. A true motion radar uses speed and course inputs from either a log and compass or an electronic position fixer to move the centre of the radar picture (the boat) across the display screen. This more accurately reflects the real-world situation by making fixed objects such as land and buoys appear to be stationary. This, however, is not quite such a big advantage as it seems, and can even be counterproductive because it makes assessing collision risks considerably more difficult.

Measuring bearings

The radar set which could provide only a picture of its surroundings might be of casual interest but it would be of little practical use: it is radar's ability to *measure* ranges and bearings that makes it a valuable tool for navigation and collision avoidance.

On all modern radars, bearing is measured by means of an electronic bearing line (EBL) –

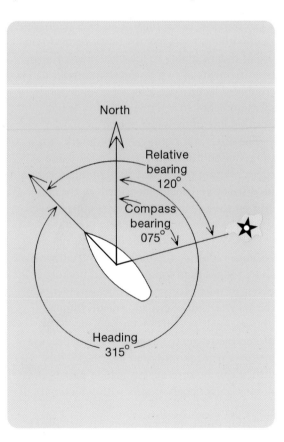

Fig 99 A head-up radar measures bearings relative to the boat's heading. To convert relative bearings to true bearings, the heading must be added to the relative bearing.

a straight line rather like a duplicate heading marker, which is anchored to the centre of the picture but can be swept around the screen like the second hand of a clock. Controls on the front panel of the set allow the radar operator to position the EBL so that it points straight at any contact on the screen, while the bearing of the EBL is displayed in a data window – usually in one corner of the main display. Radars which are interfaced to a corrected electronic compass usually offer the option of having the bearing displayed in either true or compass, but for head-up radars the indicated bearing is relative to the boat's heading, measured clockwise: a bearing of 010° (R) means '10° off the starboard bow', while a bearing of 330° (R) means '30° off the port bow'. To convert a relative bearing to a compass bearing, add the ship's heading to the relative bearing and subtract 360° if necessary, for example:

Relative bearing	120° (R)
Heading	315° (C)
	435° (C)
	– 360°
Compass bearing	075° (C)

When taking bearings by radar, especially when using a set with a small scanner, it is important to remember the effect of beamwidth, which enlarges both sides of every contact by approximately half the beamwidth. For small contacts such as ships and buoys, this means the EBL should be positioned so that it cuts through the centre of the contact. When taking the bearing of islands or headlands, the EBL should be positioned just inland of the edge of the contact by an amount equal to half the beamwidth. Even this is only an approximation, and if one takes into account the difficulty of getting the EBL accurately lined up with a contact on an unstabilized head-up picture, of noting the boat's heading at precisely the right moment, and the risk of arithmetical errors in converting from relative to compass, it is clear that radar bearings are unlikely to be as accurate or as reliable as those taken visually with a hand bearing compass. This means radar bearings should be used only when absolutely necessary, and even then only with some caution.

Measuring ranges

The standard display of a marine radar includes a pattern of concentric rings, equally spaced at pre-determined ranges from the centre. Their spacing depends on the operating range of the radar: on a 3 mile scale, for instance, the rings are typically ½ mile apart, increasing to 4 miles when the radar is set to a 24 mile range. These fixed range rings are very useful for making a quick estimate of the range of a contact, but on the long range settings in particular they are not precise enough for accurate navigation. For this reason almost all radars have at least one variable range marker (VRM) – an extra range ring whose radius can be varied by the operator. The setting of the VRM is usually shown in one corner of the display.

Measuring the range of a contact is a simple matter of expanding or contracting the VRM, by means of controls on the radar's front panel, until it just touches the nearest part of the contact, and reading off the indicated range.

Radar is much better at measuring range than bearing: range measurements are not affected by the yawing of the boat, by compass errors or by the radar's beamwidth, and on a properly set up and well-maintained radar should be accurate to about 1% of the range scale in use.

The cursor

As small boat radars become generally more sophisticated, most are now equipped with a feature called a cursor, which effectively combines the functions of the VRM and EBL. The details of its use vary from set to set, but the cursor usually appears on the screen as a small cross which can be moved around either by means of a tracker-ball, a touch-sensitive

pad, or by up/down/left/right arrow keys. Like the VRM and EBL, the cursor's range and bearing from the centre are shown on the display, so a target's range and bearing can be measured simultaneously by placing the cursor on the contact.

Navigating by radar

The fact that the EBL can be used for measuring bearings suggests that radar could be used as an alternative to a hand-bearing compass for taking fixes based on the bearings of two or three conspicuous objects. Measuring bearings, however, is not radar's strong point, so although a position line based on a radar bearing is better than nothing, it is generally much better to make use of radar's ability to measure range. Range measurements of two or three landmarks can be combined to produce a fix, or a single range measurement can be crossed with a visual position line of the same object.

The criteria for choosing landmarks for a range-based radar fix are much the same as those relating to a visual fix: landmarks should be distinct and easily identified on the chart and on the radar screen; they should be well spaced around the boat; near objects are preferable to more distant ones – in this case because radar is inherently more accurate over short ranges than long ones, and because it is easier to take precise range measurements on the shorter range settings. Steeply-sloping objects, such as cliffs or harbour walls, are preferable to gently-sloping beaches because – just as when taking visual bearings – it is difficult to be sure exactly which part of the radar contact corresponds with which part of the chart.

Radar range measurements can usually be taken more quickly than visual bearings, so the order in which measurements are taken is less important. Ideally, however, ranges should be measured in the opposite sequence to visual bearings: start with landmarks which are

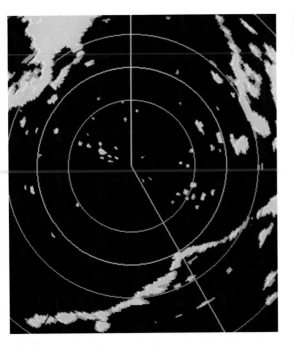
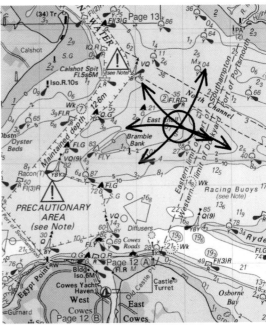

Fig 100 The radar picture was taken on a yacht heading south-westwards, so the distinctive yellow land mass in the top left hand corner corresponds to the land shown in the bottom of the chart. The green ring is the variable range marker, being used to measure the distance to the headland in the bottom right hand corner of the screen (top right of the chart). The ranges of three features can be plotted on the chart to produce a fix (see text).

almost abeam and finish with those which are directly ahead or astern.

Radar for collision avoidance

What sets radar apart from other electronic navigation aids is its unique role in collision avoidance. It is capable of far more than merely detecting the presence of other vessels, and is so important that it receives special mention in the International Regulations for the Prevention of Collisions at Sea:

*'every vessel shall use all available means …
to determine if risk of collision exists'* and
*'proper use shall be made of radar
equipment if fitted and operational'*.

It is a well-known principle of collision

avoidance that *'there is a risk of collision if the compass bearing of an approaching vessel does not appreciably change'*. Notice that the rule refers to 'compass bearing' not to 'relative bearing'. This is to remove the possibility of confusion that might arise if the boat was yawing, or slowly but progressively altering course.

In practice, however, if the boat is on a steady course and the relative bearing is steady, then the compass bearing must also be steady, so many experienced skippers back up bearings taken with a hand-bearing compass by lining up an approaching vessel with some fixed part of the boat's structure – to give a rough check of its relative bearing. A similar rough check can be carried out with a head-up radar by putting the EBL (electronic bearing line) on the approaching contact: if the contact subsequently appears to slide along the EBL towards the centre of the display then its relative bearing is

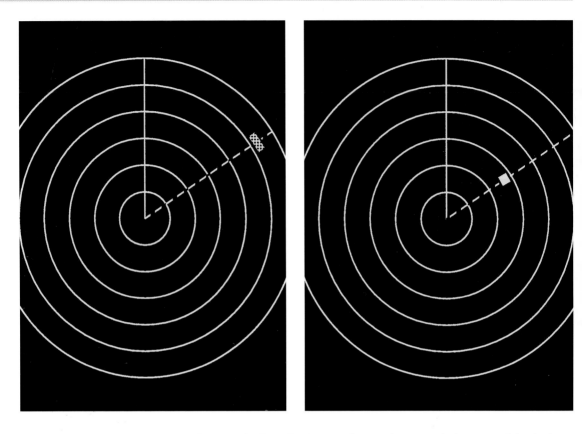

Fig 101 If a target appears to be sliding straight down the electronic bearing line towards the centre of the display, there is a risk of collision.

not changing. Doing the same thing with a stabilized (course-up or north-up) display is even better: compass stabilization means that the EBL represents a compass bearing rather than a relative one, so in this case a contact sliding along the EBL is almost certainly confirmation that there is a risk of collision.

The radar makes it particularly obvious why the steady bearing rule is such a sure fire way of assessing the risk of collision, because if a contact has been heading straight for the centre of the screen for several minutes, and neither of the vessels involved alters course or speed then it is clear that the contact will continue to move in the same direction and sooner or later will arrive at the centre of the screen. This, of course, represents your own boat, so the implication is that sooner or later you and the

other vessel will be sharing the same piece of water.

If the approaching contact is not sliding directly along the EBL then it is not heading for the centre of the screen and there is therefore no immediate risk of collision, but it could still pass uncomfortably close.

Measurements of bearing alone are not enough to predict how close such a near miss is likely to be, but with radar it is possible to work out the other vessel's closest point of approach (CPA). The principle is similar to that used in assessing the risk of collision: if neither vessel alters course or speed then the contact will continue to move across the radar screen in the same direction and at the same speed. One practical difference is that because the contact is not heading straight for the

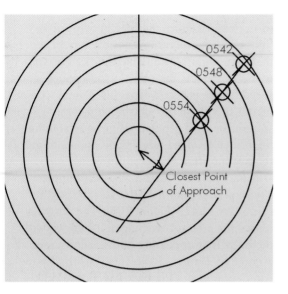

Fig 102 Recording the past movement of a contact allows its future movement to be predicted, to find its closest point of approach.

centre of the screen the EBL alone cannot be used to show its direction of movement. Instead its position on the screen must be systematically recorded – plotted – either with a whiteboard marker on the radar screen itself or on a paper representation of it, called a plotting sheet.

Ideally, successive plots should be made at regular intervals of three, six or twelve minutes, but when using an unstabilized (head-up) set, being on course is more important than precise timing. After the first few plots a trend should become clear. If neither vessel has altered course or speed the contact will appear to be moving in a straight line. If both vessels continue to maintain their courses and speeds, it is reasonable to assume that the contact will continue to move along the same straight line, so projecting it onwards past the centre of the screen gives a forecast of the contact's future

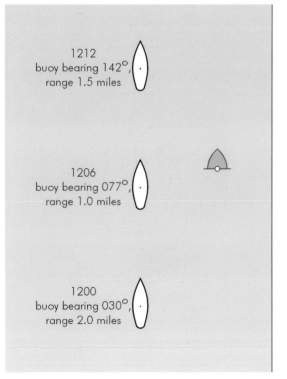

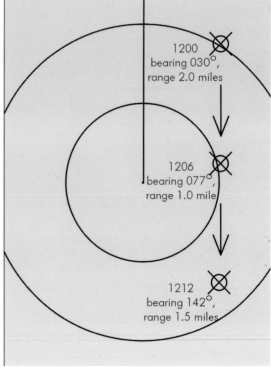

Fig 103 The contact representing a stationary target moves down the radar screen, parallel to the heading marker but in the opposite direction, and at the same speed as the boat.

movement. The point at which the line passes closest to the centre of the screen represents the closest point of approach.

If the initial plots were made at regular intervals it is possible to evaluate the contact's speed of movement, and to mark off equal distances along the projected line to give a good idea of when the target is likely to reach its CPA.

Assessing a target's course and speed

The normal steering and sailing rules of the International Regulations for Prevention of Collisions at Sea do not apply until vessels are within sight of one another so, strictly speaking, you should not have to use radar information alone to make decisions about collision avoidance. Many large ships, however, routinely travel at 20 knots or more,

so in poor visibility the time between first sighting and a possible collision may be less than five minutes. Valuable time can be gained if you can assess the other vessel's course and speed before it becomes visible. Doing so is a matter of systematic plotting and some straightforward geometry, but understanding the principles demands a good appreciation of relative motion.

It may help to think of the very simple situation of a boat in still water passing a stationary object (Figure 103). The drawing represents a boat travelling at 15 knots, with the buoy first appearing on its radar screen at a range of 2 miles, 30° off its starboard bow. After six minutes the boat has moved on 1½ miles, so the buoy is almost abeam and its range has reduced to one mile, and after another six minutes the buoy is over 1½ miles away on the starboard quarter. Translated on

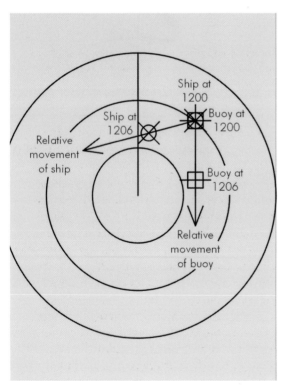
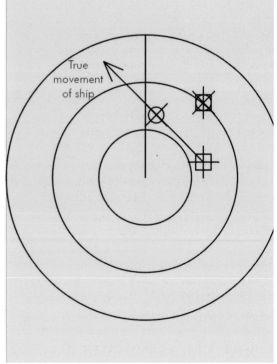

Fig 104 If a ship passes a buoy at 1200, then the difference between their 1206 positions represents the movement of the ship.

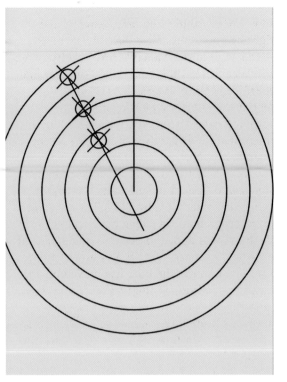

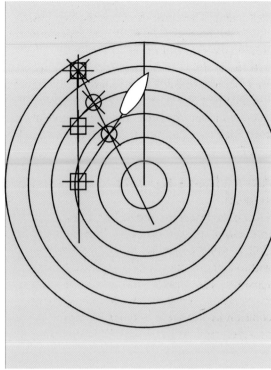

Fig 105 Knowing how the contact representing a stationary target would move on the radar screen means that a ship does not have to pass a real buoy for you to be able to work out its course and speed: you can plot the movement of an imaginary buoy instead.

to a radar screen, the buoy appears to have moved parallel to the boat's course, but in the opposite direction. Its apparent speed is the same as the boat's true speed.

Now imagine the same situation, except that this time another vessel has just passed the buoy at the same moment as the first plot (Figure 104). Six minutes later it is slightly closer and dead ahead. On the radar screen it appears to be moving from right to left, almost at right angles to our own boat's course, and to have covered one mile in six minutes. But we know that six minutes ago it was at the buoy – and the buoy is now a mile away on our starboard beam – so the target's true movement through the water is not represented by its movement across the radar screen, but by a line from the buoy to its present position.

This shows that the target is actually on a converging course and it has travelled 1.6 miles in 6 minutes, so its speed must be 16 knots. Of course, one cannot rely on approaching ships passing close to convenient buoys just when we want them to! But knowing that stationary objects always appear to move parallel to the boat's course but in the opposite direction and at the same speed, it is always possible to combine a plot of a real target with that of an imaginary buoy.

Figure 105 shows a developing near miss situation: the contact first appeared 50° off the port bow at a range of six miles and after 18 minutes has closed to two miles, with less than 10° change of bearing. At first sight this might appear to be a vessel crossing from left to right. If it had dropped a drifting marker buoy

121

at the precise moment of the first plot, the buoy contact would have moved parallel to the heading marker but in the opposite direction and at the same speed as our own – in this case 20 knots. Joining the plot of the imaginary marker buoy to the corresponding plot of the real contact shows that the other vessel is on a converging course, at a speed of about 14 knots: so it is not a give-way crossing vessel, but one that we are overtaking – placing the onus on us to keep clear.

Pilotage

On passage in open water, navigation is mainly concerned with reaching your intended destination. Fixing or estimating your position and shaping a course are simply means to this end, and hazards are avoided by taking care to pass well clear of them.

There are times, however – particularly when entering and leaving harbour – when it may be necessary to venture into more confined waters. Here, the main concern is likely to be hazard avoidance, yet the hazards may well be so close and so numerous that the methods used for offshore and coastal navigation are too slow and too inaccurate. Situations like these call for a different range of skills and techniques, together known as pilotage.

Pilotage is seldom concerned with knowing exactly where you are. More often it involves following a clearly defined track – you should know that you are 'on track', without necessarily knowing exactly how far you have progressed along it.

Buoy-hopping

One of the most obvious ways of marking a channel is by means of buoys or beacons. In narrow rivers and estuaries, where the marks are closely-spaced and positioned very close to the edge of the channel, they give an immediate visual indication of the line to be followed, so steering along the channel is simply a matter of passing each mark on its correct side.

It is important to be aware, however, that the presence of buoys or beacons does not necessarily indicate that there is enough water in the channel at any particular time: some well-marked channels are only passable for a short period around high water.

In more major channels, where the marks have been laid mainly for the benefit of ships, the buoys or beacons are likely to be larger, but further apart, and there may be quite large

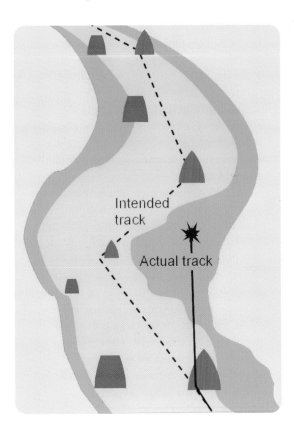

Fig 106 Be careful not to cut corners when buoy-hopping: make sure you know the bearing and distance of each buoy from the one before.

areas of water outside the marked channel which are still quite deep enough for small craft. In this situation, there is a lot to be said in favour of passing on the 'wrong' side of buoys, in order to keep out of the way of larger vessels using the main channel. This calls for a slightly different, more carefully-planned technique – often known as buoy-hopping – which involves steering from one buoy to the next, then on to the next, and so on – in other words, treating each buoy as a waypoint.

It sounds simple, and usually is, but there are a couple of pitfalls to avoid. One of these is the risk of missing a buoy – thereby cutting a corner, and possibly going aground on the very hazard the missed buoy was intended to mark.

The first line of defence against this is to plan ahead, noting the bearing and approximate distance of each buoy from the one before. This ensures that by the time you have reached one buoy, you know where to look for the next. At night, especially, it is important to know what you are looking for: the apparent brightness of a light is a very poor indication of its range, so it is possible to be seduced into going for a large, brightly-lit mark if the one you really want is relatively small and weak.

In long or intricate buoyed channels it can be very easy to lose track of which buoys have already been passed, and to either skip one or two or believe yourself to be further back than you really are. The defence against this is to record the fact that you have passed each mark as you do so, either with a note of the time on the chart – as a fix – or by crossing off the buoy on the chart, or by ticking it off on a pre-prepared list. Be strict with yourself: don't let enthusiasm push you into ticking off a buoy until you really have passed it, nor let activities associated with arrival or departure to distract you from the job in hand.

The other pitfall to watch out for is the effect of wind and tide. Although, in clearly-defined channels, the tidal streams or river currents usually set along the line of the

channel, this is not always the case. A winding channel may have been carved by river water on the ebb tide, but once the sandbanks have been covered by a rising tide, the flood stream may go straight over them – possibly flowing quite strongly, almost straight across the channel.

In this case it is not enough simply to 'aim at the next buoy', because the tide will push the boat sideways, forcing the helmsman to alter course slightly to keep the buoy ahead. Unless he aims uptide of the mark, however, he will never make up the ground already lost,

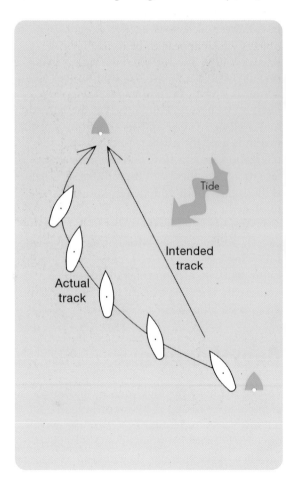

Fig 107 If there is a strong wind or tidal stream setting across your intended track, it is not enough just to aim at the next buoy: the wind or tide will push you sideways on to a curving track.

and as the process repeats itself, the boat's actual track will be a curve, bulging downtide of the intended straight line. This curving track could come to an abrupt halt on the sandbank the buoys were intended to mark! Alternatively, it could be disorientating to find yourself arriving at a buoy from the 'wrong' direction.

The best way to prevent this from happening is to look beyond the buoy for some kind of landmark – any kind of fixed and recognizable object. It does not have to appear on the chart: anything will do, ranging from houses or beach huts to a distinctive bush or even a parked car. In Chapter 4, it was pointed out that two objects which appear to be in line form a particularly useful position line. In this instance the buoy and landmark also form a transit, which – even if it cannot be plotted on a chart

– coincides with the intended track. If the buoy and landmark appear to drift apart, then the boat must have moved off the transit, and therefore off the intended track. It is a reasonably simple matter to alter course to keep the two in line: if the buoy appears to be drifting left of the landmark, alter course to port; and if it appears to be drifting to the right, alter course to starboard.

Leading lines

The use of an impromptu transit in buoy-hopping suggests that long straight channels could be very effectively marked without using buoys at all, by setting up transit marks especially for the purpose. Such marks are called leading marks, or leading lights. As with

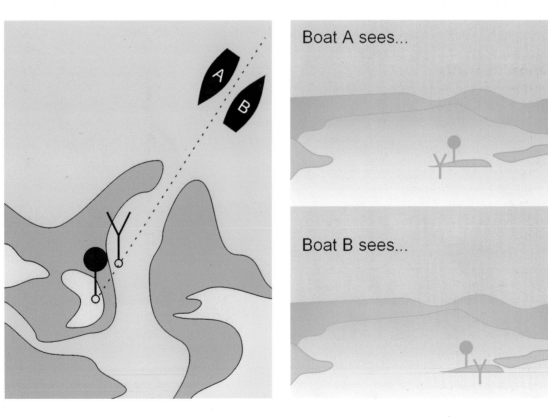

Fig 108 Boat A – inbound – sees the front marker to the left, so she should alter course to port to get back on the leading line. Boat B – outbound – sees the back marker to the left, so she should also alter course to port.

most navigation aids, however, they should only be used in conjunction with a chart, partly because the presence of leading marks is not, in itself, a guarantee that the channel is of any specific depth, and partly because there are local variations. In the Channel Islands for instance, some transits are called 'striking marks', because if you follow the transit you will strike one of the 'heads' of underwater rocks. The safe water is anywhere *except* on the transit line!

If, as is usually the case, leading marks are set up on shore, then yachts heading into the harbour will be steering towards them, so the same rule applies as for the impromptu transit used in buoy-hopping – if the nearer (front) mark appears to be drifting left, steer more to port, and vice versa. Craft leaving harbour will, of course, have the leading marks astern. Now the rule has to be reversed: if the further (rear) mark appears to be drifting left, steer more to port.

'Open' transits

A variation on the transit theme is known as an 'open' transit. This is most often used in relation to natural landmarks which are nearly – but not quite – in the right place, because a

transit is described as being 'open' when the marks are not quite in line with each other.

Compass bearings

A leading line is essentially just a position line which coincides with the intended track. In theory, any kind of position line would do so long as it is sufficiently accurate and reliable, and in practice it is quite common to come across circumstances in which a compass bearing will serve the purpose, because there is a suitable landmark right on the intended track.

Having found such a landmark on the chart, and noted what its bearing should be, the

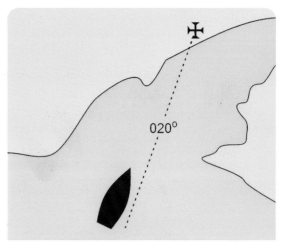

020°

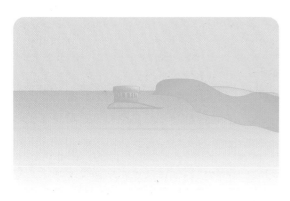

Fig 109 An 'open' transit is one where the two marks are not quite in line with each other. Here, the fort would be described as 'just open to the left of the headland'.

Fig 110 A compass bearing can be used as a leading line, so long as absolute accuracy is not essential.

easiest way to use a compass bearing as a leading mark is either to use the hand bearing compass to look along the intended bearing, or to turn the boat briefly on to that heading. If the mark is then to the left of your line of sight you need to come to port to get back on track, and vice versa.

Clearing lines

Leading lines, especially those marked by transits, are generally extremely precise: it is easy to see at once if you have strayed off the line. That, however, is not always a good thing.

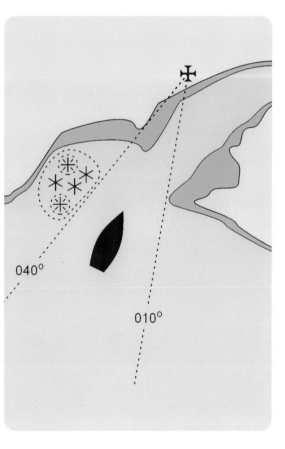

Fig 111 Clearing lines are position lines which have been planned in advance to define the edges of a safe approach corridor. In this case, the bearing of the church must be not more than 040° and not less than 010°.

Sailing yachts cannot beat to windward in a straight line, and if inbound and outbound vessels meet on a transit line, both are likely to stay as close to it as possible, thereby reducing the gap between them as they pass.

In many cases, the width of the channel is such that a high degree of precision is unnecessary – the channel is not like a single, narrow tightrope with dangers on each side, but a wide corridor. Clearing lines are position lines which have been planned in advance to make the edges of the safe corridor visible. A typical situation is illustrated in Figure 111, in which a wide bay is bordered by underwater hazards. Lines drawn from the church at the head of the bay divide it into three areas – a safe, funnel-shaped corridor with hazardous areas on each side.

So long as the navigator of the approaching yacht sees the church on a bearing that is between 010° and 040°, then the boat must be somewhere within the safe sector bounded by the 010° and 040° lines of bearing.

Although visual bearings are probably the commonest type of clearing line, they are not the only possibility: any type of position line can be used so long as it can be plotted on the chart in advance. In some places, for instance, transits have been set up specifically to mark the edges of hazards. Nor do clearing bearings have to be used in pairs. If the only hazard is on one side of the intended track, then a single position line is all that is required to avoid it.

A single clearing line can be particularly useful in the early stages of pilotage, between making a landfall and entering harbour, when the navigator is faced with the conflicting needs of going close enough to the coast to be able to identify the inshore marks, whilst staying far enough offshore to be safe until the way in has been positively identified. In this situation, a clearing bearing on a single major landmark is enough to set a definite limit to how close it is safe to go without having found the inshore marks.

Sectored lights

Sectored lights are a relatively high-tech variation on the idea of clearing lines, which use directional lights to make the edges of the safe corridor visible without even a hand-bearing compass. A typical example is shown in Figure 112.

Even more sophisticated versions have five sectors, rather than three, with a white light showing over the main channel, alternating green and white and red and white showing along its edges, and plain green and red outside the channel.

Sectored lights make pilotage so easy that their main disadvantage is that they are – with a very few exceptions – useless by day. Using sectored lights still calls for some care, though, as the fact that the colour of a directional light varies depending on where it is being seen from means that you need to be careful in identifying it.

Soundings

No matter where one goes, it is almost inevitable that until you are secured to an alongside berth, the closest solid ground will be the seabed, directly below. This too can be used to provide a position line, and can, therefore, be used as a clearing line – simply by deciding, for instance, that 'I will not go into water less than five metres deep'.

The snag with using depth contours in this way is that they are not straight lines, so when the echo sounder reading reduces to the chosen limit, it may not be obvious which way to turn

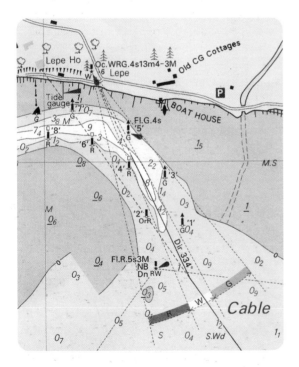

Fig 112 A sectored light shows different colours over different arcs. Usually (but not always) a vessel in the deepest channel will see a white light, and one outside the channel will see a red or green light.

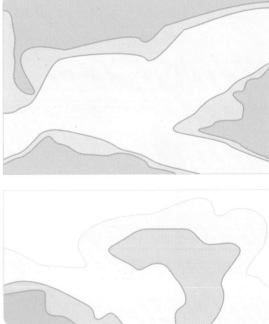

Fig 113 An echo sounder can be used to follow depth contours, but beware of forked channels (top) and hooked contours (bottom).

in order to get back into deeper water.

It is important to plan pilotage by contour as carefully as pilotage by any other method, to avoid traps such as the hook-shaped contour and the forked channel shown in Figure 113. Once planned, however, contour pilotage lends itself to short-handed operation, because the echo sounder's deep and shallow alarms can be set to give an automatic audible warning of when to alter course.

Head-up radar

At its most basic, a head-up radar can be treated rather like a video game: you pick a feature to head for, such as a buoy or a gap between two islands, and alter course until the heading mark is pointing straight at it. The principle can be modified slightly, in order to pass a set distance off a headland, for instance, by using a chinagraph pencil or a whiteboard marker to draw a line on the screen parallel to the heading marker and the appropriate distance from it. Then it is simply a matter of steering the boat so as to keep the headland sliding along the marked line.

These techniques, though, are no more than the radar equivalent of aiming for the next buoy by eye, and suffer the same drawbacks if there is any wind or tidal stream setting across your intended track.

Unfortunately, radar's poor bearing discrimination and its inability to pick out specific landmarks ashore mean that the problem cannot be overcome by using clearing bearings.

The principle of clearing lines can still be used with radar, in the form of clearing ranges.

Figure 114 shows a harbour entrance encumbered by shallow patches. The gap between the shoals is just under 100 metres wide, and lies between 0.29 and 0.33 miles off the shore. In other words, a boat would be in danger of grounding if it got closer than 0.29 miles to the shore or more than 0.33 miles from it. By setting VRMs or guard zones, or by drawing chinagraph or whiteboard marker circles on the screen at the appropriate distance from the centre, it's possible to see at a glance if the boat strays outside these limits.

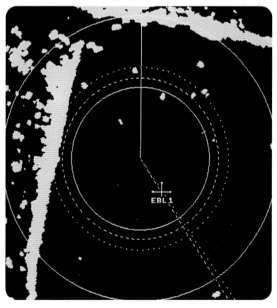

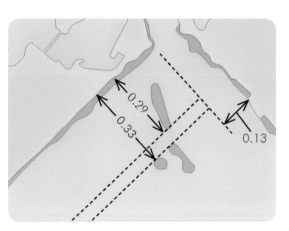

Fig 114 Clearing ranges can be used to find a safe passage between shallows, and to show when to turn.

Fig 115 Here is the radar picture of the same situation with guard zones (shown by dotted lines) used to mark the relevant ranges.

129

In this case, another clearing range could be used to decide when to make the bold turn to port towards the harbour entrance. The shoal patches are no closer than 0.13 miles from the eastern side of this funnel-shaped entrance, so once the boat is with 0.13 miles of the coastline ahead, her navigator knows he must be clear of the shallows and that it is safe to alter course.

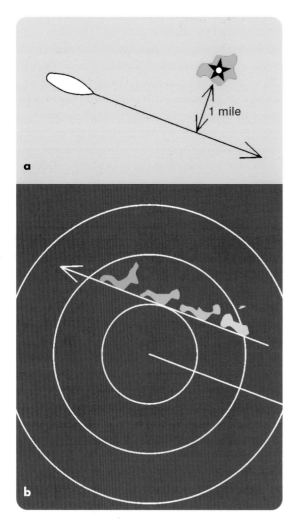

Fig 116 Parallel indexing is a powerful pilotage technique, but can only be applied on a north-up radar display. It involves plotting the intended movement of a fixed reference target in advance.

North-up radar

North-up radar is an even more powerful pilotage tool, particularly because of a technique known as parallel indexing. This is based on the fact that on a stabilized radar it is possible to predict how the contact representing a stationary object will appear to move across the screen, assuming that the boat follows a pre-determined track.

Figure 116(a) shows a yacht's planned track past a small island. Its track is 110°(M) and it passes 1 mile from the island. Figure 116(b) shows how the same situation appears on radar: the contact representing the island moves across the screen on a reciprocal (opposite) track of 290°(M), passing a mile from the centre of the screen. If the contact fails to behave as predicted, then the assumption must be that the yacht is not on her planned track: if the island is too far from the centre, for instance, then the yacht needs to alter course towards the island, in order to reduce the range, and vice versa.

As with traditional pilotage, one of the main keys to success is preparation:

1 Choose a suitable target (the 'index target') that will be within range when the radar is set to a range scale that gives sufficient accuracy, that will show up on radar, and that can be positively identified. Large shore-based structures such as jetties are better than buoys, which can easily be confused with other boats.
2 Measure the range and bearing from any point on the planned track to the index target.
3 Set the VRM and EBL (or the cursor) to this range and bearing, and mark this point on screen with a chinagraph pencil.
4 Set the EBL to the direction of the intended track, and draw a straight line parallel to the EBL, passing through the mark made in step 3.
5 Write the range scale used in the planning

on to the screen in chinagraph, and on to the chart, to reduce the risk of using a different scale when you put the plan into effect!

The parallel indexing technique can be taken a stage further, by repeating the process for each leg of the intended track. The end result should be a pattern of lines on the radar screen which copy the intended track drawn on the chart, but inverted. This means, incidentally, that a quick and effective check against major blunders is to turn the chart south-up, and compare it with the chinagraph lines!

Blind pilotage by radar is not easy: it requires great care in the planning stage, a well set-up radar, and an operator who is thoroughly familiar with it, so it is well worth practising in good conditions.

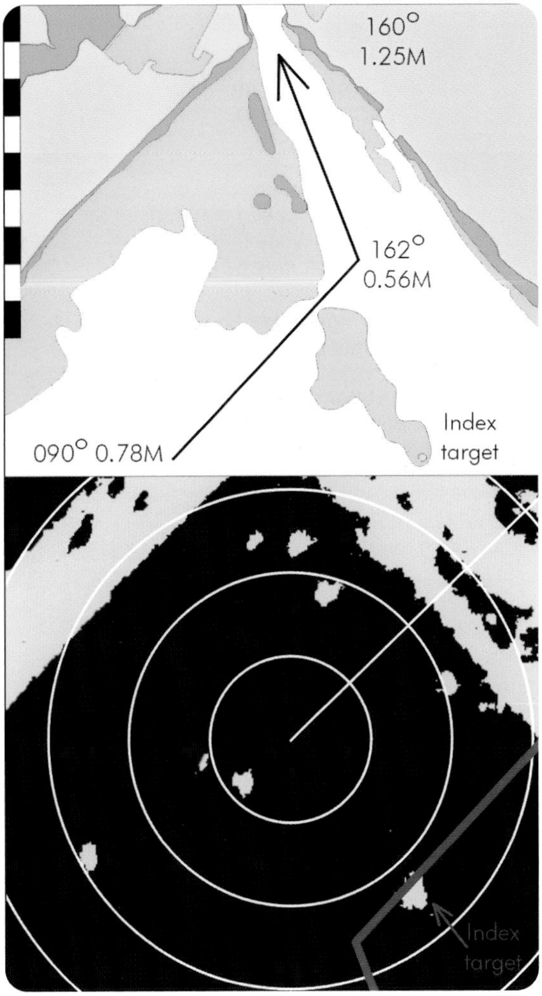

Eyeballing

These precise, formal pilotage techniques will cover most situations, but there may still be occasions when there are simply no marks available. Even this does not necessarily make pilotage impossible – it just calls for more

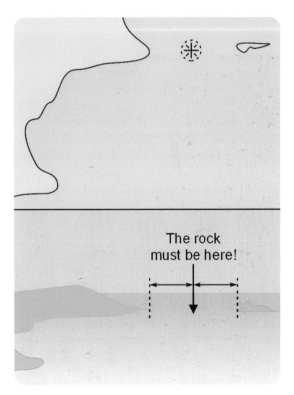

Fig 117 Parallel indexing can be applied to more complicated pilotage situations. Notice that the reference line drawn on the screen is the same shape as the intended track on the chart, rotated through 180°.

Fig 118 In simple situations, it may be possible to steer by eye, relying on an informed guess about the position of hidden hazards.

inventiveness, flexibility and intuition.

One might, for instance, be faced with a gap between an island and the shore, with an underwater rock in the middle (Figure 118). Even with no other marks available, it is clear that the rock can be avoided by sticking closer to one side of the channel than the other.

Similarly, if there were shoals on each side but a deeper channel through the centre, the channel could be found simply by steering for the middle of the gap.

Planning pilotage

The whole point of pilotage is that it enables a boat to be navigated accurately but quickly, without spending time on chartwork, so it defeats the object if the skipper or navigator tries to carry out pilotage 'on the fly' – searching the chart and pilot books for information when the boat is already moving through confined waters.

Planning is essential, but there are no hard and fast rules: every harbour is different, and the plan for each one may well vary depending on the size of the boat, the state of the tide, the weather and visibility, and whether it is day or night. The first stage of the process is likely to be gathering information, in particular from the pilot book and tidetables. Knowing the height of tide is almost always important, because it enables you to take a more intelligent look at the large-scale chart of the area. What appears to be a winding channel between rocks and sandbanks may turn out to be a straightforward approach across open water if the tide is high enough to cover the hazards; conversely, half tide or low water may reveal enough of the sandbanks to make a channel obvious, or make useful landmarks out of rocks that would be hidden hazards at high water.

At a fairly early stage in the planning process, it is as well to establish any constraints which are likely to affect your freedom of movement – things such as locks or

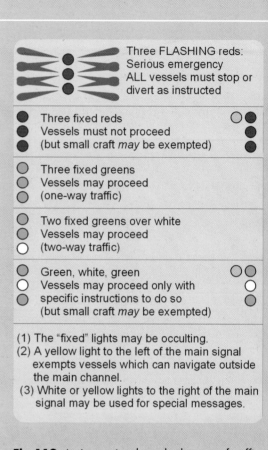

Three FLASHING reds:
Serious emergency
ALL vessels must stop or
divert as instructed

Three fixed reds
Vessels must not proceed
(but small craft *may* be exempted)

Three fixed greens
Vessels may proceed
(one-way traffic)

Two fixed greens over white
Vessels may proceed
(two-way traffic)

Green, white, green
Vessels may proceed only with
specific instructions to do so
(but small craft *may* be exempted)

(1) The "fixed" lights may be occulting.
(2) A yellow light to the left of the main signal exempts vessels which can navigate outside the main channel.
(3) White or yellow lights to the right of the main signal may be used for special messages.

Fig 119 An international standard system of traffic control signals is gradually being introduced.

HARBOUR REGULATIONS AND BYELAWS

In general, the movements of all vessels in ports and harbours are governed by the same rules as apply at sea – the International Regulations for the Prevention of Collisions at Sea. The increasing size and speed of many commercial vessels, however, mean that in most ports Rule 9 assumes overwhelming importance:

'A vessel of less than 20 m in length or a sailing vessel shall not impede the passage of a vessel which can safely navigate only in a narrow channel or fairway.'

Whilst it may not be easy to decide exactly what constitutes 'a narrow channel or fairway', it is fair to assume that a buoyed channel used by ships will be regarded as a narrow channel or fairway by ships' masters and by the harbour staff! Staying out of it, if at all possible, not only conforms to the collision regulations, but is safer and less worrying for all concerned.

In many ports, the spirit of Rule 9 is repeated in Harbour Byelaws, or in recommendations published by the Harbour Authority. Southampton's rules, for instance, clarify the meaning of 'shall not impede' by defining an 'exclusion zone' around particularly large vessels, in the shape of a rectangle extending 1000 metres ahead of the ship and 100 metres each side; Harwich extend the 'shall not impede' rule to cover the approaches to wharves, piers and jetties, and recommends specific routes for pleasure craft moving in and around the harbour; while Portsmouth has a compulsory 'small boat channel' just clear of the main channel through the entrance.

Most busy harbours now make increasing use of VHF radio to control shipping movements. Very few have the capacity – or the need – to handle incoming calls from yachts except in emergencies, but most recommend that all vessels equipped with VHF keep a listening watch on the port operation channel, so as to be aware of shipping movements.

As well as rules like these, many harbours with particularly narrow entrances or locks have a system of traffic lights. The international system shown in Figure 119 is slowly being introduced, but many harbours still use their own codes, not all of which are quite as obvious as 'red for stop and green for go'.

The increasing number of rules and regulations mean that researching them must now be an integral part of any pilotage plan. Sources of information include booklets and brochures published by the Harbour Authorities, as well as charts and pilot books. It is worth remembering that pilot books, in particular, are seldom right up to date and charts can give only very brief details, so be prepared to accept instructions from harbour patrol launches.

Most yachtsmen's pilot books are written primarily for sailing craft, so almost all ignore the existence of speed limits. Motor cruiser navigators therefore need to keep their eyes open for warning notices on buoys, piles or harbour walls, and in any case try to keep their wash down when passing other craft.

bridges which open only at certain times, sand bars or marina cills which can only be crossed with a given rise of tide, and any harbour regulations that prevent you from entering certain areas.

Having established a 'feel' for the area, the chances are that one or more routes will present themselves as possible ways in (or out). In some of the most complicated situations, it may be difficult to decide which to choose, but pilot books often give useful advice, such as:

'On a first visit to Chausey, the approach is best made from the southward, as the leading marks for the northern entrance are not so easily picked up and much of the channel dries out.'

Having chosen a channel – or at least narrowed down the choice – it is possible to

start making a more definite plan. Assess the hazards, and the marks that are available to help avoid them. Here, too, pilot books and almanacs can be a great help, offering 'potted' pilotage plans that may include almost everything you need. Even so, it is a mistake to rely entirely on the pilot book alone – at the very least, its suggestions should be checked against the chart.

Without such a 'potted plan' you will need to devise your own strategy from scratch, based on the various techniques described earlier in this chapter. If possible, try to avoid depending entirely on a single technique: a crucial buoy may have broken adrift, or a leading mark may be obscured by trees, so it is always useful to have a back-up method in reserve, even if it is only a compass course and an idea of the distance to go.

Having decided on your strategy, write it

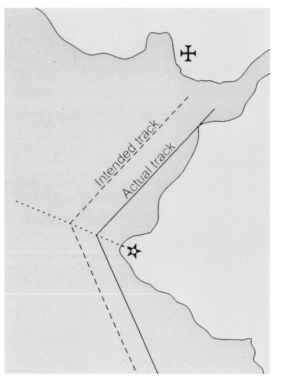
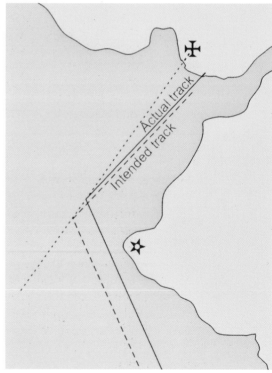

Fig 120 When using a compass bearing to decide when to alter course, it is better to use a landmark which will be directly ahead or astern on the new course than one which is abeam.

down, either on the chart or on a notepad, or both. This written plan is not intended to be a reproduction of the pilot book or a record for posterity: it should consist of working notes sufficient to stop you having to refer to the chart at every alteration of course. It will almost certainly include the expected height of tide, and the range and bearing of each landmark from the one before, together with a description of it.

'From green conical No 43 315° 400 m to green conical No 45 – LEAVE TO PORT'

for instance, is far more useful than

'LEAVE No 43 and 45 to port',

because it tells you what to look for and where to look for it, as well as what to do when you've found it.

A common difficulty is deciding where to start and stop the pilotage plan, and the common mistake is to start too late and finish too early. It is important to be certain that the first mark, or starting point, of the plan can safely be located by conventional navigation, and to end the plan at your intended berth or mooring.

Turning marks

The essence of pilotage is that it involves sticking to a pre-planned track, so it is often important to make an alteration of course at a specific point. It is very tempting to use a bearing of something abeam for the purpose – 'we'll turn when the beacon tower is abeam'. Although this may seem very precise, because the bearing of objects abeam changes relatively quickly, it does not actually serve the purpose: as Figure 121 shows, if you are already off track, then using a mark that is abeam virtually guarantees that you will still be off track after you have altered course. It is far better to use a mark that will be directly ahead or astern on the new course.

Transferred turning marks

A transferred position line, like that used to produce a running fix, can be used in much the same way, though with less accuracy. It is particularly useful when trying to find an inconspicuous harbour, when the only obvious landmark is on a headland a few miles along the coast.

Again, the key to success is to make sure that the transferred position line is on a bearing that is the same as (or the reciprocal of) the new course. Draw in the required line of bearing to cut through the charted landmark, and measure along the initial track to find the distance you will have to travel from the bearing line to your intended turning point. Note the log reading when the landmark is on the pre-drawn bearing and – allowing for tide – make the turn when you have run the required distance.

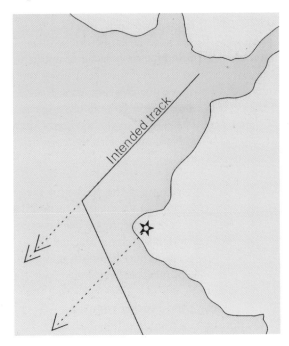

Fig 121 A transferred position line can be used to determine when to turn – to find an inconspicuous harbour entrance, for instance – but for greatest accuracy, it is important that the bearing used is parallel to the boat's new course.

Pilotage in practice

Having devoted time and effort to planning, good pilotage should mean no more than sticking to the plan. This, however, is itself a two-stage process, involving identifying the marks for each leg, and guiding the boat accurately along the intended track. This, ideally, calls for good teamwork between the helmsman and navigator, rather than one person trying to do it all.

The navigator should be looking at least one step ahead, locating and identifying the marks for the next leg, while the helmsman concentrates on steering the boat. Then, as they approach a turning point – a buoy, or a change from one transit to another – the navigator should point out the new marks to the helmsman.

As the helmsman turns the boat on to the new course, the navigator should first check that the new heading corresponds with the plan, and that the helmsman is, indeed, steering by the correct marks, before setting about the job of finding the next set of marks.

One exception to this principle of being one step ahead is when using clearing lines. It is difficult, if not impossible, to take bearings at the same time as steering, so the navigator may well have to involve himself with the current leg, as well as looking for the marks for the next leg.

The other exception is if the marks for the next leg are so difficult to see that they cannot be identified in time. In this case, if you can be absolutely certain that you have reached the correct turning point, it may be worth making the turn on to the planned heading, and looking for the marks directly ahead – as though using the boat itself as a hand-bearing compass.

Do not, however, underestimate the advantages of using binoculars, especially at night. They can make all the difference between seeing and not seeing a critical mark.

Back bearings

Steering by compass alone in the general direction of an unseen buoy or transit can be unnerving in pilotage waters, especially if there is a strong cross-wind or tidal stream setting the boat off track. A useful double-check can be made by taking bearings of a buoy or landmark astern.

If, for instance, your plan involves following a track of 045° from one buoy to the next, then so long as the first buoy is astern, on a bearing of 225° – the reciprocal (opposite) of the intended track – then the boat must be on track. In practice, using a back bearing is very similar to using the bearing of a single landmark ahead as a leading line: it is better to look along the correct bearing than to take a bearing of the mark in the usual way. One important difference is that if a back-mark is to the left of your line of sight, you need to come to starboard to get back on track.

A backbearing like this has the important advantage that, because you have just passed close to the object concerned, it is easy to make a very positive identification of it, but it is much more difficult for the helmsman to use as a point of reference than a mark which is ahead. To overcome this problem, then, once you are on track, it is a good idea to find some object – even one that is not on the chart, such as an oddly-shaped tree or a parked car – for the helmsman to aim for.

Fig 122 When using a back bearing, it is usually easier to sight along the correct bearing to see whether the mark is to the left or the right than to take a bearing of the mark and try to figure out the implications.

10 Passage-making

The idea of simply setting off into the sunset to cruise wherever and whenever the fancy takes you, has a certain romantic appeal. Were one to try it, however, the chances are that the first night might be spent fighting a foul tide, and the second searching for a cashpoint to get the right currency for wherever you've landed – or worse!

Cruise planning factors

Any journey, no matter how simple, requires some degree of planning. When you get up in the morning, you may not consciously think 'I want to go down to the kitchen ... that means going downstairs and through the dining room ... I can't put the lights on, because that will wake the children, but I have to avoid the dog basket in the hall', but a plan along those lines must be in your mind. Almost all journey plans include:

- an objective;
- constraints – which limit your freedom of operation;
- hazards – to be avoided;
- aids – that will help you achieve your objective;
- a route – based on the other four.

In practice, the first phase of any passage plan is likely to involve gathering information, from charts, pilot books, tidetables, and tidal stream atlases. For major cruises it may also be worth adding guidebooks, ferry timetables, and the RYA booklet *Planning a Foreign Cruise*.

Even at this stage – before the objectives have been decided – some of the constraints are likely to come into play. There is little point, for instance, in planning a Baltic cruise from the south coast if you only have a week to do it in, unless you are prepared to make other plans for getting the boat there and back: time, speed, and distance are important factors to consider. A very common mistake is to over-estimate the average speed made good and the time that will actually be spent under way.

Cruise planning may well be carried out so far in advance that reliable weather forecasts are not available. Pilot books – especially Admiralty pilots – often include weather statistics which can be used as a guide to the likely conditions, and in particular to how many days should be deducted from the time available to allow for bad weather. In setting objectives, it is also important to remember more mundane matters, such as the need to take on food, water and provisions.

Family holidays are often constrained by the need to get the boat home by a given date. A good overall plan for this type of cruise is to start with a short passage to 'shake down' and get used to being at sea, followed by a longer trip to one of the most distant ports of call. This leaves most of the time available for the return journey, which can be broken up into short passages, giving the opportunity to skip one or two stopovers if time is running out.

The cruise plan usually boils down to a set of objectives – a list of ports of call – which break the cruise into a number of separate passages. Each passage can then be planned in more detail, usually working on larger scale charts. The breadth and depth of detail required depends largely on the speed of the boat concerned. It could be said that a sailing boat has to be navigated from wherever it happens to be *towards* where it is trying to go, whereas a motorboat can be navigated from where it was, *to* its destination.

To be more explicit, a sailing boat is so much affected by tide and wind that it cannot hope to stick rigidly to a set plan. Indeed, one of the commonest mistakes made by inexperienced navigators is to regard an 'intended track' drawn on the chart as though it were a railway line, and devote too much time and effort to slogging uptide or upwind in order to stay 'on the rails' . For sailing yachts – and slow motorboats – it is far better to accept that you will have to re-assess your situation from time to time, and adapt your passage plan accordingly. Fortunately, at speeds in the order of 5–10 knots, the slow boat navigator usually has the luxury of time in which to make decisions.

By contrast, a fast boat – at speeds of 20 knots plus – is relatively little affected by tidal streams, and small variations in wind speed or direction make almost no difference to the boat's speed. The chances of being able to stay close to the intended track are therefore good – and it is important to do so because there is little time available to adapt the plan, especially if lively motion or lack of navigation facilities are making chartwork difficult. Navigation at speed is less a matter of decision-making than of monitoring progress to ensure that the passage is going according to plan. Of course, the fast boat navigator always has the option of slowing down if things go awry, but that makes the initial plan even less valid, and puts him in much the same situation as the slow boat navigator.

Sunrise and sunset

The effect of sunrise and sunset is, quite literally, as clear as day. Simply operating the boat at night demands more skill and expertise; coastal navigation and pilotage become more difficult; and unlit harbours are effectively closed to strangers altogether. Having said that, many people enjoy night passages, and for sailing boats there is the strong possibility that a night at sea may be the only way to complete a passage longer than about 50 miles.

One positive feature of darkness is the operation of lighthouses, which can make it easier to identify parts of an unfamiliar coastline by night than by day. For this reason it is common practice for cruising yachtsmen to time passages across the North Sea, Celtic Sea, and the wider parts of the English Channel so as to make their landfall just before dawn, to have the benefit of the lighthouses as they approach the coast, and daylight to enter harbour.

CONSTRAINTS

Many different factors can limit your freedom of action, not necessarily preventing movement, but certainly influencing your decisions. These include:

- sunrise and sunset
- tidal height

- locks and bridges
- tidal streams
- weather and sea-state
- boat and crew strength
- traffic separation schemes
- domestic requirements
- fuel

The times of sunrise and sunset do not vary significantly from day to day or over short distances, so for passage planning during a cruise, detailed calculation is unnecessary – you are likely to have a good idea of when it gets dark. For advance planning the 'lighting up times' given in many diaries are a rough guide, but more accurate times can be found in yachtsmen's almanacs. *Reeds* includes a table showing the time of sunrise and sunset at 3 day intervals throughout the year, and at different latitudes. From the extract in Figure 123, for instance, it is easy to see that the time of sunrise at 48° North on 5 July must be somewhere between 0407 and 0409, so 0408 seems like a reasonable estimate. On adjoining pages of the almanac, there are similar tables for other latitudes, and by interpolating between them, it is possible to come up with a

reasonable estimate for any latitude.

But the reason the sun appears to rise and set is because the Earth is spinning, not because the Sun is moving, so sunrise and sunset both happen later as you move westwards. The simple rule is to add 4 minutes for every degree of easterly longitude.

Finally, remember that the tables are in Universal Time (GMT) so you may need to add an hour to convert to BST.

Tidal height

The entrances of many natural harbours are partly obstructed by bars, formed where the out-flowing river water slows down on meeting the sea, and drops the sand and silt it has been carrying. The depths over such a bar can be considerably less than those inside the harbour, so it acts as a natural barrier, which can only be crossed when there is sufficient height of tide.

In onshore winds the shallowness of the water over a bar makes the waves higher and steeper, perhaps even to the extent of forming breakers. In such conditions, the troughs of the waves reduce the effective depth still further, so an extra margin for safety needs to be included in your tidal calculations. Breaking waves are particularly dangerous, but they are almost impossible to see from seaward, so it is essential to heed any relevant advice in the pilot book before tackling a bar in a fresh or strong onshore wind, especially on an ebb tide.

Many marinas, especially in areas with large tidal ranges, have *cills* across their entrances. A cill is a wall, intended to retain water inside the marina basin, when the water level outside falls. Like bars, cills can only be crossed when there is sufficient height of tide. As they are almost invariably protected by an outer harbour, there is no need to allow much safety margin for wave troughs – most have a tide gauge showing the actual depth available.

Bridges and overhead cables impose similar constraints, with the obvious difference that in this case you can only pass underneath when

LATITUDE 48°N						
	Rise	Set	Rise	Set	Rise	
	JANUARY		FEBRUARY		M	
1	07 50	16 17	07 29	16 59	06 4	
4	07 50	16 20	07 25	17 04	06 3	
7	07 49	16 23	07 20	17 09	06 2	
10	07 48	16 27	07 16	17 13	06 2	
13	07 47	16 31	07 11	17 18	06 1	
16	07 45	16 35	07 06	17 23	06 1	
19	07 43	16 39	07 01	17 28	06 0	
22	07 40	16 43	06 55	17 32	05 5	
25	07 37	16 48	06 50	17 37	05 5	
28	07 34	16 53	06 44	17 42	05 4	
31	07 30	16 57			05 4	
	JULY		AUGUST		SEF	
1	04 05	20 03	04 36	19 35	05 1	
4	04 07	20 02	04 40	19 31	05 2	
7	04 09	20 01	04 44	19 26	05 2	
10	04 12	19 59	04 48	19 21	05 3	
13	04 14	19 57	04 52	19 16	05 3	
16	04 17	19 54	04 56	19 11	05 3	
19	04 21	19 51	05 01	19 06	05 4	
22	04 24	19 48	05 05	19 00	05 4	
25	04 28	19 45	05 09	18 54	05 5	
28	04 31	19 41	05 13	18 48	05 5	
31	04 35	19 37	05 17	18 43		

Fig 123 *Reeds Nautical Almanac* gives the time of sunrise and sunset at various ports at different latitudes, at three-day intervals.

the tide has fallen far enough. The headroom is marked on the relevant chart – remember that the charted headroom, like the elevation of a light, is measured from Mean High Water Springs, so there will usually be more room than given on the chart. In addition, bridges are often fitted with tide gauges, showing the available headroom.

Locks and swing bridges

Locks and swinging or lifting bridges are subject to human control, rather than being governed solely by the height of tide, but the tide still has a part to play: low air-draft motorboats may be able to pass underneath a bridge without it opening if the tide is low enough; and the opening times of locks are often related either to the time of high water or to a specified height of tide.

Tidal considerations apart, locks and swing or lifting bridges may open on demand at any time, on demand during specified working hours, or at set times. It is worth checking with as many sources of information as possible, because policies can change – and a lock-keeper who has gone home for supper is unlikely to open up just for a yachtsman who quotes a ten-year-old pilot book at him!

Tidal streams

Around much of the coast of the UK and northern Europe, the tidal streams are strong enough to have a major effect on the speed over the ground of a displacement motor cruiser or a sailing yacht. This is particularly true when beating to windward, when the VMG (velocity made good) upwind is likely to be only about two-thirds of the boat's speed through the water (Figure 124).

A favourable tidal stream could, in many areas, double this, whilst a contrary tide could bring the boat almost to a standstill. It makes sense, therefore, to plan a passage so as to make best use of favourable tidal streams, and to minimize the effect of contrary ones. Tidal streams tend to be stronger around headlands

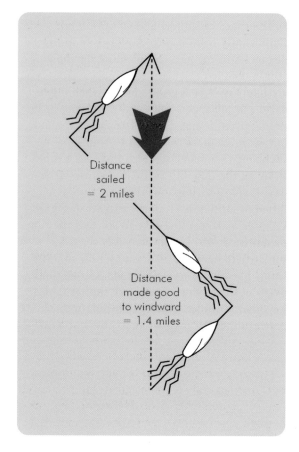

Fig 124 The overall progress of a sailing yacht beating to windward is approximately two-thirds of her speed through the water, and will be significantly affected by tidal streams.

and in narrow channels than in more open water, so these areas are sometimes described as 'tidal gates' – because they effectively block the passage of low-speed boats altogether at certain times.

Tidal streams can also have a significant effect on sea-state: a fast-flowing tide creates overfalls over a shallow, broken seabed, and makes the waves larger and steeper when it is flowing against the wind. Overfalls can be avoided either by going round them, or by passing through the area concerned at or near slack water, whereas wind-against-tide conditions can only be avoided by timing. Sea-state, of course, affects all boats, but its consequences are most pronounced for planing motorboats, which may be forced to reduce to displacement speed in wind-against-tide conditions.

A good example of the way tidal streams affect passage planning is in the passage south west from Alderney to Guernsey. The prevailing winds in this area are south westerly (ie blowing from the south-west), and the tidal streams flow strongly in a SW/NE direction. Sailing yachts, faced with a beat against the SW wind and a tidal stream of three knots or more, have no real option but to leave Alderney in time to catch the fair tide, and put up with the wind-against-tide sea-state. Their time of departure is further constrained by the need to leave near slack water, in order to avoid the overfalls around Alderney.

In calm conditions, the navigator of a motor cruiser might well opt for the same strategy, using the tidal stream to increase the boat's speed over the ground. In fresher conditions, however, sea-state assumes greater importance, and it becomes worth considering making the passage when wind and tide are together, on the NE-going tidal stream.

Weather and sea-state

The weather is much less predictable than the tide, so even the best weather forecast can only be regarded as a guide. Nevertheless the weather plays such an important part in the comfort and safety of the boat and crew that it would be foolhardy to ignore the forecast. There are many possible sources of weather information.

During a cruise, for instance, the more 'heavyweight' newspapers may be used as a source of weather maps, to keep an eye on changing weather patterns, whilst the apparently glib forecast of 'another hot sunny day on the beaches' from a local radio station is a strong hint that sea breezes are likely to develop in the afternoon.

More useful forecasts are tailored for marine use, such as Marine call (telephone), Metfax (fax) and the Shipping Forecast on BBC Radio 4.

Around the UK, HM Coastguard regularly issue repeats of the shipping forecast, and reports of actual weather conditions, all by VHF radio.

Navtex and Wefax both provide weather information by radio, but need specialist receiving equipment to display their text messages (Navtex) or graphic images (Wefax), while the Internet offers a huge mass of information which can be accessed by anyone with a computer on board and a suitable communications link (such as a mobile telephone or satcom system).

Visibility

Visibility is usually classified as:

- good (over 5 miles);
- moderate (2–5 miles);
- poor (1100 yds–2 miles) or
- fog (under 1100 yds).

Its effects are almost self-evident: moderate visibility may affect coastal navigation by making visual fixes difficult or impossible; poor visibility is likely to have a serious effect on inshore navigation and pilotage; while fog almost rules out any kind of visual navigation altogether. Visibility also plays a part in collision avoidance, so the risk of collision must be assumed to be greater in fog or poor visibility. It may well be worth thinking about adapting a passage plan to avoid shipping lanes or ferry routes if the visibility is forecast to be 'poor' .

Wind

Wind not only provides the motive power for sailing yachts, but also has a significant effect on the sea-state – something that affects everyone, sail or power. Generally speaking, increasing sea-states (ie larger waves) make conditions on board less comfortable, increase the power required to maintain any given speed, and may well set an upper limit on the speed that can be achieved or maintained. What constitutes 'calm', 'pleasant', 'rough', or 'survival' conditions, however, varies from boat to boat and crew to crew, so it is important to be realistic about the conditions your particular boat/crew combination can handle.

Although the wind creates most of the waves we encounter at sea, the size and length of the waves is related not only to the strength of the wind, but also to the depth and nature of the seabed, the direction and rate of the tidal stream, how long the wind has been blowing, and the **fetch** – the distance it has been blowing over clear water.

The effect of fetch can be dramatic, especially in an offshore wind. In a force 6 – the strength at which strong wind warnings are issued – the typical wave height in open water is likely to be around 10 ft (3 m), with many waves spontaneously breaking into foam at their crests. It is quite appropriately called 'a yachtsman's gale', because few family cruisers would choose to be at sea in such conditions. Inshore, the 'shelter' of the land to windward may lower the wind speed by only a few knots, but the reduced fetch is likely to keep the wave height down to a couple of feet. The implication of this, for motorboats especially, is that in wind strengths above about force 3 it may be worth planning a passage that hugs the coast, rather than one that hops from headland to headland.

Boat and crew strength

A 70 foot maxi-rater, with a crew of fit professional sailors, can race around the world, but it is pretty obvious that a 17 footer crewed by an eight-year-old and her 70-year-old grandfather could not. This – admittedly extreme – example proves that the boat and crew strengths impose limitations on the passage plan. Those constraints are, however, extremely difficult to quantify, simply because there are so many variables, but with

experience of the boat and a knowledge of the individuals involved, most people find it becomes almost instinctive to set themselves some kind of weather and endurance limit. Having recognized your limitations, it is often possible to think of ways round them.

A crew of fit young adults, for instance, might sail to Spain from the UK in one hit. A 70-year-old couple would probably choose not to – but because they do not have to go back to work in two or three weeks, they could still go to Spain in a series of relatively short coastal 'hops', with days in port in between. A family with young children might shorten the

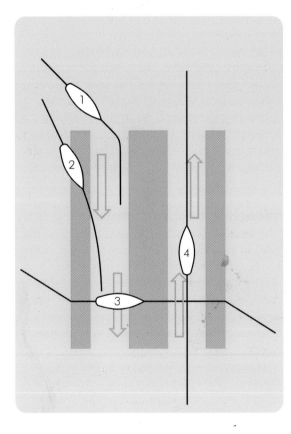

Fig 125 The rules governing traffic separation schemes are simple: (1) join and leave at the ends if possible; (2) otherwise, join at a shallow angle; (3) cross on a course – NOT a track – at right angles to the flow; and (4) travel in the appropriate lane. Small craft are well-advised to stay out of TSSs whenever possible.

cruise, but could still cope with a Channel crossing by making most of the 'boring' passage at night with the children asleep, perhaps with the assistance of another adult either to spread the watchkeeping while under way, or to entertain the children while the parents catch up on sleep the next day.

Traffic Separation Schemes

Traffic Separation Schemes have been set up in many busy sea areas, in order to reduce collision risks by channelling ships into clearly defined shipping lanes. Various special rules cover the behaviour of yachts and small craft in Traffic Separation Schemes. From the passage planning point of view, the most significant are:

- If you are following a Traffic Separation Scheme, you must be in the right lane – just as you would on the road.
- If you are joining or leaving a separation scheme, you should aim to do so at the ends; otherwise join or leave it at a shallow angle – like the slip roads on and off motorways.
- If you are crossing a separation scheme – probably the most common situation for pleasure craft – you must steer a course at right angles to the traffic flow, without allowing for tidal streams or leeway.

Domestic requirements

It may be tempting to dismiss domestic requirements as trivial. Nevertheless, details such as having fresh milk on board can make a major difference to the overall success of a cruise, so it is worth allowing for them in the planning process. Don't assume you can get going at 0830 and sail for 8 hours every day!

Fuel

The observation that 'there are no petrol stations at sea' is trite, but it makes the point that the distance you can cover under power is limited by your fuel capacity and consumption. As a working guide, one should never rely on being able to use more than 80% of your tank's capacity.

Consumption is a much more complicated calculation, with several different formulae in use. Any calculation is bound to be an approximation because it will be affected by several unmeasurable factors, but as a crude rule of thumb:

- a diesel engine uses about 1 gallon per hour per 20 hp
- a petrol engine uses about 1 gallon per hour per 12–14 hp
- a two-stroke engine uses about 1 gallon per hour per 8–10 hp.

The power used is approximately proportional to the cube of the shaft speed – shown by the graph in Figure 126.

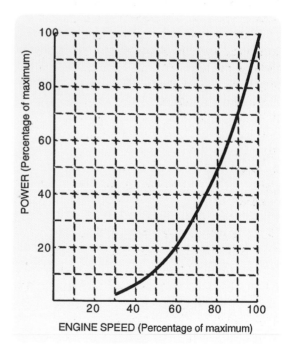

Fig 126 The power used – and hence the fuel consumption – is roughly proportional to the cube of the shaft speed.

As an illustration of how these calculations might work in practice, a motor cruiser with two 200 hp diesels would produce 400 hp at full power, and would therefore burn about 400 ÷ 20 = 20 gallons per hour. Reducing to cruising speed of, say, 80% of maximum revs reduces the power produced to just over 50% of maximum, reducing the fuel consumption to about 11 gallons per hour.

A sailing boat powered by a 6 hp outboard would burn 6 ÷ 8 = ¾ gallon per hour at full throttle, or about 0.4 gallons per hour at 80% of maximum rpm.

Hazards and aids

Hazards, such as rocks and shoals, are generally fairly obvious – at least on the chart – though the height of tide and prevailing weather conditions need to be borne in mind to determine a sensible under-keel clearance. By day, in clear weather, above-water objects scarcely rank as hazards, because if you can see them it is easy enough to steer round them. In fog or at night, however, it is a different story: even unlit buoys and beacons – which by day would be classed as aids to navigation – become hazards to be avoided.

Aids and hazards need to be considered together, because it is the aids available that determine the safety margin that should be allowed around each hazard. The safety margin should never be less than the level of accuracy available – in other words, you

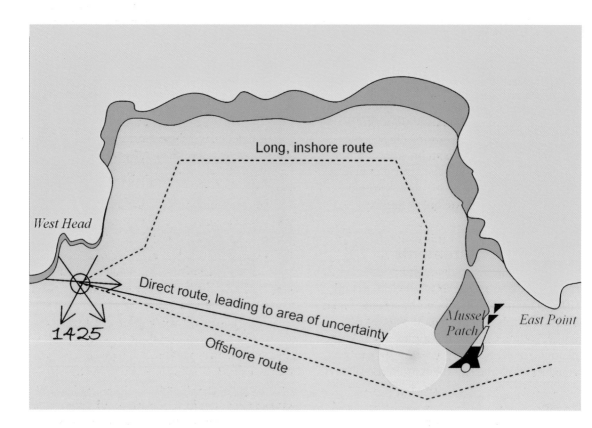

Fig 127 You should never approach a hazard more closely than the level of your navigational accuracy. With 20 miles since the fix, the navigator of an eastbound yacht in this situation could not guarantee to find the buoy before hitting the bank.

should not aim to pass within 50 metres of a hazard if your navigational accuracy is 'only' 100 metres.

Figure 127 shows a shoal patch close to one side of a deep bay. A boat crossing the bay from east to west would have a good position fix rounding East Point, so it could safely aim straight for the Mussel Patch buoy, knowing that with only five miles to go, the buoy will be in sight before there is any serious risk of hitting the bank.

Without electronics, the navigator of an eastbound yacht is faced with a more complex decision, because on the 20 mile leg from West Head to Mussel Patch, an EP could easily be over a mile in error, making it quite possible to pass inshore of the buoy without seeing it. In good visibility (over 5 miles) it might still be safe enough to aim for the buoy, with a clearing bearing on East Point as a double-check. In moderate or poor visibility (1100 yards to 5 miles) this would be impossible, because East Point would be out of sight. One option would be to go inshore, to stay in sight of landmarks ashore. The alternative would be to aim at least a mile offshore of the Mussel Patch.

Bolt-holes

The chances of anything going badly wrong on the simple journey from bedroom to kitchen that introduced this chapter are fairly small. That is not the case at sea: a sailing boat can be delayed by lack of wind, and miss a tidal gate as a result; or a motorboat might suffer engine trouble, so on any passage likely to last more than a few hours or to cover more than about 10 or 20 miles it is a good idea to give some thought to bolt holes – harbours or anchorages in which to find shelter, carry out repairs, or simply await a favourable tide.

At the very least it is worth looking at what the pilot book has to say about any potential bolt-holes, to find out whether they are affected by any weather or tidal constraints,

and whether the pilotage involved is easy or difficult. Then, if things do go wrong, you can make a quick decision about where to head for, rather than having to hunt for the information.

If you know circumstances are likely to be difficult – when short-handed, or on a boat with limited navigation facilities, for instance – it may be wise to take this 'what if' planning a stage further, and prepare pilotage plans for bolt-holes as well as for the intended destination, or even to amend the intended route so as always to be within easy reach of at least one safe harbour.

The finished plan

The object of all this research is to produce a plan of how the passage should go, which can be summed up by drawing the intended track on to a chart. Mark on it any critical timings such as tidal 'gates', and useful information such as the name and number of the next chart. For night passages, many navigators like to draw circles showing the visible ranges of major lighthouses, while fast-boat navigators often highlight key landmarks and hazards by circling them with a thick soft pencil. The pages of the tidal stream atlas can usefully be labelled with the clock time to which they refer.

If you are going to be using an electronic position fixer, each waypoint should be clearly marked and labelled on the chart, written down on a separate list, and carefully 'entered' into the navigator. Most electronic navigators are capable of displaying the range and bearing of one waypoint from the one before: comparing this with the bearing and distance on the chart gives a useful cross-check that the positions entered by lat and long were correct. Without this facility, it is almost essential to regard entering waypoints as a two-person job, with one reading from the list while the other keys in the position, then swapping roles so that one reads the stored data from the navigator while the other double-checks it on the chart.

Navigating on passage – traditional methods under sail/at low speed

Once on passage, the first requirement for any navigational decision is a knowledge of your present position, so fixing should become a regular routine. How often you should fix your position is largely determined by the proximity of hazards: as a very rough guide, the interval between fixes should be no more than the time it would take you to reach the nearest hazard.

Whatever fixing method you use there is always the possibility of gross errors, so it is essential to get into the habit of cross-checking by using a mixture of position-fixing methods, and by comparing each fix with an EP based on the fix before. If a position fix cannot be obtained, then of course you will have to fall back on to EPs alone, but even these can often be cross-checked, roughly, by comparing the charted depth in the vicinity against the echo sounder.

Slow boat navigation often involves quite a lot of chartwork, so by the time you have worked out a few EPs, plotted a few fixes, and shaped a new course each time, the chart can quickly become very cluttered. This is especially true if you use the chart itself as a surface on which to jot down bearings, courses, log readings, and so on. It is much better to keep a notebook for rough jottings, and a proper **decklog** for everything of navigational significance. This need not be a pre-printed log book: an exercise book or even a loose-leaf binder will do, so long as you record the right information.

As a bare minimum, this means that whenever something significant happens – such as an alteration of course, change of sails, or a fix – you should record the time, log reading, course steered (since the last log entry) and 'remarks'. A simple test of whether your log-keeping is adequate is to ask yourself whether it would be possible to re-work all your chartwork using the information in the deck log alone, but there is also some merit in including columns for estimated leeway, wind, weather, and engine hours. Over the course of a season or two the deck log will then build up into a record of the boat's performance in various conditions that can be very useful in deciding which sails to set, or what the fuel consumption is likely to be.

Wind and tide routeing

The shortest distance between two points is a straight line, but the straight-line route is not necessarily the fastest or most efficient. Wind and tide routeing involves adapting the straight-line route so as to maximize the effect

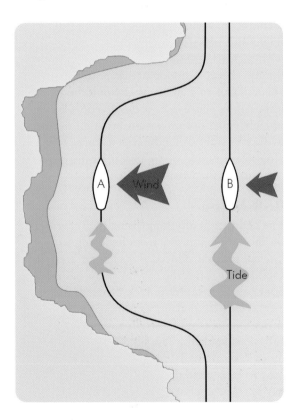

Fig 128 The optimum route may be influenced by wind and tidal streams. Boat A has the advantage of a sea breeze but is out of the tidal stream. Boat B has less wind but more tide. Which is best depends to some extent on the boat!

of favourable tidal streams, minimize the effect of contrary ones, and sail in the optimum wind.

A typical example might occur on a sunny afternoon when sailing across a bay, with a favourable tide and a very light onshore breeze (Figure 128). One option would be to stay slightly offshore of the straight-line route, to make the most of the favourable tide, but an equally valid alternative would be to go inshore – sailing further and losing the tide, but making the most of the sea breeze on the coast. Which of these two is actually better depends on a number of factors – not only the strength of the tide and the anticipated sea breeze, but also the characteristics of the boat. A lightweight, high-performance boat might well do best on the inshore route, whilst a long keel, heavy-displacement cruiser will fare better offshore. It would almost certainly be a mistake for either of them to 'hedge their bets' by taking the middle line – far enough into the bay to lose the tide but too far offshore to pick up the sea breeze.

In different circumstances, however, that might well be the optimum route. Crossing the same bay against the tide, the offshore route would have nothing to recommend it, while on a dull day with no possibility of a sea breeze there would be no merit in adding distance by going right inshore.

Beating to windward

Beating to windward under sail inevitably involves a significant departure from the straight-line route, with the boat's course largely determined by the direction of the wind. It is still, however, up to the navigator/skipper to decide which is the best tack to be on at any particular moment.

If we sailed on tideless waters, and with perfectly consistent winds, 'which tack' would be an academic question: both tacks would be equally favoured. Nor would there be much to be said in favour of short tacking to stay close to the straight-line route: if anything, it might

be better to make fewer, longer tacks to avoid losing speed on each tack. In the real world, things are different: not only do wind and tide vary from place to place and from time to time, but they interact with each other.

Apparent wind

The wind you feel, and which generates drive on the sails of a boat under way, is not the same as the 'true wind' which would be registered by the wind indicator and anemometer of a stationary boat.

Imagine, for a moment, a boat at anchor on a perfectly windless day. Her anemometer reads zero, and her wind indicator points nowhere in particular. Now imagine that she weighs anchor and starts motoring at seven knots.

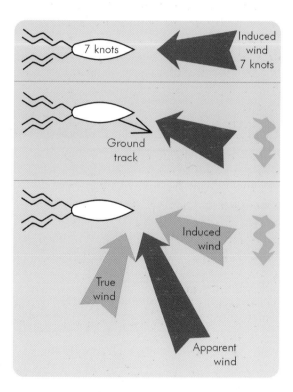

Fig 129 An induced wind is created by the boat's movement (top). It is parallel to the boat's ground track, so it is affected by the tidal stream (middle). The apparent wind is a combination of the induced wind and the true wind (bottom).

Because she is now moving through still air, her crew will feel the sensation of wind, and her instruments will show a 7-knot breeze, dead ahead. Much the same would happen if she was drifting in a strong tidal stream instead of motoring: the crew and instruments would register an 'induced wind', equal in speed to the boat's speed over the ground, but in the opposite direction.

If it was not a calm day, but there was, instead, a true wind of ten knots, then this would be felt as well as the induced wind: the two would combine to produce what is usually called the 'apparent wind'. What follows from all this is that the apparent wind that creates drive from the sails and determines the boat's close-hauled course is dependent on six factors:

- True wind speed
- Boat's speed
- Tidal stream speed
- True wind direction
- Boat's course
- Tidal stream direction

Faced with so many interrelated variables, even the most conscientious navigator might be forgiven for throwing in the towel and deciding to 'tack when we've all finished our tea'! Fortunately, however, racing navigators have developed a number of strategies to simplify the decision, some of which can usefully be adopted by cruising sailors.

The cone and corridor strategies
The cone strategy is a simple device that is mainly intended to hedge your bets, to avoid the temptation to hang on to one tack for so long that you risk being caught out by an unexpected wind shift when sailing towards a destination to windward. Prepare it by drawing a line on the chart, extending directly downwind from your intended destination. Then add two more lines, at an angle of 15°, one on each side of the downwind line, so as to form a 'cone' or funnel-shaped approach.

Start by sailing close-hauled into the funnel, then tack whenever you reach one of the limiting lines, so as to stay within the approach cone.

One drawback of the cone approach is that on a long passage the first few tacks may be so long that a fresh and enthusiastic crew become bored, while at the end of the trip the tacks are so short that a tired crew become irritated. A variation is to modify the cone into a 'corridor', with limiting lines drawn parallel to the downwind line, but a mile or two away from it.

Electronically-assisted cone and corridor
The cone and corridor strategies both lend themselves particularly well to electronic navigation. In the case of the cone strategy, the edges of the cone are defined by straight lines

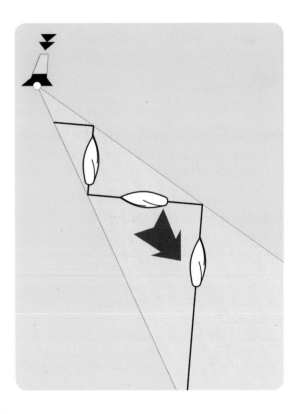

Fig 130 A cone strategy can be used when beating to windward, to avoid being caught out by wind shifts.

radiating outward from the waypoint. In Figure 130, the cone's edges are 320° and 290°. Using the Bearing to Waypoint display of an electronic navigator makes staying inside the cone a simple matter of tacking whenever the bearing to waypoint increases to 320° or reduces to 290°.

The corridor strategy is more difficult to set up, but is even easier to use. Essentially, you need to set up a waypoint somewhere on the downwind line, so that the navigator regards the downwind line as one leg of your route. Then, once you've crossed the downwind line, 'tell' the navigator to skip the extra waypoint, and guide you to the next one – the one you were really interested in all along. Finally, switch to the Cross Track Error display, and tack whenever the cross track error reaches the limit you have set yourself.

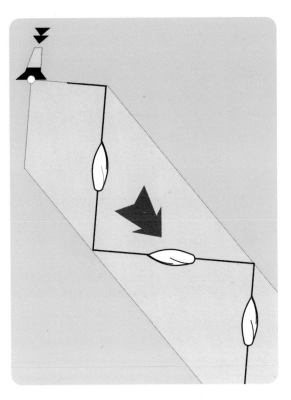

Fig 131 A corridor strategy uses the same principle as the cone strategy, but gives more evenly-spaced tacks.

The purpose of the initial jiggery-pokery with the extra waypoint is simply to make sure that the cross track error is measured from the downwind line, rather than from the line between your two genuine waypoints. On many electronic navigators there are easier ways of achieving the same effect: it is well worth reading the manual.

Steer towards wind shifts

The cone and corridor strategies are both pessimistic, damage-limitation plans, aimed at minimizing the risk of being caught out by an unexpected wind shift. If, however, you have good reason to expect a wind shift, and you know which way it is likely to go, it is possible to adopt a much more constructive approach by using a strategy aimed at taking advantage of the shift.

The idea is very simple indeed: you set off on the tack that takes you as close as possible to the direction of the forecast wind. This means that if the wind is expected to veer (eg from west to north-west) you should initially favour port tack: if it is expected to back (eg from west to south-west) you should opt for starboard tack.

Lee-bowing the tide

The lee bow strategy is intended to make sure that the shifts of apparent wind caused by changing tidal streams are always in your favour.

Although the principle is somewhat complicated, applying it is simple: you should choose the tack that puts the tidal stream on the lee bow of the boat. Having the tidal stream on the lee bow creates an induced 'tidal wind' on the windward quarter, which moves the apparent wind further aft – allowing the boat to point slightly closer to the true wind. The effect is most pronounced in light winds and strong tides, and especially when wind and tide are at right angles to each other.

The lee bow strategy is simple and effective, but it needs to be applied with some caution, especially if it conflicts with the 'steer towards wind shifts' policy; a shift in the true wind that is large enough to have been forecast is almost certain to be more significant than the apparent shift created by a lee bow tide.

Lay lines

Despite a name that sounds as though it has something to do with crop circles or parapsychology, a lay line is simply a line that represents the optimum close-hauled track to a windward mark. In other words, once you have crossed the lay line, you can lay the mark without having to tack again.

In non-tidal water, finding the lay line is reasonably straightforward, so long as you know your boat's tacking angle in the

prevailing conditions. Suppose, for example, that your tacking angle is 90°, and that you make 5° leeway. If your close-hauled course on port tack is 310°, then on starboard tack it should be 310° – 90° = 220°. The 5° of leeway will give a water track of 220° – 5° = 215°. With no tide, the ground track will also be 215°, so when your destination (or waypoint) is bearing 215° or less, it is time to put in your last tack.

In tidal waters, the situation is a little more complicated, because you will have to work out your likely ground track allowing for the tidal stream. One way of doing this is to work out an EP as though you had already tacked, using your estimate of the new water track and speed. The process of working out an EP gives

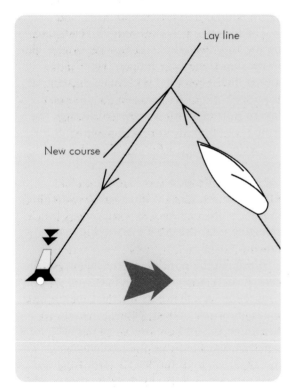

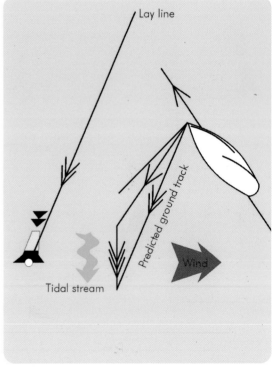

Fig 132 The lay line is the line of approach that will just reach a windward destination on one tack. In non-tidal waters, it is a line drawn through the destination, parallel to the boat's predicted water track.

Fig 133 In tidal waters, the lay line must be adjusted to allow for the tidal stream: it is parallel to the boat's predicted ground track.

you the expected ground track, which can be measured and transferred across the chart to pass through your intended destination, when it becomes the lay line (Figure 133).

A neater method, but one which is slightly less easy to remember, is shown in Figure 134:

1 Estimate your new water track and boat speed as before.
2 Find the rate and direction of the tidal stream from tidal diamonds or the tidal stream atlas.
3 Draw a line from your destination, pointing directly uptide.
4 Choose a suitable time interval (such as one hour), and measure along the tide line the distance the boat would drift with the tide in that time.

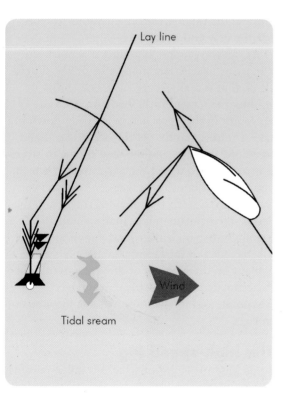

Fig 134 The lay line can be found by a technique similar to those used for plotting an EP and shaping a course (see text).

5 From the end of this measured distance, draw a line along the reciprocal (opposite) of your expected water track.
6 Measure along this line a distance corresponding to the distance you would expect to cover through the water in your chosen time interval.
7 Join your intended destination to this point with a straight line. This represents your lay line.

Navigating on passage – traditional methods at high speed

In all but the calmest conditions, the motion of a planing motorboat makes the traditional routine of plotting EPs, taking fixes, and shaping courses almost impossible. Unless you are prepared to rely entirely on electronics, this means that navigation at speed has a lot in common with pilotage, with buoy-hopping very much the favoured technique. In other words, the plan for a high speed passage should, ideally, consist of a number of relatively short, straight 'legs' from buoy to buoy.

The big difference between this and a pilotage plan is that the distances involved in a coastal or offshore passage may be very much greater. You can't expect to see a buoy (even a large one) at a range of more than a mile or two, but there is no great secret about finding a buoy that is too far away to see: it is simply a matter of travelling in the right direction for the right distance. The navigator's main task, therefore, is to check the compass and log.

In practice, however, it is much easier to steer accurately by aiming for some fixed object ahead, so if there is land visible beyond the buoy – especially if it has some conspicuous landmark – it is worth steering towards it, and using the compass as an occasional check. Equally, as most motor cruisers' logs show speed much more clearly than distance travelled, it is a good idea to work out your estimated time of arrival at the next mark, based on speed and distance, rather than relying on the distance reading itself.

Allowing for tidal streams

Many people make the mistake of assuming that the speed of a planing boat renders it completely immune to the effects of tide. That is not the case, though on a passage made up of very short legs or at very high speeds it may seem to be so, because the effect of the tidal stream over a short period will be so small. Over longer distances or at lower speeds, however, it becomes more noticeable: on a ten mile 'hop' between buoys, a three knot tide setting across the intended track is enough to push a twenty knot boat far enough off track for it to pass out of sight of the second buoy. If you have a decent chart table, it's quite possible to use the classic method of working out a course to steer (page 97) to good effect. On a RIB or open cockpit sports cruiser, it may be better to use the One in Sixty Rule. Whichever you choose, it's worth working out your speed over the ground as well as your course to steer.

Estimating time to go

The reason speed over ground is important is because it allows you to estimate when you can expect to reach your next waypoint. This reduces the risk of overshooting and, conversely, stops you worrying about having not seen a buoy when, in reality, you have not yet reached it.

The basic arithmetic is simple: you don't need to be a mathematical wizard to work out that if you are doing 20 knots and have 10 miles to go it will take half an hour. Without a calculator the problem seems much more difficult if, for instance, you are travelling at 23 knots and have 17 miles to go. One solution is to think in terms of tenths of an hour – or 6 minute intervals.

It is easy to see that in 6 minutes, a boat

travelling at 23 knots will cover 2.3 miles, and that in half an hour it will cover 11.5 miles. Combining these two gives:

$$11.5 + 2.3 = 13.8 \text{ miles in 36 minutes}$$

$$13.8 + 2.3 = 16.1 \text{ miles in 42 minutes,}$$

$$16.1 + 2.3 = 18.4 \text{ miles in 48 minutes} \dots$$
and so on.

From this, it is obvious that it will take about 45 minutes to cover the distance. (The right answer, incidentally, is 44 minutes 21 seconds!)

Reaching a waypoint

Shortly before reaching a waypoint, then, the navigator should check on the planned track, and use the tidal stream calculations to work out the new course to steer.

At the waypoint – assuming it is marked by a buoy or nearby landmark – he or she should check that it really is the right one, either by reading the name off the buoy or, if it is a waypoint in the open sea, by slowing down to take a traditional fix. At this stage it is useful to record the time and the new course to steer; it is too easy to forget the exact time at which you passed a buoy, or to get confused between the course to steer, the intended track, and the course the helmsman is actually steering!

Finally, as you leave the waypoint and have a better idea of the speed you are likely to achieve on the next leg of the route, work out the estimated time of arrival at the next waypoint, and if necessary reassess the course to steer.

The high-speed log

Some kind of record of what has taken place is just as important in high-speed navigation as it is at the more sedate pace of a sailing yacht, yet the factors that make chartwork difficult – the lively motion and (often) the lack of space – also make it difficult to maintain a traditional deck log. There are a number of

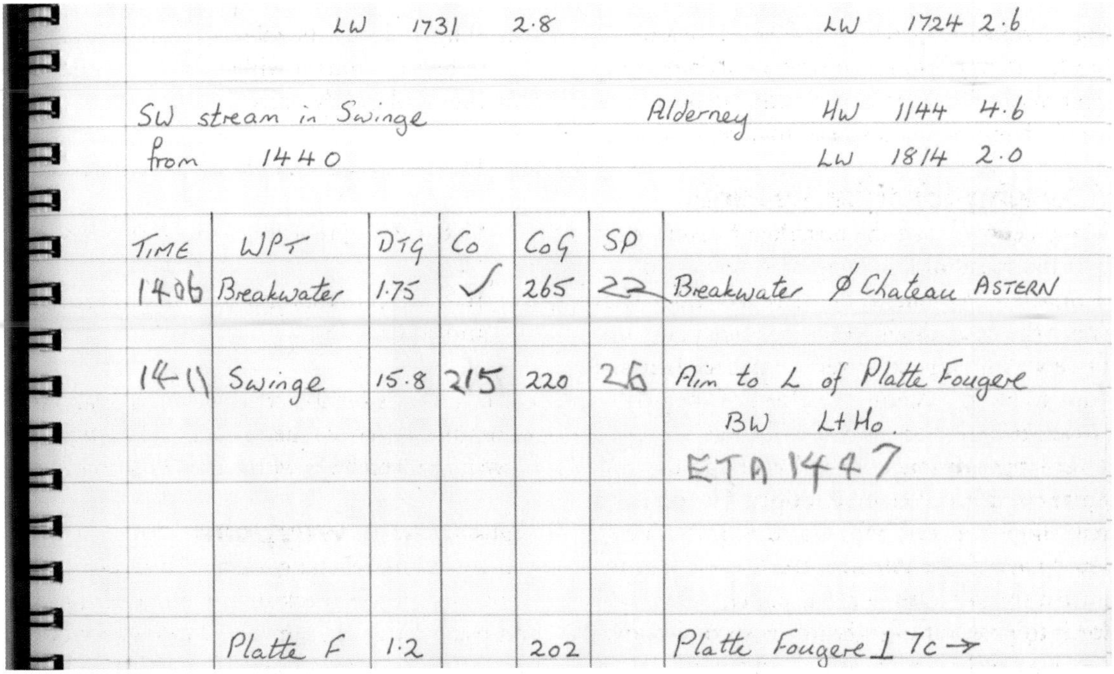

	LW	1731	2.8		LW	1724 2.6

SW stream in Swinge
from 1440

Alderney   HW   1144   4.6
         LW   1814   2.0

TIME	WPT	DTG	Co	CoG	SP	
1406	Breakwater	1.75	✓	265	22	Breakwater ∅ Chateau ASTERN
1411	Swinge	15.8	215	220	26	Aim to L of Platte Fougere BW Lt Ho. ETA 1447
	Platte F	1.2		202		Platte Fougere ⌐ 7c →

Fig 135 Fast boat navigators can combine the passage plan and deck log, reducing the writing involved on passage by leaving spaces in the passage plan for information to be filled in as the passage progresses.

possible alternatives, each with advantages and disadvantages.

The pre-written log

As a high speed passage has to be planned in considerable detail, and with the expectation that it will go almost exactly according to plan, there is no reason why most of the information that would traditionally be recorded en route should not be written down in advance. Much of it – including positions (waypoints), intended tracks, and possibly even courses to steer – are part of the plan anyway. To use the written plan as a pre-written log, it is only necessary to leave spaces for the details such as times, log readings, speeds and actual courses steered that cannot be planned in advance.

The log-on-chart

The log-on-chart method is exactly what it says it is: the most important pieces of information that would traditionally be recorded in a separate logbook are written directly on the chart itself. It is important to be methodical and as neat as possible, otherwise the chart quickly becomes an unintelligible mess. But if you can discipline yourself to stick to a system, such as writing the time, log reading and course to steer alongside each waypoint as you pass it, the intended track and distance to run alongside the track, and the estimated time of arrival alongside the next waypoint, it has the dual advantages of keeping all the navigational information together and reducing the amount of paper that has to be kept under control.

The tape recorded log

The use of a pocket dictating machine in place of a written log is the most controversial option, and is based on the assumption that everything will happen exactly according to plan, and that the log is kept only as a last resort – to be referred to if an expected buoy doesn't show up on time. The obvious

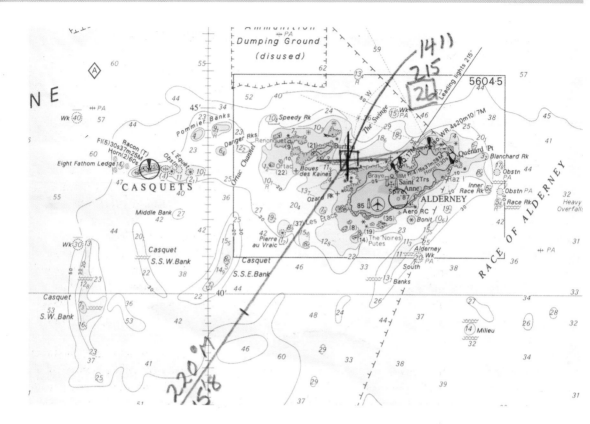

Fig 136 The information that would traditionally be recorded in the deck log can be written on the chart, but it is important to be as neat and methodical as possible.

drawbacks are that it is difficult to find specific pieces of information quickly, and that a machine intended for use in an office environment is unlikely to be 100% reliable at sea. On the credit side, in very lively boats, or when operating short-handed at very high speeds, it may be the only means of keeping any sort of log at all.

Between waypoints

Between waypoints the fast-boat navigator, as well as continuing to keep an eye on the boat's speed and course, is mainly concerned with monitoring its position relative to the intended track. Traditional position-fixing may not be practical, or necessary: the information required is not 'Where am I?', but 'Am I on track?' and 'How am I progressing?'

Answering the question 'Am I on track?'

requires only a single position line, so long as that position line lies along, or nearly parallel to, the intended track. Any kind of position line will do, such as a depth contour line, a radar range from a coastline or feature passing abeam, or a visual bearing of a landmark almost directly ahead or astern. The position line does not even have to be plotted on the chart: if you know, for instance, that your intended track follows the 10 metre contour, and the echo sounder reading (corrected for the height of tide) is 8 metres, then it is reasonably obvious that you need to turn out towards deeper water in order to get back on track. Similarly, if your intended track lies 2 miles off the coast but the radar shows the coastline to be 2½ miles away, then you need to turn inshore until the coastline touches the 2 mile range ring.

For this purpose, visual bearings can be taken without using a hand-bearing compass, simply by pointing the boat at the landmark for a few seconds, and reading the heading from the steering compass. This has the advantage of being easier to read, generally more stable, and corrected (or correctable) for deviation. Assuming you have chosen your intended track and landmark carefully, so that the landmark lies very close to the intended track or on a continuation of it, then the bearing should be the same as the intended track. If the measured bearing is low – 240°, for instance, when it should be 250° – then you need to steer lower still, to (say) 230°, to get back on track. If the measured bearing is higher than it should be, then the opposite applies, and you need to steer higher still to regain your intended track.

Using a back bearing, such as the buoy you have just left, is more difficult: it is likely to involve using a hand-bearing compass, and the bearing should be the reciprocal of the intended track (track ± 180°). The rules for getting back on track are reversed, too: if the bearing is high, you steer lower, and vice versa.

Monitoring progress also requires only a single position line – this time roughly at right angles to the intended track. Again, any kind of position line can be used, including depth contours which cross the intended track, radar ranges of objects ahead or astern, or visual bearings. In this case, visual bearings are often the easiest, because it is usually possible to keep an eye open for conspicuous landmarks, and to note when they pass abeam. With experience, and at ranges up to two or three miles, it is possible to do this quite accurately enough by eye. At longer ranges it is again possible to use the boat's steering compass, rather than a hand-bearing compass, by sighting along some fixed part of the boat such as a seat-back or bulkhead, and adding or subtracting 90° to or from the compass reading when the landmark crosses your line of sight.

Using electronics

A navigator who chooses to rely entirely on traditional tools and techniques is likely to find that quite a significant proportion of his time and effort has to be devoted to finding out where he is – either by taking and plotting fixes or by working up EPs. Electronics, of course, can do that particular job almost continuously with considerable accuracy and precision and without human intervention.

This does not, however, mean that the navigator has nothing to do. The electronic navigator still needs to go through the same planning process as his traditional counterpart. His preparation may well need to be rather more thorough, because he may need to mark up waypoints on the chart and store them in the GPS or chart plotter.

Of course, he reaps the benefit once the boat is under way. Even here, though, electronic systems can only provide information: it is still up to the human skipper or navigator to make decisions.

Example 1

A fleet of yachts was racing across the Celtic Sea to the Fastnet Rock. They had just cleared Lands End when the weather forecast predicted that the SW wind would shift to the NW in about 12 hours time. On one of the leading boats the PC plotter incorporated weather routeing software which took this shift into account, and suggested a route well north of the rhumb line. Most of the fleet, however, carried on along the rhumb line.

In this case, the skipper overruled the plotter because she had reservations about the reliability of the weather forecast, and was unwilling to jeopardise a good position by breaking away from the main fleet.

Example 2

A motor cruiser was due to leave Alderney, bound for St Peter Port, Guernsey. Her PC plotter suggested that the optimum time to leave Alderney was at about the time of local low water.

Her skipper decided to overrule the plotter, because its plan would have taken him through the Alderney Race when the SW tide was at its strongest, and likely to be producing rough conditions against a SW wind. Also, arriving at St Peter Port soon after LW, he would not have been able to go straight into the marina.

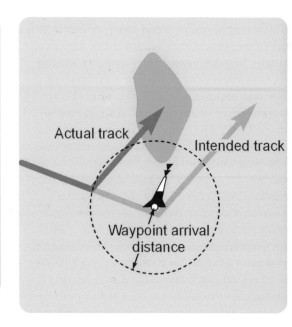

Fig 137 It is important to be aware exactly what an electronic navigator's waypoint arrival alarm means, especially if it is linked to an autopilot.

Waypoint arrival

Of course, it is important to be certain that waypoints have been entered correctly, but there is another more subtle piece of information that an electronic navigator needs if it is to guide you along the planned route; you have to tell it how to decide when you have reached a waypoint. Some of the more sophisticated devices offer a range of alternatives, but most use waypoint arrival distance as the main criterion. This is usually found in one of the menus dealing with alarm settings, because arrival at a waypoint usually triggers an audible alarm, as well as switching the instrument's attention to the next waypoint.

The waypoint arrival distance can be set to anything from zero to several miles. If it is set to a very small distance, then it may be almost impossible to get close enough to the waypoint to convince the navigator that you have actually arrived. On the other hand, if the waypoint arrival distance is too large, then the navigator will switch to the next waypoint too early, and you will find yourself cutting the corner. The appropriate setting depends on how precisely you need to follow your planned route and on the accuracy you can expect from

your position fixer. It is seldom necessary or desirable to use an arrival distance of much less than about 0.05 mile, or greater than about 0.25 mile.

Monitoring progress

The apparent precision of an electronic display makes it tempting to try to steer by the cross track error display, aiming to keep it to zero. This is particularly true if you are using the popular 'rolling road' or 'highway' display, but it's akin to driving a car by looking out of the driver's door at the white line: it is almost invariably better to be guided primarily by the bearing to waypoint display, and to steer by compass, referring to the cross track error display at intervals to see if there is a clear and continuing tendency for the boat to slide off track in one particular direction.

Finally, remember that whilst traditional navigation usually involves a range of different tools and techniques, electronic navigation tends to put all your eggs in one basket, in which errors can pass unnoticed, and in which the whole system can fail if a single wire breaks or a fuse blows. To guard against this it's important to keep some kind of backup system ticking over, ready to take over if things go wrong. This could, perhaps, be a second electronic system, but for most people it's more likely to be traditional navigation. It is a good idea to get into the habit of using traditional methods to cross-check your electronics at regular intervals – by noticing, for instance, when you cross a transit or depth contour, or when you pass a headland or buoy. Keep a deck log of some sort, whether it's in the form of notes added to the passage plan, a log-on-chart system, or a tape recorder.

Example 3

A large cruise ship left Bermuda bound for Boston, Massachusetts. Her integrated bridge system automatically compared the output from the GPS with a DR position, calculated automatically by means of log and compass inputs.

About an hour after leaving Bermuda the antenna cable became disconnected from the GPS, which automatically switched to DR mode. The integrated bridge system was then comparing the DR position that had been calculated by the GPS set with the DR position that it had calculated for itself. Not surprisingly, there was no difference between the two, so it did not trigger its position fix alarm.

Thirty four hours later, the ship ran aground, having recently passed several buoys, and within sight of a lighthouse.

The Marine Accident Investigation Branch (MAIB) report of the incident pointed out that 'a fundamental rule of navigation is always to check the primary method of navigation by an independent source'.

Example 4

A 28 foot yacht was approaching Plymouth after a channel crossing. It was late in the season, it was dark, and there was a force 7-8 blowing. Four of the five man crew succumbed to seasickness, leaving the skipper effectively singlehanded for the last 4 hours of the passage. He had GPS, but no chart plotter, and was not able to leave the cockpit to plot his position on the chart, so he resorted to local knowledge and eyeball navigation.

The yacht grounded on unlit rocks just off the eastern entrance to Plymouth Sound, and quickly broke up. Four of the crew survived, but the owner/skipper did not. The GPS set was subsequently recovered, and the position data it had recorded was used by accident investigators to reconstruct the yacht's movements during her final few minutes.

Getting lost, and 'finding yourself'

Logs sometimes under- or over-read, compass deviation can change without being noticed, and electronics can fail – and all human beings make mistakes occasionally. So there can be very few experienced navigators who have not, at some stage, been 'uncertain of their position'.

There are two distinct types of being 'lost', of which by far the most dangerous is being misplaced – being convinced (wrongly) that you know where you are when you are really somewhere quite different. This is the kind of 'lost' that leads to boats running on to rocks, to yachts being pounded on to lee shores, and to motor cruisers leaving their sterngear on sandbanks. It happens when you can see something, but convince yourself that it is something else, or 'fudge' a fix by adding a few degrees to one of the bearings because you

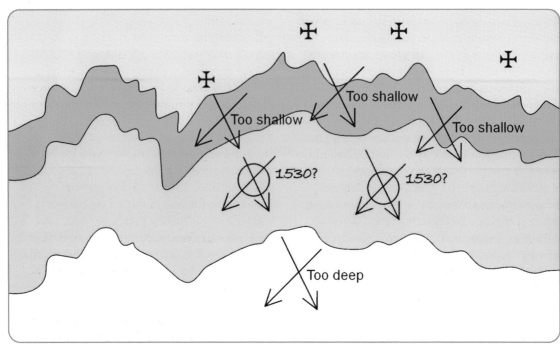

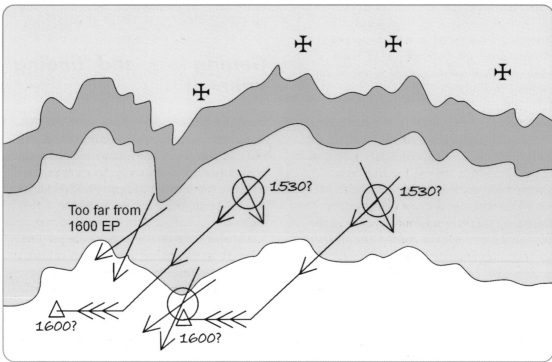

Fig 138 Finding yourself, once lost, is often a matter of gathering every available clue and eliminating the positions that are impossible. It is important, however, to be very careful not to eliminate possibilities just because you don't like them, or to 'bend' facts to suit what you believe.

would rather believe that you remembered the wrong numbers than accept that you have just taken a bearing of the wrong object. It is important never to believe that what you can see is what you want to see, unless you have some real evidence to support it.

The other kind of 'lost' is a gradual realization that something is 'not quite right', usually brought about by not seeing something when you expect to, by seeing something you were not expecting, or by a succession of larger-than-usual cocked hats that don't quite agree with your EP.

The first job is to prevent the situation getting worse. Generally, this means slowing right down, if possible reducing your speed over the ground to zero by anchoring or by altering course and speed to stem the tide. Once you know you are not rushing towards an unseen hazard you have time to think and to study the chart.

The main exception to this general advice is if staying where you are would increase the danger: if, for instance, you are already in shallow water and the tide is falling or the weather deteriorating. In that case, it may be better to turn and head back the way you came until the boat is in a safer position.

Having stabilized the situation, it is time to take stock of your assets. Foremost amongst these is your last reliable fix; from this, it should be possible to work out an EP. This is why keeping some form of deck log is so important, because without a record of the time of the fix, and the courses and distances since, it is impossible to produce an EP. The EP may not be right (if it is, then you are not really lost!), but it is a good basis to work on, because you can now set about deciding why it is wrong.

You may, for instance, have noticed that the log has stopped working, in which case it would be reasonable to assume that you have travelled further than the EP suggests; or you may have a 'gut feeling' that the helmsman has been allowing the boat to yaw further one way than the other; or that your estimate of leeway could have been optimistic. This should narrow down your possible position to somewhere within a more or less definite area. If, for some reason, you have no deck log, you still need to try to narrow down your position somehow, even if it is based on little more than rough guesses such as 'I think we must have been drifting north-east for almost an hour after the mainsail blew out' or 'That must have been the Roscoff ferry that passed us.'

Limiting the possibilities should make it possible to start using more conventional navigational clues, such as visual bearings of landmarks. A visual bearing of an unidentified church crossed with one of an unidentified headland does not provide a fix, but plotting the bearings on every possible church and headland in your general vicinity will narrow down your possible position still further. Some of these false fixes can then be eliminated by using other clues, such as the depth of water, or their proximity to other landmarks.

Once all the available clues have been used, you will have to move in order to gather more information, but by this stage you should have a relatively limited number of possible positions. Choose a course which would be safe from any of the possibilities, and set off – this time keeping a meticulous log, so that you can plot an EP based on each of the tentative 'fixes'. After a while you may be rewarded by a new and easily identifiable landmark. If not, try taking bearings of the same objects as you used before, comparing each of the new 'fixes' with the 'EP' based on the corresponding old 'fix': a new 'fix' which agrees with the corresponding 'EP' is probably right. It is still a matter of eliminating the impossible, however, not a question of convincing yourself that the 'best' of several dubious possibilities must be right.

Finding yourself calls for more skill and ingenuity than not getting lost in the first place. There are no hard-and-fast rules, other than to make sure you have used every piece of information available to you. It calls for clear thinking, so it is important not to panic, but work methodically, and avoid distractions. Above all else, though, it is essential to avoid any temptation to bend the facts to support your supposition about where you are. Giving in to that temptation only makes matters worse because you will then be misplaced, rather than merely uncertain of your position.

If necessary, you must be prepared to accept defeat. Approaching the Brittany coast, for instance, where there are dangerous ledges of rocks extending several miles offshore, it would be reckless to close the coast without having a good idea of where you are. If you cannot find yourself, the only option might well be to make for the English coast, where you stand a better chance of being able to go close enough to identify landmarks without running into danger.

Landfalls

Making a landfall after a passage in open water is always a special moment, though electronics have removed much of the excitement from the occasion. One waypoint is just like any other, and the mere fact that one is within sight of land makes very little real difference. For the traditional navigator, however, there is always a sense of uncertainty about a landfall. The satisfaction of finding land and the anticipation of arrival is mixed with some of the anxiety that is associated with being lost, and an almost overwhelming temptation to believe that what you can see is what you were expecting to see.

In some ways, the navigational tasks associated with making a landfall are very similar to those involved in finding yourself, but you start off with a number of inbuilt advantages – including an EP which you believe to be reliable, rather than one which has been proved wrong! Another big advantage is that you have no real choice about where

you get lost, whereas you can plan a landfall in advance, so as to make the job relatively simple. The easiest possible landfall is on a safe stretch of coastline with a few conspicuous and readily-identifiable features. In this case, the best plan is usually to aim straight for the most conspicuous feature, because that way, even if your EP is a few miles out, you can still expect to see your chosen target before you get close enough to have to worry about knowing exactly where you are.

At the other extreme are flat or featureless coastlines, with off-lying hazards. In this case, when land first appears, it can be almost impossible to identify anything with certainty. If your destination is not directly ahead of you, you will – quite literally – not know which way to turn. The solution is to 'aim off', usually aiming for a position a few miles up-tide of your final destination. Then at least you know which way to go, and can close the coast at an angle, looking for identifiable features whilst using a depth contour as a clearing line to stay away from possible hazards.

This approach does not work if you are approaching a coastline made up of deep bays, because by 'aiming off' you could find yourself heading into the wrong bay! In this case, it may be better to make sure of getting the right bay by aiming for the middle, and rely on seeing the headland on one side or the other as you go in.

Fog

Navigating in fog is, even with electronic aids, more difficult, dangerous, and unpleasant than under almost any other conditions. By far the best way of dealing with it, if you have the choice, is not to go out in it. Being caught out in fog is a very different matter: heading for port is only one option, and not necessarily the best.

Staying offshore carries with it the risk of colliding with a ship or of running out of fuel, water, food, or stamina before the fog lifts. Going inshore reduces the risk of collision, but increases the chance of going aground. Heading for port is a high gain/high risk option, combining an increased risk of collision with other vessels using the harbour with the risk of going aground on your way inshore, but offering virtually guaranteed comfort and safety once you are in. A low risk alternative is to head for shallow water, and anchor. Which of these strategies is best depends on the boat and crew, the type and density of other traffic, the navigation aids available, and the weather – in particular, the type of fog and its likely duration.

Having decided on a strategy, navigation in fog is almost easier than in good visibility, simply because there is less information available. Electronic position fixers, of course, are unaffected, as is radar, but for the traditional navigator, the primary task is to maintain a meticulous EP. There are limits, however, to the accuracy which can be expected of an EP, particularly if it has to be maintained for several hours, and it may deteriorate to such an extent that it can no longer be relied upon for inshore navigation.

Buoy-hopping

The accuracy of an EP depends to a very great extent on the time that has elapsed since the last fix: an EP that is based on a fix 15 minutes ago is likely to be four times as accurate as one that has been run for an hour. So, in well-marked waters, one fairly obvious way of making safe progress inshore in fog is to amend the passage plan by breaking it down into very short 'hops' from one buoy to the next.

If a buoy does not show up when it is expected, it is futile to try searching for it, or to press on in the hope of finding the next one. As time goes by, the quality of your EP will be getting worse, not better, so having failed to find one buoy virtually guarantees not finding the next, so you will end up completely lost. In that situation it is better either to anchor or to head offshore.

Contours

Echo sounders work just as well in fog as in any other conditions, so depth contours can be a valuable source of position lines – possibly enough to allow a passage to be continued into harbour when it would otherwise be impossible. They are especially useful in areas where the seabed has a gentle, reasonably consistent slope, because this means that a pair of contours – such as the 5 m and 10 m contours – can be used as the boundaries of a corridor, which can be followed by zigzagging between the two. The angle between the legs of the zigzag depends on how straight the contours are, but should typically be about 30°. Zigzagging between contours is far more satisfactory than trying to follow the twists and turns of a single contour: it is less nerve-wracking; it is unlikely to increase the total distance travelled by very much and it allows an EP to be maintained with a reasonable degree of accuracy.

Do I need to navigate?

Unless you are prepared to trust to luck to decide whether you end up parked on a sandbank, wrecked on a rock, or roaming the seas like some latter-day Flying Dutchman, the answer to this question is an emphatic 'Yes'. That is not to say, however, that you always need to use the 'formal' methods covered in this book, any more than you would use an Ordnance Survey map and compass to get to your corner shop.

Navigation is only a part of effective skippering, and there are times when it is a relatively low priority. A good example of this would be on a short-handed sailing boat on a Channel crossing in bad weather. Trying to keep a reliable EP going is doomed to failure, because the boat cannot be steered accurately and the log may well be over- or under-reading

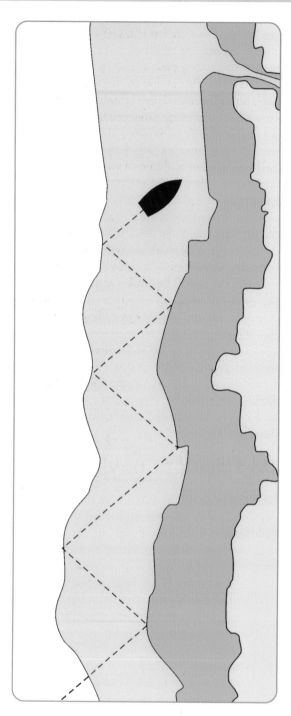

by 10%. In mid-Channel it hardly seems worth making yourself sick for, because there is nothing around to hit.

In theory, you could estimate the extent of all the possible errors, and use this information to define an area on the chart which you know must include the boat's position. This area, which is usually oval in shape, and expands with the passage of time, is sometimes called the 'pool of errors'. You may not know where you are in the pool, but so long as you are not sharing it with a hazard, that does not matter. Working out the size and shape of the pool of errors would be difficult and time-consuming, but in practice it is enough to have a rough idea of it – enough to be able to say, for instance, that 'if we keep going generally north, we should see Devon at about breakfast time', as opposed to 'if we steer 350° we shall reach Dartmouth at 0845'. This kind of navigation is

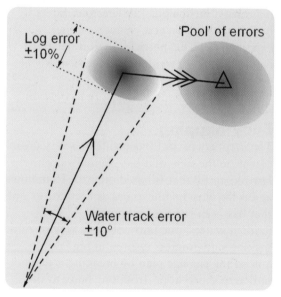

Fig 140 As the time since your last fix increases, your position becomes less accurate: it is somewhere inside an ever-expanding 'pool of errors', but so long as you are not sharing that pool with a hazard, you are safe. In extreme conditions, it may be more practical to estimate the size of the pool of errors than to be meticulous about plotting a position.

Fig 139 In poor visibility, well-defined contours may be the best way to continue the passage to a safe harbour: aim off to one side of the harbour, then zigzag between two contours along the coast.

not to be recommended, because it has obvious risks, but so long as you have assessed the risks it may at least be acceptable.

The other situation in which formal navigation can safely be abandoned could hardly be more different: it is when you are in familiar waters and good conditions. To stop familiarity breeding contempt, however, it is worth running through a mental checklist:

- Am I sure of continuing good visibility and daylight?
- Do I have complete confidence in my local knowledge of landmarks and hazards?
- Is there enough deep water around me to make a knowledge of my precise position irrelevant?
- Have I allowed for the state of the tide and the direction and rate of the tidal stream?

Do I need a passage plan?

A significant change in international law came into effect in 2002, when some of the requirements of the Safety of Life at Sea convention were extended to vessels of less than 150 tons, including private pleasure craft. One of its regulations (Number 34) requires the master of vessel to ensure that the intended voyage has been planned using appropriate charts and publications, according to official guidlines and recommendations.

The UK's Maritime and Coastguard Agency has said that it does not expect small craft skippers to produce written passage plans, and certainly does not intend that official 'approval' has to be obtained before setting off on a passage, but it recommends that a suitable passage plan should include:

- an up to date weather forecast
- tidal predictions
- an assessment of the limitations of the boat and crew
- navigational dangers
- a contingency plan
- details left with a responsible person ashore

Appendix

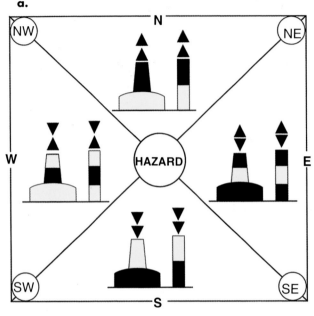

a. *Cardinal marks are used to mark hazards. The buoy shapes can vary widely, but their colour schemes and top-marks conform to this pattern. Lights – when fitted – are always white, and conform to the 'clock' rule (see text).*

b. *Lateral marks are used to mark clearly-defined channels. In the IALA A region port hand buoys are red and can-shaped or with cylindrical topmarks; starboard hand buoys are green and conical or with con-ical topmarks. Lights – when fitted – correspond to the colour of the buoy.*

c. *Preferred channel marks indicate forks in well-defined channels. A buoy which is to be treated as the first port hand buoy of the major channel has most of the characteristics of a port hand buoy – its shape, topmark, and predominant colour – and vice versa for one that is to be treated as the first starboard hand buoy of the major channel.*

d. *Miscellaneous marks are used to mark i.hazards entirely surrounded by navigable water; ii.the entrance or centreline of a channel; and iii.the boundaries of waterskiing areas, yacht racing marks, etc.*

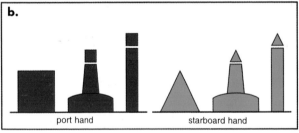

port hand   starboard hand

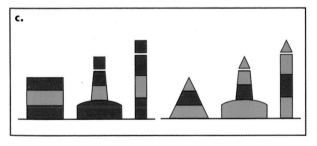

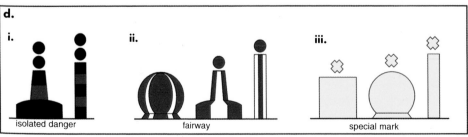

isolated danger   fairway   special mark

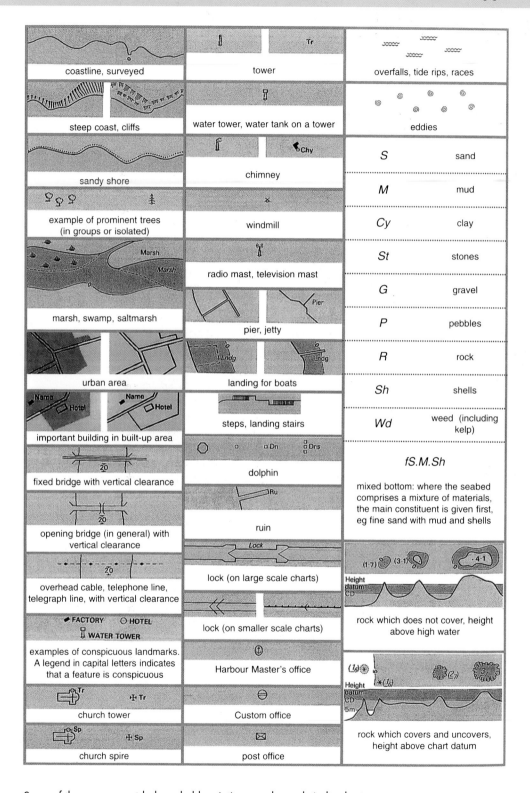

coastline, surveyed	tower	overfalls, tide rips, races
steep coast, cliffs	water tower, water tank on a tower	eddies
sandy shore	chimney	*S* sand
example of prominent trees (in groups or isolated)	windmill	*M* mud
		Cy clay
marsh, swamp, saltmarsh	radio mast, television mast	*St* stones
		G gravel
	pier, jetty	*P* pebbles
urban area	landing for boats	*R* rock
important building in built-up area	steps, landing stairs	*Sh* shells
		Wd weed (including kelp)
fixed bridge with vertical clearance	dolphin	*fS.M.Sh*
opening bridge (in general) with vertical clearance	ruin	mixed bottom: where the seabed comprises a mixture of materials, the main constituent is given first, eg fine sand with mud and shells
overhead cable, telephone line, telegraph line, with vertical clearance	lock (on large scale charts)	
examples of conspicuous landmarks. A legend in capital letters indicates that a feature is conspicuous	lock (on smaller scale charts)	rock which does not cover, height above high water
church tower	Harbour Master's office	
church spire	Custom office	rock which covers and uncovers, height above chart datum
	post office	

Some of the common symbols and abbreviations used on admiralty charts

165

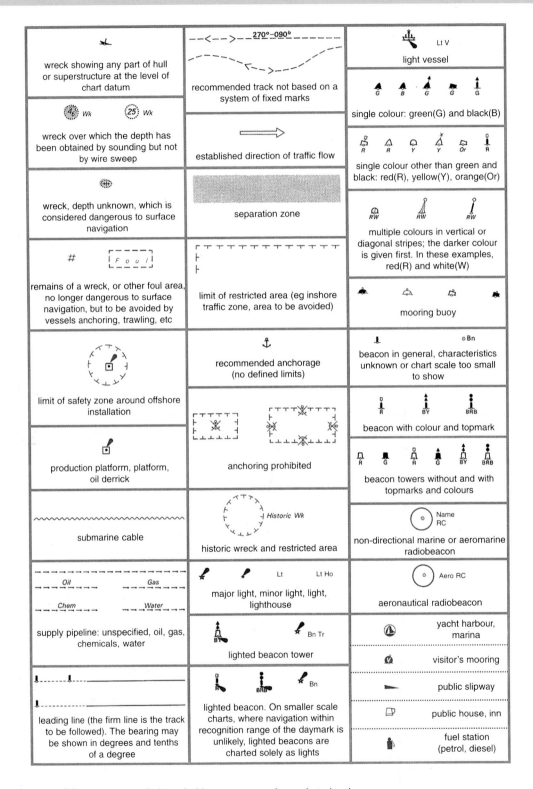

Some of the common symbols and abbreviations used on admiralty charts

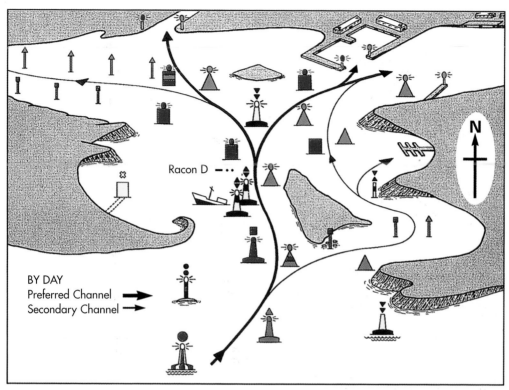

BY DAY
Preferred Channel ➡
Secondary Channel ➡

A fictional harbour by day and by night, showing how IALA system A can be applied in practice

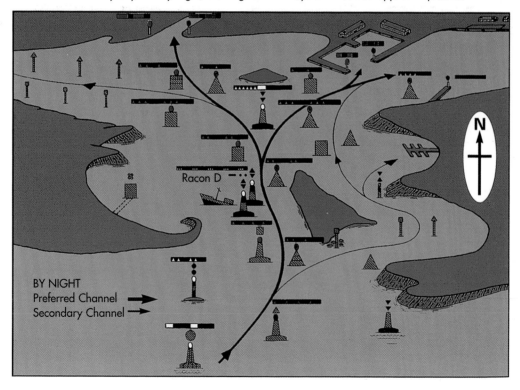

BY NIGHT
Preferred Channel ➡
Secondary Channel ➡

Index